THE IMPACT OF PRE-RETIREMENT EDUCATION :

A LONGITUDINAL EVALUATION.

BY

CHRIS PHILLIPSON   and   PATRICIA STRANG.

DEPARTMENT OF ADULT EDUCATION

UNIVERSITY OF KEELE,

1983.

ISBN   O   903160   13   7

CONTENTS

v

Acknowledgements

The Keele research project on pre-retirement education lasted from April 1979 to September 1982. During this period the two researchers had the support of many individuals and organisations. Throughout the work, a project team was available to give advice and assistance in areas of methodology and administration. This group consisted of Professor Roger Dyson and Dr. Frank Glendenning (both of the Department of Adult Education at Keele University and, respectively, Chairman and Secretary to the Project Advisory Team); three academic consultants (Professor Alastair Heron, Dr. Ian Russell and Mannes Tidmarsh); and two representatives from sponsoring organisations (Tom Blamey of the National Coal Board and Barry Collins of Shell International Limited). The assistance given by this group was crucial to the completion of the research and each individual was extremely generous with their help and advice.

The project team was supplemented by a steering committee consisting of all the sponsoring organisations. This group was itself highly supportive. We are particularly grateful to John Cammack (DES), Arthur Creber (Beth Johnson Foundation), John Evans, HMI (DES), John Deacock (British Airways), Keith Hughes (Legal and General), Graham Hoey (Scottish Retirement Council), Tom Stuchbery (Mars Ltd.) and Dr. Alastair Weir (Scottish Retirement Council).

A key figure in the work of the project was its secretary, Jill Phillips. Her commitment and enthusiasm was sustained throughout the research and we are very grateful for the high quality of her work.

Bill Bruce (Director) and David Jones (General Secretary) of the Pre-Retirement Association of Great Britain and Northern Ireland were consistently helpful and responded quickly and efficiently to requests for information.

Throughout the life of the project the researchers have benefited from discussions with a number of individuals and organisations. The following list is necessarily selective, but many thanks to all those who gave us their thought on the current state of PRE: Allin Coleman, Aleda Erskine, Professor Harvey Friedman, Molly Heath, Marion Hilbourne, Fred Mack, John Rogers, Kay Rothwell, Barbara Spiers and Cynthia Wyld.

The following individuals provided help in the organisations where interviews were conducted: Bob Elderfield (Shell International Ltd.), John French (National Coal Board), Bill Garmston (EMI Ltd.), Rose Gowlett (British Airways), Ivor Gray (Bristol Retirement Council), George Hurst (Carborundum Ltd.), Wyn Puttock (Mars Ltd.) and Daryl Shaw (Jaguar Ltd.). Social and Community Planning Research (SCPR) undertook the bulk of interviewing for the project. Jane Ritchie of SCPR provided valuable help and assistance at various stages of the research and we owe her a considerable debt of gratitude. The SCPR interviewers were sensitive and understanding about the aims of the project. We are particularly grateful to John Bastow, Bill Howard, Joy Hill, Margaret

Newns and Nick Quinton. Margaret Cunningham (formerly of the Scottish Retirement Council) assisted with the interviews in Scotland.

Dr Francis Glamser, who had undertaken an important American research project on PRE, was generous in providing material from his work.

The Library and Computer Centre staff at the University of Keele and the librarians at the Centre for Policy on Ageing were immensely helpful. Hamish Strang provided welcome advice on a particular statistical technique used in the analysis of results.

Finally, Marion Rhodes produced an excellent final copy from a very untidy final draft. We are grateful for her hard work.

Chris Phillipson
Patricia Strang

January 28 1983

Department of Adult Education
University of Keele.

Project Team and Sponsoring Organisations

Director and Senior Research Fellow: Dr Chris Phillipson BA

Research Assistant: Patricia Strang MA M.Sc
                                                       (Econ)

Secretary to the Project: Jill Phillips

Project Advisory Team

Professor Roger Dyson   (Chairman)

Dr Frank Glendenning   (Secretary)

Professor Alastair Heron)
)
) Academic consultants
Dr Ian Russell   )
)
Mannes Tidmarsh   )

Tom Blamey   )
) Representatives of sponsoring
Barry Collins   )   organisations.

Sponsoring Organisations

Department of Education and Science, The Department of
Health and Social Security, together with Shell Inter-
national Ltd., British Petroleum Ltd., Unilever Ltd.,
Mars Ltd., the Thompson Organisation Ltd., National Coal
Board, British Airways, Legal and General Assurance
Society Ltd., Choice Magazine, Scottish Retirement
Council and the Beth Johnson Foundation.

SECTION 1

In this section we outline the scope and methodology of our research. We also provide a historical analysis of the development of pre-retirement education, focusing upon the organisation of courses in Britain and America.

CHAPTER 1

INTRODUCTION TO THE KEELE REPORT

1. Introduction

The Keele Project started its work in April 1979. The finance of the research was the result of three years work by a committee drawn from the academic world, the pre-retirement movement and private and nationalised industries.[1] This committee set a number of tasks for the research: first, to analyse current objectives in the provision of retirement education; secondly, to evaluate a range of programmes within a longitudinal survey; thirdly, to prepare individual evaluation reports on a range of programmes; finally, to develop recommendations on future practice in retirement education.

Support for the project stemmed from doubts about the effectiveness of current programmes and concern over the limited amount of innovation which had occurred since the development of courses in the 1950s. Given the absence in this country of any evaluative work on PRE, basic research was necessary to establish the adequacy of current programme designs. Our task was, therefore, to provide a provisional assessment (subject to continuing research) about the efficacy of retirement programmes. Many claims are made to justify both PRE and particular course designs, our concern was to test these claims using the methods and techniques of evaluative research.

1.1. The Presentation of the Report

In writing this report, we have tried to achieve a balance between two objectives: first, an evaluation of the effectiveness of PRE meant a detailed statistical analaysis, a theme which occupies Section 3 of our report. Through the advice and assistance from our project steering committee we have tried to make this analysis as accessible as possible, believing that many of our findings illuminate the kind of problems currently facing PRE. Secondly, we have attempted to make a practical contribution to current thinking within the movement, a concern which occupies the final section of the report. Striking a balance between analysis and recommendations is never easy and it is undoubtedly the case that a greater proportion of research time has concentrated on questions of methodology and data analysis. However, we hope that our descriptions of the process of PRE and the suggestions concerning 'good practice', are seen as a positive contribution.

1.2. Current problems in retirement education

Throughout the research, we have been made aware of two crucial elements in the organisation of PRE: First, the voluntary element in the organisation of courses; secondly, the trend towards earlier retirement. Much of the impetus behind retirement education comes from a voluntary commitment from workers within the community. This aspect is most obviously true of the retirement councils, but it is also present in industry and education - responsibility for retirement education

often being adopted as a supplement to other work roles.
In writing this report we have tried to recognise the strength
of this voluntary commitment whilst, at the same time, acknowl-
edging the pressures to which it has been subjected. A product
of these pressures has been the current lack of enthusiasm for
experimenting with new programmes. Our interpretation of the
history of the movement is that after an initial period of
exploratory work (at Rubery Owen and elsewhere), the impetus
for innovation was lost. Instead, PRE became institutionalised
around a particular structure and pattern which was applied to
an increasingly heterogenous population entering retirement.

The problems faced by voluntary workers come from a number
of sources. In Britain at least, contributions to PRE from
adult education and the social sciences have been depressingly
few. As a consequence, the practice of retirement education has
evolved separately from theories and insights into how adults
learn and the type of attitudes which have developed towards
leaving full-time work. Financial resources have also been
disbursed on a limited scale, a feature which has encouraged
the development of short and unimaginative courses. Without the
stimulus of research and adequate financial resources, the
voluntary ideal has struggled to survive. Indeed, given the
second factor which has influenced our work - the growth in early
retirement - many organisers have been engulfed by a dramatic
upturn in demand.

Early retirement has affected our work in a number of ways.
At a practical level, we often had to work hard to identify
stable populations of men and women from which we could draw
our sample. Lists of retirement dates would quickly become out
of date as early retirement packages prompted many to withdraw
from work ahead of time. Moreover, we sometimes encountered
suspicion amongst employees about the nature of our work - PRE
being viewed as a method of softening the impact of labour
policies which discriminate against older workers.[2]

The phenomenon of early retirement also influenced our
thinking about the kind of courses which PRE needs to develop.
Thus, with increasing numbers of people retiring in their fifties,
major reforms are necessary in the way in which PRE organises its
work - changes which, as we observe in Section 4, will create a
range of course designs radically different from those currently
in use.

The problems created by PRE's isolation and the growth of
early retirement have been crucial to many of the observations
made in this report. Our work will inevitably be seen as a
critique of existing theories and methods within the movement.
However, we hope that our arguments will be taken as supporting
the aims and ideals of PRE, whilst, at the same time, urging
radical changes to the existing structure and content of
programmes.

We conclude this chapter with a cautionary point for the
reader. The central message of this report is for more research
on PRE and more experimental work in developing newtypes of
courses. Our discussion should be seen as a starting point for

a debate on making retirement education relevant for the 1980s.
We hope that people will use this report as a resource for
examining the problems they face in their own localities. We
do not offer immediate solutions to these problems. Instead,
we urge people to develop an attitude towards PRE which allows
for continual self-criticism and re-appraisal, this being a
significant way of improving and expanding the existing network
of provision.

CHAPTER 1

FOOTNOTES AND REFERENCES

1. The list of sponsoring organisations is given on page vii.

2. For a discussion on this issue see Oliver, C.
   Older Workers and Unemployment, Unemployment Alliance
   1982.

CHAPTER 2

PRE-RETIREMENT EDUCATION: THE BRITISH
AND AMERICAN EXPERIENCE

2.   INTRODUCTION

In this chapter we explore the historical background to
the development of pre-retirement education (PRE). We also
examine projects which have evaluated the effectiveness of
PRE, placing our own work within a broader (mainly North
American) research tradition. It will be argued that the
industrial and economic environment from which PRE emerged
has been crucial in influencing the development of courses.
To illustrate this view, material will be drawn from both
Britain and America (America being the first country to
organise preparation for retirement courses).[1]

2.1. The Origins of Pre-Retirement Education

Judgements about the value of retirement education are
closely related to a range of ideas about the relative value
of work and leisure. They are also connected to perspectives
on retirement itself, e.g. its costs to society, the benefits
to the individual. These perspectives are subject to considerable change, depending on fluctuations in the national
economy and the presence or absence of mass unemployment. As
historical studies of retirement have suggested, the immediate
post-war setting - in Britain at least - was one which
emphasised both the economic necessity of work (for the nation
and the individual) and the problems arising from 'too much
leisure'. Images of people 'dying in their armchairs', the
spectre of the 'sudden death syndrome', were part of a sustained
policy debate designed to encourage 'useful' work rather than an
'idle' retirement.[2]

It is against such a background that the early pre-retirement
courses were developed.[3] In this country, the first course
appeared in 1955 and in the same year a preparation for retirement
Study Group was established by the National Old People's Welfare
Council (now Age Concern). In 1956 the Rubery Owen Company
initiated their work on preparation for retirement, the first
course being held in 1958. Also in 1958, an experimental week-end
course was held by the NOPWC to test out ideas arising from the
work of the study group:

"The course was attended by twenty-eight resident members
and there were two non-resident speakers. The participants
came from widely differing walks of life. The programme
included a session on 'Planning to Enjoy Retirement' by
Dobson and Young, two talks on 'Employment and Retirement'
by Alastair Heron, a talk on 'Changes in Social Relations'
by Dr A.N. Oppenheim, one on 'The Spiritual Aspects of
Ageing' by the Rev. L.P.B. Pain, and a talk on 'Health in
Mind and Body' by Professor R.E. Tunbridge. Frequent
informal disucssions were held throughout the weekend on
the content of the talks, on the ways in which participants
spent their own leisure and on what they themselves thought
about the course".[4]

Even at this early stage there was some experimentation in respect of the timing of courses. At Rubery Owen, for example, work was concentrated on those at the age of 50, with provision for subsequent follow-up at 55, 60 and 64. By contrast, activities at the Glasgow Retirement Council (established in 1958), concentrated on workers within three months of retirement. According to Molly Heath: "This was not an attempt to change the 'cultural habit' or the 'attitudes' of the participants but to give them a boost to get them through the first months of retirement, when anxiety, depression and introspection might do infinite harm, and to give them all the practical, factual help they might require".[5]

These activities in England and Scotland had been preceded by work on preparation for retirement in America. From the late 1940s onwards there had developed an interest in providing educational programmes for retirees (the passing of the Social Security Act combined with the high numbers of younger people entering the labour market providing a convenient environment). A number of universities (Chicago and Michigan in particular) started offering information and advisory programmes for retirees, and this area was gradually adopted by some of the larger organisations. A survey by Tuckman and Lorge of the 113 largest concerns in the US posed the question: "Does your company have any programmes, formal or otherwise, to help prepare employees for the problems they will have to face upon retirement?" Of those responding, nearly 40 per cent claimed to have some type of programme already in operation.[6] Subsequent research was to confirm this growth in interest, although optimism was tempered by the limited scope of many of the programmes implemented.[7]

Description of this American work was provided in some of the early publications of the pre-retirement movement in this country;[8] and Molly Heath notes that an American course was used as a basis for the Rubery Owen programme.[9]

Notwithstanding the American influence there are some distinctive features about the British work on pre-retirement in the fifties and early sixties. For example, a network of voluntary advisory groups at national and local levels emerged to provide support for pre-retirement education. The NOWPC Study Group was to evolve into the Pre-Retirement Association of Great Britain and Northern Ireland - an important development in stimulating the growth of courses. As Woodrow Hunter remarked in the first cross-national study of pre-retirement education: "Nothing of this sort has developed in the US despite the fact that Americans have been in the business of pre-retirement education for a much longer period of time".[10]

Moreover, as Hunter's study concluded, British programmes were much less standardised than their American counterparts, and there was greater emphasis on viewing each new programme as an experiment in "objectives, content and method".[11] Yet despite these advantages British programmes developed in a hesitant way after the initial burst of activity. Only around five per cent of workers who retire every year receive a course.[12] Allin Coleman's survey of PRE in England and Wales summarised provision as "non-existent in some places, inadequate in others".[13] Public

knowledge about the existence of programmes remains deficient.[14]
Comparisons between British and American programmes show
British courses to be closer to the actual date of the individual's retirement and to have lower rates of employee participation.[15]   Finally, the sense of experimentation described by
Hunter was lost in the 1960s and 1970s, and a movement towards
greater standardisation in course design became apparent.

There are three main reasons for the modest development
of PRE in this country: (a) cultural resistance to retirement;
(b) the under-development of British social gerontology;
(c) economic conditions in post-war Britain. We shall now
discuss each of these factors.

2.2. Cultural Resistance to Retirement

Retirement has taken much longer to be accepted in Britain
than in American society (the reasons are complex but economic
differences - see below - may be of key importance). Whilst
in the US the growth of a retirement industry (books, educational
films, retirement communities) can clearly be identified in the
1950s (and even earlier), in this country it surfaces in a more
oblique way. In the fifties we were largely tied to a view of
old age as a period of peace and serenity, with elderly people
themselves being the object of vast charitable endeavours. The
publications of this period abound with phrases from Greek
philosophers testifying to the dignity of old age, but it is the
dignity of quiescence and acceptance of one's fate. The message
of an active retirement - outside occupational structures - took
much longer to penetrate and required more generous financial
provision before it could emerge.

2.3. The Under-Development of British Social Gerontology

In the fifties we find the development in the US of a
number of intellectual frameworks for understanding ageing and
retirement. Publications such as Cavan et al. on personal
adjustment[16] and Friedmann and Havighurst on the variety of
meanings attached to retirement,[17] explored the range of attitudes
and behaviours that might be encountered amongst older people.
On the other hand, in Great Britain, we find a more avowedly
pathological view concerning the 'burden' and 'anxiety' arising
from the loss of work.[18] Whilst undoubtedly accurate for a
substantial section of the retired population in the fifties,
this approach gave little indication that attitudes to retirement
might substantially alter (and that attendance at a pre-retirement course could itself be influential in this process).

These contrasting intellectual traditions had important
implications for PRE. The early American programmes (e.g.
those developed at the Univerities of Chicago and Michigan) drew
heavily on social scientists in those institutions who had pion-
eered research into social gerontology (e.g. Ruth Cavan, Robert
Havighurst and Clark Tibbitts). This relationship between PRE
and social science ultimately led to a number of projects
designed to evaluate the effectiveness of programmes (for early
examples see Burgess, Hunter and Mack).[19] In Britain, on the
other hand, PRE developed from a community and industrial base
(although key figures had an academic background); and in an

environment where the sociology of ageing was in its infancy. Without the input from the social sciences (and in a rather hostile economic climate) there developed disinclination to explore alternative course models or even to modify a pathological view of retirement. Within this context (and given the limited enthusiasm being expressed towards PRE) it was perhaps inevitable that questions about the value and effectiveness of courses should go unanswered. Unfortunately, when the economic and cultural environment did take more interest, it found a movement both insecure and lacking in direction - a product of nearly twenty years of isolation.

2.4. Economic Conditions in Post-War Britain

Economic factors may go some way to explaining the difficulties encountered by PRE. American industry, in the twenties and thirties, had come to view the older worker as a marginal element in the labour force - a combination of the technological environment (the spread of assembly line methods of production) and the recession, both of which fostered debates on how to remove the 'inefficient' older worker from industry.[20]

Despite the more favourable economic climate in the fities, a steady supply of younger workers meant there was little need radically to change the policy of discouraging older people from involvement in work. In Britain, however, we find a much clearer reversal of the policies of the depression years, with exhortations to the elderly to remain at work, an important aspect of labour policy. Underlying this were fears of a larger retired population acting as a burden upon the economy - a burden which would hold back the growth necessary for post-war reconstruction.[21]

2.5. PRE in the 1960s and 1970s

The interaction between the economic, sociological and cultural factors we have described, meant a hostile environment for the fledgling PRE movement. To sum up: although the spread of compulsory retirement and the growth of occupational pensions schemes made some form of PRE a necessity, external pressures were influential in depressing the spread and scope of courses.

On the positive side, in Britain, the local, regional and national organisation of PRE gradually consolidated its position;[22] publications such as Retirement Choice substantially increased their circulation;[23] the number of handbooks showing the way to an active retirement increased enormously;[24] and a large number of organisations have continued to demonstrate a keen commitment to PRE.

In America, where around 10 per cent of the labour force are served by programmes, PRE continued to expand throughout the sixties and seventies.[25] In 1964, and again in 1974, the Industrial Conference Board surveyed a cross-section of major corporations, examining the extent of pre-retirement assistance they made available. The 1964 survey indicated that such assistance was available in only 65 per cent of the companies surveyed (633 out of 974); in 1974, the figure was 88 per cent (704 of 800). Only 12 per cent of the companies surveyed offered no assistance, and these were largely firms with no pensions and/or a young work force.[26] However, these figures must be treated with caution. Commenting on this survey, Virginia Boyack noted that only one-quarter of the companies offered "in-depth pre-retirement programmes". She went on to argue: "Most companies offer only financial advice, as such relates to company benefits. Despite the increased emphasis which business and educational institutions are placing on sound planning for retirement, there is evidence that most employees start planning too late to provide themselves with the most effective option for their retirement years".[27]

Arguably, until PRE manages to demonstrate more clearly its value to the retiring worker, the modest growth in programmes is likely to continue.[28]

In this respect the slow growth of research into the effectiveness of courses remains a matter of concern. In Great Britain evaluation research in this field has been non-existent. In the US, however, a number of important studies have been carried out in the post-war period. What conclusions can be drawn from their findings?

2.6. Pre-Retirement Programmes - How Effective Are They?

This is not a question which can be answered in a definit-ive form. In Britain, the absence of evaluation studies has already been noted; in America, methodological defects in the studies which have been completed limit definite conclusions. Evaluation is also made difficult by the "confusion of goals" apparent in many programmes:

"...Typically....programmes are conceived and charged with... a ...counselling function (i.e. to change attitudes and promote adjustment) but the overwhelming majority are only brief lecture series which barely fulfil the function of disseminating useful information to participants. The existing programmes simply are not designed in terms of format or content to focus on basic attitude change, so it is unreasonable to condemn retirement preparation programmes for failure to achieve this goal".[29]

The above argument is supported in virtually all the evaluation studies. The work by Glamser and De Jong found that both a group discussion programme and an individual briefing approach were "generally ineffective in the area of attitude change".[30] Bowman's work at Drake University and Hunter's longitudinal research indicated a lack of sustained attitude change as a result of participation in a programme.[31] According to the latter:

"Most of the significant gains by experimental subjects were achieved during the first year of retirement and they tended to persist into retirement, but at a somewhat diminishing level of significance. Further study is needed to deter-mine whether gains of these sorts persist during the first five years of retirement or whether all subjects, those who participate and those who do not partic- ipate in a pre-retirement programme, eventually achieve equal levels of adjustment to retirement". [32]

Glamser returned to his subjects six years after initial contact and found no substantive differences between experi- mental and control groups.   He concluded that the impact of pre-retirement courses may be of short duration, with their primary value coming in the pre-retirement phase.[33]   More fundamentally, Charles was to question whether altered state- ments on questionnaires really did represent a change in behaviour.   Few studies, he felt, offer us any more evidence than "altered responses to questionnaires or test items". [34]

2.6.1. The Characteristics of Participants

One explanation for the apparent inability to document attitude change lies in the characteristics of people who attend courses.   Most participants are volunteers and may already have taken steps to prepare themselves for leaving work. Indeed, their factual knowledge about retirement issues may be considerable and they may already exhibit a high degree of adjustment to their retirement.[35]   In line with this, the research at Drake University suggested that individuals do not come to courses so much for new information: "as they do to have their thoughts, ideas, and current information confirmed by someone's expertise".[36]   Indeed, as Kasschau was to point out: "people with negative or neutral attitudes subject to potential influence are simply unlikely to expose themselves to the programme".[37] Confirmation of these points came in a study by Cokinda of the differences between participants and non-participants to the Chrysler-UAW programme in Michigan. Among the findings were that males tended to participate more than females; that participants had a higher level than non-partici- pants of formal education; that less-skilled personnel tended towards non-participation.   Participants were also much more like- ly to have heard about the programme before receiving their letter of introduction and to have already started making plans and thinking about retirement several years ahead.[38]

The problem for course tutors and lectures is that if they operate on the assumption - as many do - that very few people in the class will have done anything about their retirement, they may simply present information which is already known to the worker. On the other hand, attempting within the same group to cater both for those with substantial knowledge about retirement and those who have given it little thought poses significant educational dilemmas.

2.7. Structure and Content

Remarkably little is known about the role of factors such as length of course in helping to change retirement attitudes. Lorna Hubbard, one of the pioneers in the pre-retirement field, has suggested that intensive courses run the risk of inform- ation overload, whilst those run at weekly intervals allow both for a better absorption of information and time to discuss the implications with family and colleagues.   A day seminar, on the other hand, she sees as a useful stimulant for further

enquiry by the individual e.g. via public libraries and
retirement councils. We do not, however, have systematic
evidence on these areas.[39] Those constructing courses more
often choose a particular structure according to available
resources or existing training procedures, as opposed either
to educational criteria or the wishes of their retirees.

Another important area - one which has attracted much
comment - concerns the social composition of pre-retirement
classes. One line of argument suggests splitting courses
along occupational lines because of variations in financial
resources and because of conflicts in experiences and expectations amongst men and women from different social classes.
Walker, in his study for the Tennessee Valley Authority, found
that there was some objection to top management being grouped
with others, since lower-level salaried personnel "seemed
inhibited by their presence".[40] Hunter concluded that the
experiences of American programmes indicated that group homogeneity encouraged participation.[41] In this country, on the
other hand, there is a stronger tendency to open courses to
all layers of personnel, arguing that conflict between groups
within the organisation can be resolved within the atmosphere
of the pre-retirement class.[42] Again, we need some basic
research on this area. It might be argued that the lower
take-up of British courses[43] reflects an unwillingness on the
part of some employees to discuss matters of finance, personal
relationships, etc. with people who have been in positions of
authority over him/her for much of their working life.

Limitations regarding the form in which material is
presented is another problem area in PRE. Since the 1950s,
when Alastair Heron's six points were developed, there has
been remarkably little innovation in this area.[44] The six
points (presented in the form of six or seven lectures) still
form the foundation of numerous courses in this country and,
despite the utility of this type of approach, it seems
surprising that more development has not occurred. Research
work in this area has emphasised the merits of discussion
programmes and the use of learning modules. Molly Heath, for
example, in a British study, has put the case for:

"More flexibility and innovation in the design of
courses, so as to promote active learning: modular
forms, for example, with sections spaced out over time
and held in different places; planned transitions from
the security of work-based courses to the more open
stimulus of an educational centre; personal and independent counselling to reinforce the discoveries and self-
assessments made on a course; elements of self-programmed
learning as a step towards personal autonomy. All these
are present somewhere, if only in embryo; they need to be
generalised".[45]

Innovation along these lines will require, however, a
substantial degree of commitment towards pre-retirement education - much more than is needed when operating a simple standardised course. How far companies will be willing to give this
degree of commitment remains uncertain.

2.8. The Benefit of Pre-Retirement Education

So far attention has been drawn to the rather negative findings of research work. However, the picture is not entirely gloomy. Even if the findings are unequivocal in showing the failure of PRE to have any significant impact on attitudes, more positive results are found if we look at its ability to give individuals a greater sense of confidence about their future life. According to Virginia Boyack:

"Pre-retirement planning programmes can provide the individual with insights and awareness so as to avoid the potential 'role shock' and subsequent demoralisation that follows an abrupt termination of major roles associated with earning a living. Further, a pre-retirement programme may provide an individual with his or her first exposure to serious consideration of retirement living problems. It has been found that, after participating in a planning programme, respondents reported less concern about: financial insecurity; contact with friends; boredom in retirement; and growing old".[46]

Hunter's longitudinal study, although containing the reservations about long term attitude change noted earlier, credited the programme with: "...having had a significant effect of reducing dissatisfaction with retirement, of reducing worry over health, and in encouraging participants to engage in all kinds of actitivities including social activities with family and friends".[47]

Glamser's longitudinal research also concluded that pre-retirement programmes seemed to have little significant impact on the subsequent experience of retirement. However, he suggested that there was still a strong case in favour of PRE:

"Upon programme completion, a solid majority of the participants in both (discussion and individual briefing) groups reported feeling better as a result of the programme, and nearly 90 per cent felt that their respective programme was helpful as a way of preparing for retirement. This would seem to indicate that most older workers desire assistance in preparing for retirement, and they appreciate such assistance when it is rendered. Thus, the true value of retirement preparation programmes appears to lie in the help that can be provided when it is needed - during the pre-retirement stage".[48]

2.9. Policy Recommendations

Arising out of research described above there have been various proposals aimed at improving both the effectiveness and the quality of courses. Such proposals are particularly important given the increase in the number of employees who see it as company policy to help prepare them for retirement;[49] and the continuing problem of low take-up on many courses (particularly those in Britain).

2.9.1. Increasing Effectiveness

A central argument in proposals for increasing effectiveness concerns the timing of courses. Rives and Siegel,
for example, see the time-frame of British programmes as
alarmingly short. They contend that:

"Psychological adjustment often requires a lengthy
time period, and employees certainly begin to
concern themselves with the transition to retirement
well before its actual occurrence .... Organisations
surveyed in this study seem well aware of the need for
an early start to retirement preparation. Yet over
half of them introduced employees to pre-retirement
programmes within only one year of retirement". [50]

The argument for widening the time-frame of courses
has led to a range of proposals. We find Rives and Siegel
urging organisations to make "greater efforts to initiate
preliminary counselling well before retirement and to continue counselling for an extended time period". [51] With this
approach, then, the 'one-off' course would be abandoned, and
a much longer transitional period would be built into the
preparation programme. These proposals might also be linked
to the emergence of phased retirement and to a range of
occupational policies designed to improve the conditions
experienced by older workers.[52] In sociological terms, they
represent a broadening in the transitional period, a structural
change which may reduce the psychological trauma of retirement
as an immediate and sudden departure from the world of work.

Such suggestions, although still relatively under-
developed in practical terms, involve rather less problems
as regards implementation than other policy proposals. Although
adopting a scheme of phased retirement and extending counselling over the final year at work may cause some organisational
difficulties, considerable benefits may be gained in respect
of removing anxiety about retirement and reducing the workload
of personnel departments.

More controversial, however, are research findings which
suggest bringing retirement planning back to middle-life and
even earlier. Kasschau cites a number of authorities recommending retirement preparation 15-20 years ahead of the event;
and research at Drake University suggested the age range 56-57
as the most influential time for changing attitudes.[53] In
Britain, Arthur Stock has suggested that the type of life-style
developed in early middle-age (between 35 and 40) is crucial
for the wellbeing of the individual during retirement and old
age. He argues:

"This is the phase when new interests which will be
vital for personal independence and flexibility in
later years should be carefully nurtured. Indeed this
is the stage when true 'pre-retirement courses' should
begin - though not necessarily labelled as such - and
certainly not concentrating, as some for the 60 year
olds do, on a series of first-aid measures for the
imminently disadvantaged". [54]

But the implications of these arguments - for individuals and for organisations - are immense. At the ages of 40 or 50 individuals may be unreceptive to discussions about their retirement, particularly where:

(a) they still view themselves as climbing the occupational ladder;

(b) they see it as an attempt by the organisation to impose early retirement.

For the organisation, policies designed to assistant adjustment to retirement (e.g. relating jobs to physical capacities and mental changes) may demand huge upheavels if implemented in mid-life. Indeed, they may pose fundamental issues about the direction and philosophy of a firm's labour and welfare policies. Existing research can only give limited guidelines as to how recommendations for planning at mid-life can be implemented. Without more detailed work it seems unlikely that, in Britain at least, the development of such courses will take place on any large scale (although the spread of early retirement may stimulate a modest increase).

2.9.2. Improving the Quality of Courses

A number of points have emerged in respect of improving the quality of courses. One consistent theme concerns the need to base courses more directly around the needs and wishes of those participating. The argument here is against the standardisation of programmes, with a suggestion that control over course design should be devolved towards the retirees' themselves. O'Rourke and Friedman, for example, feel that the failure of many courses to produce predicted changes in knowledge and attitude is partly due to the repetition of facts already known to the participants. They argue:

"The attitudes of workers towards retirement and their levels of knowledge about retirement should be ascertained before a training programme is contructed. In this way, the programme content may be designed for and aimed at those areas of attitudes and knowledge most critical for the worker".[55]

This argument cuts across existing practice whereby a set formula once developed and found "successful" is repeated over a number of years, despite changes in the attitudes and material circumstances of retirees. However, in the attempt to 'democratise' pre-retirement education, it will be essential to give a key role to the Trade Unions and to shop stewards within factories and offices. Hitherto, these groups have often been excluded in the development of programmes, a factor which partly explains the suspicion and lack of enthusiasm with which pre-retirement is often greeted.

2.10. The Role of Trade Unions in Pre-Retirement Education

It is sometimes suggested that the slow development of PRE can be partly attributed to the limited interest shown by trade unions. This viewpoint needs, however, to be questioned. It is true that the early history of retirement education provides

examples of union hostility towards towards programmes. In
America, for example, Breckenridge, writing in the early
1950s, noted that: "Opposition to programmes of preparation
for retirement is sometimes encountered from representatives
of labour unions because they associate programmes of such
preparation with the implementation of compulsory retirement
policies". [56] However, American trade unions were also
amongst the first organisations to initiate programmes (e.g.
the United Automobile Workers, the International Association
of Machinists and the Upholsterers International Union). In
the case of Britain, the 1971 TUC Congress adopted a resolution
calling for the development of educational facilities: "to
ensure that workers nearing retirement are able to prepare for
this during the later period of their employment".[57] More
recently, USDAW's research and economics department has issued
a paper discussing elements of a union policy for retirement.
The paper argued that: "Facilities to prepare for retirement
should be the right of every member of staff. Both Management
and Union should positively encourage staff to attend a course,
regardless of initial reluctance on the part of the member of
staff and regardless of them being 'indispensable'".[58] ASTMS
has an agreement on preparation for retirement (signed with
APEX) covering staff at its head and district offices. Amongst
the provisions are: "The Association will make known to
employees the details or source of details of TUC, WEA, local
authority and any other courses which may be available to assist
people in preparing for retirement .... (and) will meet the
course fees, travelling and subsistence expenses in connection
with courses on, for example, handicrafts, languages or hobbies,
which may not be directly related to retirement training".[59]

Despite these initiatives there remains an underlying
tension between trade unions and the pre-retirement movement.
We can cite three main reasons for this: first, in respect of
their older members, the dominant concern of trade unions has
been with securing improvements to state and occupational
pensions (the work of the T and GWU has been particularly import-
in this area); barring significant improvements to the state
pension this emphasis is likely to continue.

Secondly, the organisation of PRE may have discouraged
active involvement by trade unions. Inside companies, PRE
is usually regarded as the concern of welfare, personnel or
training departments. Representatives from these departments
will usually organise programmes and suggest any changes to
their structure or content. Trade unions may only have peripheral
involvement in this process, a fact which may reinforce any
initial suspicion about retirement education.

Thirdly, the pressure of early retirement and unemployment
has created problems for the image of PRE. Is it a genuine
attempt to provide support for those faced with a difficult
period of adjustment? Or for those seeking information about
state or occupational pensions? Alternatively, is it a measure
designed to sweeten the pill of compulsory or premature
retirement? In a period when considerable growth in PRE might
have been envisaged, cynicism remains about the value and
effectiveness of programmes: doubts which have been sharpened
in a context of job insecurity.

2.11. Conclusion: The Historical Experience of Retirement Education

The problems faced by retirement education must
be related to our earlier discussion on the historical background. When retirement education first emerged, relatively
few people left work before the statutory retirement age.
Moreover, attitudes towards retirement were, at least in
British society, still fairly negative. As late as 1968,
for example, a major cross-national survey of older people
(Shanas et al.) found that the British working class failed
both to miss work or to enjoy anything about retirement.[60]
In this environment, then, the relatively modest form taken
by PRE was in line with the low aspirations of many retirees.
The situation now, however, is rather different. Whilst the
courses in the 1950s and 1960s were homogeneous in terms of
the age, sex and attitudes of course members, courses in
the 1980s will be far more heterogeneous, with a mixture
of early- and normal-age retirees, a large number of women
participants, and a greater spread of attitudes, from the
highly positive to the highly negative. There is little
doubt that this will represent a highly unstable mixture,
and that unless major changes are made, in course content
and structure, there will be increased dissatisfaction with
PRE. A constructive response to this problem will, however,
require the integration of PRE with both adult education and
the social sciences. Retirement education must develop a
theory and practice based upon the kind of teaching methodology best suited to those in mid-life and older and an
understanding of the sociology and psychology of retirement.
The application of these areas could do much to transform
the existing shape of PRE. We shall explore this theme in
more depth in later chapters of this report.

CHAPTER 2

<u>FOOTNOTES AND REFERENCES</u>

1. An earlier version of this chapter appeared in <u>Ageing and Society</u>, Vol.1, Part 3, 1981, pp. 393-413.

2. For an analysis of the emergence of retirement see Phillipson, C., <u>Capitalism and the Construction of Old Age</u>, MacMillan Books, 1982; for an American study see Graebner, W.A. <u>History of Retirement</u>, Yale University Press, 1980.

3. For descriptions of the development of the Rubery Owen course see Heron, A., <u>Preparation for Retirement: Solving New Problems</u>, NCSS, London, 1961; Heath, M., Pre-Retirement Courses as an Instrument of Self-Fulfilment in Retirement, M.Ed. (University of Manchester 1976).

4. National Old Peoples' Welfare Council, <u>Preparation for Retirement or Adjusting to Ageing,</u> NCSS, 1959.

5. Heath, M., <u>op. cit.</u>, pp. 16-17.

6. Tuckman, J. and Lorge, I., "Retirement Practices in Business and Industry", <u>Journal of Gerontology</u>, Vol.7. 1952.

7. See Wermel, M.T. and Beidemann, G.M., <u>Retirement Preparation Programs: a study of company responsibilities</u>, Californian Institute of Technology, Industrial Relations Section, 1961; Franke, W.H., "Preparing Workers for Retirement", <u>ILIR Bulletin</u>, No.27, University of Illinois Bulletin, Vol.59, No. 53., 1962; Siegel, S.R. and Rives, J.M., "Characteristics of Existing and Planned Pre-Retirement Programs", <u>Aging and Work</u>, Spring, 1978.

8. See Groombridge, B., <u>Education and Retirement</u>, National Institute of Adult Education, 1960; Heron, A., <u>op.cit.</u>

9. Heath, M., <u>op. cit.</u>

10. Hunter, W., <u>A Cross National Appraisal of Pre-Retirement Education,</u> Division of Gerontology and the Institute of Labor and Industrial Relations, The University of Michigan, Ann Arbor, 1965, pp.55.

11. Hunter, W., <u>ibid</u>, pp.78-80.

12. <u>Growing Older</u>, Command 8173, HMSO, 1981.

13. Coleman, A. edited by Groombridge, J., <u>Preparation for Retirement in England and Wales: A National Survey,</u> National Institute of Adult Education in association with the Pre-Retirement Association, 1982.

14. Parker, S., Older Workers and Retirement, OPCS, HMSO, 1980.

15. Rives, J.M. and Siegel, S.R., "Out to Grass: A Transatlantic Look at Pre-Retirement Programmes", <u>Personnel Management</u>, February, 1980.

16. Cavan, R.S., et al., _Personal Adjustment in Old Age_, Science Research Associates, 1949.

17. Friedmann,E. and Havighurst, R.J., _The Meaning of Work and Retirement_ ", University of Chicago Press, 1954.

18. See, for example, Townsend, P., "The Anxieties of Retirement", _Transactions of the Association of Industrial Medical Officers_, April, 1955; Anderson, W. F. and Cowan, N., "Work and Retirement: Influences on the Health of Older Men", _Lancet_, December 29th, 1956.

19. Burgess, E. W., _A Case Study of a Retirement Preparation Program_, Chicago Plan, U.S. Department of Health Education and Welfare, 1961; Hunter, W., "Preparation for Retirement of Hourly Wage Employees in Niagara Falls", New York: University of Michigan, Division of Gerontology, _mimeo_, 1957; Mack, M. "An Evaluation of a Retirement Planning Program", _Journal of Gerontology_, Vol. 13, pp.198-202, 1958.

20. See Howe, R., "Industry and the Aged", _Harvard Business Review_, Vol. 8, 1934.

21. This theme is illustrated by _Report of the Royal Commission on Population_, Command 7695, HMSO, 1949; see also the Phillips' Committee, _Economic and Financial Problems of the Provision for Old Age_, Command 9333, HMSO, 1954.

22. Membership of the Pre-Retirement Association by companies and other organisations stood at 100 in 1969; by 1980 this had grown to 477. Membership by individuals in this period has grown from 101 to 1,144.

23. Pre-Retirement Choice magazine was launched in 1972 with a circulation of 10,000. By April 1980 this had reached 110,000.

24. For two recent examples, see Kemp, F. and Buttle, B., _Focus on Retirement_, Kogan Page, 1979; Erskine, A., _The Time of Your Life_, Help the Aged in association with the Health Education Council, 3rd edition, 1982.

25. The figure of 10 per cent is given by Monk, A. and Donavon, R.,in "Pre-Retirement Preparation Programmes", _Aged Care and Services Review_, Vol. 1, No. 5/6, 1978-79, pp.1-7.

26. Ossafsky, R., "Retirement Preparation: A Needed Addition to the Pension Plan", _Urban Social Change Review_, Vol. 10, No. 2, 1977.

27. Boyack, V. L., "Preparation for Retirement: Crisis or Challenge?" _Testimony to the US House of Representatives Select Committee on Aging_, Subcommittee on Retirement Income and Employment, Washington, 1978.

28. For information on the European scene see: Council of Europe, _Preparation for Retirement_, Strasbourg, 1977; Gilmore, S., _Report on Educational Aspects of Preparation for Retirement in the European Economic Community_, Department of Continuing Education, University of Stirling, 1978.

29. See Kasschau, P., "Re-evaluating the need for retirement preparation programs", _Industrial Gerontology_, Winter, 1974. pp. 42-55.

30. Glamser, F. and DeJong, G., "The Efficacy of Pre-Retirement Prepara-

tion Programs for Industrial Workers", <u>Journal of Gerontology</u>, Vol. 30, No. 5, 1975, p.600.

31. Bowman, D. L., <u>A Longitudinal Comparison of Attitudes and Activity Involvement of Persons who have Completed a Pre-Retirement Planning Program</u>, Ph.D. Thesis, Iowa State University, 1974.

32. Hunter, W., <u>A Longitudinal Study of Pre-Retirement Education</u>, Division of Gerontology, University of Michigan, 1968.

33. Glamser, F., "The Impact of Pre-Retirement Programs on the Retirement Experience", <u>Journal of Gerontology</u>, Vol. 36, No. 2, pp.244-250, 1981.

34. Charles, D.W., "Effect of Participation in a Pre-Retirement Program", <u>The Gerontologist</u>, Vol. 11, No. 1, 1971., pp. 24 - 28.

35. O'Rourke, J. and Friedman, H., "An Inter-Union Pre-Retirement Training Program: Results and Commentary", <u>Industrial Gerontology</u>, Spring, 1972., pp. 49 - 64.

36. Drake University Pre-Retirement Planning Center, <u>op.cit.</u>, p.34.

37. Kasschau, P., <u>op.cit.</u>, p.34.

38. Cokinda, R. M., <u>An identification of differences between participating and non-participating automobile workers in a pre-retirement program</u>, Ph.D. dissertation, Wayne State University, 1974.

39. Hubbard, L., "Too Little, Too Late", <u>Industrial Society</u>, July-August, 1979, pp.5-6.

40. Walker, R. W., <u>An evaluation of a pre-retirement planning program - the TVA experience</u>, Ph.D. dissertation, Cornell University, Ithica, New York, 1959.

41. Hunter, W., "Pre-Retirement Education and Planning", in Grabowski, S. M., and Mason, W. D., (Eds.), <u>Learning for Aging</u>, Adult Education Association of the USA and ERIC Clearinghouse on Adult Education, 1974.

42. Benson, B., "Banking on a Successful Retirement", <u>Choice</u>, March, 1981, p.85.

43. Rives, J. M., and Siegel, S. R., <u>op. cit.</u>

44. For a re-examination of the Six Points, see Heron, A., "Preparation for Retirement: Some Crucial Problems", in <u>Preparation for Retirement - its Significance and Present Status in Europe</u>, Norwegian Institute of Gerontology, Oslo, 1978.

45. Heath, M., "Education for Retirement - Objectives and Practice", <u>Studies in Adult Education</u>, Vol. 11, No. 1, 1979.

46. Boyack, V. L., <u>op.cit.</u>

47. Hunter, W., 1968, <u>op.cit.</u>, p.43.

48. Glamser, F., <u>op.cit.</u>, p.44.

49. See Fillenbaum, G., "Retirement Planning Programs - At What Age and for Whom? <u>The Gerontologist</u>, Vol 11, No. 1, 1971; Greene, M.R., et al.

<u>Pre-Retirement Counselling, Retirement Adjustment and the Older Employee</u>, University of Oregon, Graduate School of Management 1969; McGoldrick, A., <u>Early Retirement</u>, Department of Management Sciences, UMIST, 1979.

50. Rives, J. M., and Siegel, S. R., <u>op. cit.</u>, p.44.

51. Ibid., p.44.

52. Council of Europe, <u>op. cit.</u>

53. Bowman, D. L., et al., <u>How Pre-Retirement Planning Works</u>, Drake University Pre-Retirement Planning Centre, Des Moines, 1970.

54. Stock, A., "Learning in Later Life: A Life-Cycle Approach to Educational Provision", Paper to the British Association for the Advancement of Science: Symposium on Ageing, September, 1977.

55. See, for example, O'Rourke, J., and Friedman, H., <u>op. cit.</u>, p.61.

56. Breckenridge E. L., <u>Effective Use of Older Workers</u>, Wilcox and Follet, 1953, (reprinted Arno Press, 1980), p.154.

57. <u>Industrial Relations Review and Report No. 108</u>, July, 1975, p.7.

58. USDAW, <u>Research Bulletin</u>, No. 4, August, 1980, p.6.

59. <u>Industrial Relations Review and Report No. 270</u>, April, 1982, p.16.

60. Shanas, E., <u>Old People in Three Industrial Societies</u>, Routledge and Kegan Paul, 1968.

CHAPTER 3

EVALUATING PRE-RETIREMENT EDUCATION:
A REVIEW OF RESEARCH METHODS

3.   INTRODUCTION

In our review of the literature, we noted the methodological defects of many of the American evaluation studies. The main problems we can cite are: (1) no control groups; (2) self-selected samples in the research designs; (3) no longitudinal element to examine long-term effects (Table 3:1 lists the design of some of the main studies). In the Keele survey we considered a variety of approaches to meet these criticisms. The purpose of this chapter is to describe how the research methodology was developed, how the courses were selected and the advantages and disadvantages of particular approaches to the research.

3.1. Prospective or Retrospective Research?

The basic concern of the study was to evaluate the effectiveness of a range of retirement programmes. We initially debated whether to select a group of people already retired (for a period of, for example, five years), and examine whether their involvement in PRE had affected their experience of retirement (a retrospective design). Alternatively, we could follow groups of subjects forward in time, assessing the impact of PRE during the transition to retirement (a prospective design).

The arguments in favour of a retrospective design were as follows:

(1)   Control groups would be easier to form with a retrospective model.

(2)   By looking at individuals who have experienced at least five years retirement, we can examine the benefit of PRE for long-term adjustment.

(3)   By concentrating on the long-term effects of PRE we would avoid the disturbance created by the initial impact of retirement.

In the case of PRE we could simply compare attenders with non-attenders within a number of private and nationalised firms. Moreover, our close involvement with a range of companies (some of whom were financing the research), meant that access was available to lists of retired employees.

On the other hand, there were a number of arguments in favour of a prospective design:

(1) A retrospective design would have raised complex problems of data analysis, with the interpretation of results being threatened by a range of confounding variables. In practice, it would be difficult to separate the effect of the course from long-term changes in income, health and family relationships.

TABLE 3:1 METHODOLOGY OF SELECTED PRE STUDIES*

	MILLER (1973)	MACK (1958)	HUNTER (1957)	CHARLES (1971)	BOLTON (1976)	FITZPATRICK (1979)	BURGESS (1960)	TIBERI et al (1978)	BOWMAN (1974)	HUNTER (1968)	GLAMSER (1973, 1981)
PRE-TEST		✓	✓	✓	✓	✓	✓	✓	✓	✓	✓
POST-TEST	✓	✓	✓	✓	✓	✓	✓	✓	✓	✓	✓
CONTROL GROUP							✓	✓		✓	✓
LONG-TERM EVALUATION									✓	✓	✓
RANDOM ALLOCATION											

* See Appendix 5 for a list of these studies.

(2) A retrospective design would need to rely on memory of the early period of retirement. However, there may be a tendency to repress difficulties which were experienced during this period.

(3) Our basic concern was with studying the effect of courses currently available in the U.K. In most instances, attitude change will not be a primary element in the conduct of these programmes. A more substantial concern is the provision of information relevant to the change-over from work to retirement. Such information may have long-term benefits. However, the main impact is likely to be in the first months of retirement, when major decisions on finance, health and leisure are likely to be made.

(4) There is considerable uncertainty about the long-term effects of PRE. Indeed, the two longitudinal studies which have been completed (by Hunter in the 1960s and Glamser in the 1970s) produced negative conclusions on this issue. The empirical grounds for concentrating on long term effects were, therefore, open to question.

The problem of confounding variables and the possibility of no long-term effects, led us to reject the retrospective design. Instead, we decided to focus on the transition to retirement, following a group of subjects in their last year(s) at work and their first year of retirement. In this way we specified the minimum which we might expect from PRE. We said that rather than assist long-term adjustment, it should help preparation for the transfer from full-time work. In particular, individuals should feel more knowledgeable about retirement issues; feel more optimistic about the immediate future; have greater confidence about their ability to plan. If retirement programmes were unsuccessful in these areas, we argued that it was even less likely they would influence the broader question of retirement adjustment.

3.2. The Selection of Courses

Table 3:2 provides details of the courses evaluated in this study. The choice of programmes was influenced by a number of factors. Some of the organisations who contributed to the finance of the research wished to have their own courses evaluated. However, we also attempted to provide organisations and courses who could give a contrast to this group. In addition programmes were especially selected to provide a basis for an experimental approach (see below) to our work.

In terms of the structure, content and organisation of the eight programmes, they reflect dominant features of PRE nationally (this is confirmed by Allin Coleman's survey of retirement preparation[1]). A criticism that could be made of our selection is that it doesn't include a representative from the educational sector. However, some work was already being done in this area (e.g. John McCallum's research on

WEA provision[2]). Allin Coleman's work was itself likely to
provide a commentary on the quality of work in this sector.
Indeed, his final report indicated that the educational and
occupational groups were remarkably similar in terms of
programme structure, content, type of speaker, degree of
audience participation and reliance on the lecture-model.

Before outlining the type of designs used in our
research, we shall give a brief sketch of each of the eight
courses which were studied:

Bristol Retirement Council

The Retirement Council was formed in 1973 on the
initiative of the local Rotary Club. During 1980/81 it ran
a total of 54 courses, both single company programmes and
'open' courses, where participants are from a variety of
industrial and commercial organisations. We concentrated on
the latter courses for this research. The bulk of the Council's
programmes run for two or three consecutive days. There is a
strong belief in the value of mixing people of different back-
grounds and an attempt is also made to include partners on
courses.

British Airways

The history of PRE inside British Airways dates back to
1968. By 1978 the organisation was running 11 courses per
year with between 40 and 50 people attending each programme.
Since that point there has been an unprecedented rise in the
number of retirements inside British Airways, a by-product
of a major contraction within the airline industry. During
1980-81, 1833 retirees attended 28 courses (an average of 65.5
per course). In the following year, 2740 people attended 41
courses (an average of 66.8 per course). The programmes we
evaluated were those for ground staff and had a duration of
two days.

EMI (in co-operation with Legal and General)

This was the only one of our firms which did not have a
background of running courses prior to our research. With the
co-operation of the Legal and General Assurance Limited we ran
three two-day programmes as part of a randomised trial of the
effectiveness of PRE

Mars

Counselling for retirement dates back to the early 1960s
at Mars. In 1972 the company introduced a three-day course
offered three years before the individual's retirement. A
further development in 1979 was the introduction, 10.5 years
before retirement, of a half-day course concentrating on
financial planning. In 1980 the three-day course was reduced
to two days. Men and women from all occupational grades
attend the courses; partners, however, are not invited.

TABLE 3:2 : COURSES STUDIED

	B.A.	BRISTOL	EMI	MARS	NCB	SHELL	GLASGOW	JAGUAR
Length of course	2 Days	2 Days	2 Days	2 Days	3 Days	6 Days	7 Days	8 Days
Course Organiser	B.A.	Bristol Ret'nt Council	Legal & Gen-eral	Mars	Notts Pre-Ret'nt Council	Shell	Scottish Ret'nt Council	Jaguar
How close to ret-irement?	Final Year	Mostly final year.	Final Year.	3 Years	Mostly Final Year.	1 Year – 18 mnth.	Mostly Final Year.	Final Year.
Grades of workers	All Grades	All Grades	All Grades	All Grades	All Grades	Junior or Senior	All Grades	All Grades
Sex	Men + Women	Men + Women	Men + Women	Men + Women	Men	Men + Women	Men	Men + Women

National Coal Board (NCB)

This was a three-day course for miners employed in the South Nottingham area of the National Coal Board. The programme is run by the Nottingham and District Pre-Retirement Council (see Chapter 4 for further details).

Shell International

We evaluated a six day course run by the company for employees with salaries below £10,000 (see Chapter 5 for further details).

Scottish Retirement Council

This was a seven day course spread over seven weeks, participants being drawn from a number of small and medium sized firms in the Glasgow area (see Chapter 6 for further details).

Jaguar Cars

This was our longest course (eight sessions spread over an equivalent number of weeks). Participants were drawn from three Jaguar factories in the Coventry area. Partners are invited to the final session of the course.

3.2.1. The eight retirement programmes: a brief commentary

In Table 3.2. we set out the structure and content of our eight programmes. As the table suggests, they vary in contact time - from 13 hours (Mars and Bristol) to 50 hours (Scotland), in methods of presentation and in their content. Some of the programmes (e.g. British Airways) concentrate almost exclusively on disseminating factual information (about pension rights, taxation and investments). Others include a focus upon personal adjustment to retirement, with contributions, for example, from a psychologist on the Shell course and a sociologist on the Bristol course. The amount of information provided on social and leisure activities also varied, with the courses at Jaguar and Scottish Retirement Council devoting a considerable proportion of their time to this area. Only one of our courses (Shell) allowed specific periods for open discussion. In most cases lectures were relied upon as the medium for transmitting information, with a short period for discussion and question time at the end of the session. The implicit assumption on most of the courses was that participants would require relatively little help in following a 40-50 minute lecture. Only two of the programmes had active chairmen. The majority made only rudimentary use of visual aids.[3]

One final observation: most of the courses took place on company-owned premises usually in a seminar or training room. The one exception was the Scottish Retirement Council who used a Further Education College in Glasgow (the term Glasgow course is used to indicate this location).

3.3. Problems in Research Design

Given our perspective for reviewing the influence of PRE on the transition to retirement, our basic research design was as follows:-

$$O_1 \qquad X \qquad O_2 \qquad O_3$$

(First interview 2 weeks before the course).   Course   (Second inter-view, 4 weeks after the course).   (Third inter-view, 6-9 months into retirement).

The first interview gave us vital data on the attitudes of individuals before their programme; in this way, it provided baseline material against which the effects of PRE could be measured. We followed Glamser's research in allowing a four week interval between the course and the second interview. We hoped that this would give sufficient time for individuals to reflect on the value of their experience, enabling us to assess any initial action they may have taken in response to the course. Ideally, we would have liked our final interview further into retirement, thus providing a better assessment of the impact of leaving work. However, this was not possible given the constraint of the $3\frac{1}{2}$ year period available for the research. In most cases, there was a gap of 12-18 months between the second and third interview, this allowed us to collect information on the medium-term response to PRE.

The above design was applied to six of our eight groups. For two of our groups we restricted our work to just a pre- and post-test. In the case of the group at Mars, very few would have reached retirement age by the third interview. At Jaguar, we had already had problems of attrition between Phases 1 and 2. Because of this we decided against risking an even smaller sample at the third interview.

Six out of the eight groups were uncontrolled, consisting only of individuals who had received a pre-retirement course. There are a number of criticisms that can be made of this type of design:[4]

(1) Events other than the course may influence the result, e.g. retirement policies may change in significant ways between the course and the final interview; this may make it difficult to disentangle the effects of the course from wider social changes.

(2) There is the problem of maturation. Individual attit-udes may change as a function of the passage of time. In our research, a more positive set of attitudes in the final interview may be the product of particip-ation on a course; alternatively, they could reflect a softening in attitudes through the initial exper-ience of retirement.

(3) There is the effect of testing; in particular the experience gained through the pre-test (first inter-view) may influence the result of further tests (i.e. the second and third interviews).

To overcome some of these problems, we employed both quasi-experimental and experimental designs. Although the former removes most of the problems described above, important differences may still exist between the courses and control subjects. These may lead to different rates of change on important variables during the period of research. In an experimental design, subjects are randomly assigned to the course and control groups; differences on extraneous variables should thus arise only through chance. Randomisation increases our confidence in making causal inferences relating to the experience of a course and changes in knowledge levels and confidence about planning. However, it does not remove all the difficulties faced by the researcher:

"Random assignment creates focused inequalities between the ways various individuals are treated. This may exacerbate pressures on either the experimentals or controls to act atypically. Such pressures (e.g. compensatory rivalry) can obscure true differences or create effects in the control group (i.e. resentful demoralization) that may be misinterpreted as effects in the treatment group. Though random assignment does serve to make most things equal between the different experimental groups - so that selection, selection-maturation, regression, and the like are equal in each group - it does not necessarily make all things equal. The case for random assignment has to be made on the grounds that it is better than the available alternatives for inferring cause and not on the grounds that it is perfect for inferring cause".[5]

Nonetheless, it was hoped that with a range of research designs (including randomisation), we could make more accurate statements about the effectiveness of PRE generally, as well as different types of programmes.

3.4. The Development of an Experimental Approach

One of the objectives of the research was to survey a range of educational programmes. However, this had to be done via an experimental approach, with the formation of control groups of subjects. The need for a survey meant that the research embraced a wide range of institutions; by contrast, the rigour of an experimental approach imposed limitations on the number of suitable organisations. As Table 3:1 indicates, very few evaluation studies in PRE had used control subjects (none on a random basis). Given both ethical and organisation-al problems connected with an experimental design, we decided to restrict this aspect of our work to a minority of organis-ations in our total sample.

British Airways and EMI were companies where we attempted a random allocation of subjects. In the case of British Airways, the very large number of people retiring each year aroused hopes that a randomised trial of PRE might be possible. Our approach was to interview male and female subjects - based at London, Heathrow - retiring between August 1980 and March 1981. They were asked if they would become involved with a study of the effectiveness of PRE. Because we were trying to

randomise people to experimental and control groups, we had
to explain that some people would not receive a course until
after retirement, and that we were interested in seeing
whether PRE was any help in how people handled the initial
period after leaving work. We suggested that we didn't know
whether any benefit was derived through attending a course;
it was also impossible to say whether a course immediately
after retirement was any less useful than one organised just
before. We found, however, that people had expectations
that a course would be available; as a consequence, only a
minority of people were prepared to say they would forego
the opportunity, if asked, of attending a course. In this
instance, therefore, we failed to achieve randomisation and
the British Airways programme became one of our non-experimental groups.

Our experience at British Airways suggested that we should
look for a company who were interested in PRE but had yet to
organise a course. To assist our task, we were fortunate in
securing the services of   Legal and General Assurance
Limited who, through their Retirement Counselling Manager,
agreed to run three retirement courses. A randomised trial
of PRE was eventually arranged at one of the London factories
of EMI. To achieve random assignment of individuals to
control and experimental groups, we applied three conditions:

(1) It was stated that identical courses would be
    given to the control subjects as soon as the
    research period had ended (a similar technique
    was used in Hunter's Longitudinal Study).[6]

(2) Control subjects received a range of literature
    on retirement (e.g. manuals, guides on finance
    and health). The object of the evaluation was
    thus to compare the effects of a course with the
    impact of standard PRE literature.

(3) Each individual participating in the study was
    interviewed on a personal basis. At this interview
    the aims of the research were explained, together
    with the reasons for forming control and experi-
    mental groups.

With these conditions, we successfully achieved randomisation, thus creating an experimental research design.

The involvement of the National Coal Board (NCB) provided an opportunity for us to develop a quasi-experimental
approach. Here, our course and control groups were not
formed on a random basis; instead, they arose from naturally
assembled groups. The experimental subjects consisted of
miners taking a three day programme in the South Nottinghamshire area of the NCB; control subjects came from the North
Nottinghamshire area and consisted of miners retiring at
the same time as those in South Nottinghamshire. North
Nottinghamshire, however, did not provide PRE at the time of
the research.

The rest of our groups were non-experimental. In these situations we decided that, for various reasons, it was not possible to form control groups. This was especially true of the Retirement Councils, whose community-based courses (which were the subject of our research), drew participants from a range of small and medium-sized companies. We were particularly anxious to study the work of the Scottish Retirement Council, a long-established provider of PRE. As a comparison, we also examined the work of Bristol Retirement Council. The latter is a much younger organisation, running shorter courses with a different emphasis and subject-mix to those in Scotland.

The programmes at Mars and Shell provided us with an opportunity to examine two distinctive programmes within the private sector: both were organised well in advance of the individual's retirement.

Finally, the car workers (at British Leyland) switched the focus to whether a course of sufficient length (in this instance, eight days) could resolve the problems of a blue-collar group to greater effect than a short course.

3.5. The Sample Population

Table 3:3 illustrates the numbers of people in the individual samples. (See Appendix 2 for a more detailed breakdown). Except in the case of the Retirement Councils and NCB experimentals, our initial population for each group was drawn from all those workers retiring within a given period. The NCB and Retirement Council groups were drawn from individual's nominated by employers to attend the courses. With the NCB control subjects, the low response rate may reflect grievances about PRE being unavailable. This may have reduced support for the survey. However, it is worth noting that the non-response rate is not markedly higher than some other retirement studies (see, for example, Havighurst et al.).[7] Given these small numbers in each group, we were particularly fortunate in having a low attrition rate over the two phases of interviewing (a tribute both to the interviewers at Social and Community Planning Research and to the support of our respondents).

3.6. The Questionaire

Appendix 3 provides an account of the development of the questionnaire used in our study. In this chapter, we shall confine ourselves to an outline of its basic structure. The Keele research started with an important advantage in that sufficient resources were available for face-to-face interviews (the majority of PRE studies have used mail questionnaires). Interviews were shared by the research team at Keele and a market research organisation (Social and Community Planning Research). Wherever possible, the same interviewer saw the respondent he or she had interviewed at earlier phases of the project. The first two interviews were conducted at the individual's place of work; the third at his or her home.

The development of the questionnaire was preceded by a review of the instruments used on previous retirement and PRE studies (e.g. Streib & Schneider, Glamser & Hunter).[8] Some of the measures used in these studies were incorporated in

TABLE 3:3

	NCB EXPERI- MENTAL	NCB CONTROL	EMI EXPERI- MENTAL	EMI CONTROL	SHELL	GLASGOW	MARS	BRISTOL	B.A.	JAGUAR
Number of individuals approached	27	55	86		39	*	57	48	*	34
Phase 1 Interview	25	25	29	34	29	31	35	30	40	20
% of individuals approached	93%	45%	73%		74%	-	61%	63%	-	59%
Phase 2 Interview	24	N/A	24	N/A	27	29	30	29	40	14
% of individuals interviewed at Phase 1	96%	N/A	83%	N/A	93%	94%	86%	97%	100%	70%
Phase 3 Interview	23	24	24	32	20	23	N/A	27	36	N/A
% of individuals interviewed at Phase 2	96%	**96%	100%	**94%	74%	79%	N/A	93%	90%	N/A

* See Appendix.

** Control percentages calculated as a proportion of number of Phase 1 interviews.

34

various drafts of our own questionnaire. The main components of the final draft were as follows:-

(1) Social and demographic items: e.g. work experience, family structure, financial situation and contact with friends and relatives.

(2) Attitudes towards retirement.

(3) Views about planning and preparation.

(4) Images of retirement.

(5) Areas of worry or concern.

(6) Health problems.

The second interview repeated most of the questions at Phase 1, but we also examined the immediate reaction to the course. The third interview examined experiences in the transition to retirement as well as assessing the range of actions taken as a result of the course.

The questionnaire included both pre-coded and post-coded items. At the end of the interview each respondent was given a self-completion booklet containing items which assessed attitudes towards work and retirement; knowledge on retirement issues; satisfaction with life; and facts about ageing.

3.7. Conclusion: <u>The Relationship between quantitative data and qualitative data.</u>

This chapter has provided an outline of the methods used in this study of retirement education. Our attention has focused upon the production of data suitable for statistical analysis - via the medium of a questionnaire, together with the development of a research design which has enabled us to increase our confidence in making causal explanations. However, we were also interested in PRE as an interactive medium, 'good' courses being the outcome of a particular relationship between participants and course tutors and teachers. This latter aspect led us to develop a qualitative analysis alongside the survey of programmes. In practice, this meant that each course we analysed was visited by one of the researchers. Detailed notes were taken of the amount and type of interaction in the seminar room; the organisation of the course; the quality of hand-outs; the type of role given to the chairmen or course tutor. We were, therefore, able to juxtapose findings from our survey with our own description of the course (this aspect is illustrated in the case studies in Section 2). This technique was of considerable importance in clarifying a comment made by a respondent or in highlighting a statistical association. Indeed, at many points in our analysis, it was only through the knowledge gained via detailed observation, that an interpretation of survey material became possible.

CHAPTER 3

FOOTNOTES AND REFERENCES

1. Coleman, A. edited by Groombridge, J. Preparation
    for Retirement in England & Wales: A National Survey.
    National Institute of Adult Education in association
    with the Pre-Retirement Association, 1982.

2. McCallum, J. Work to Retirement: An Assessment of the
    Effectiveness of the Retirement Preparation provided by
    the Workers Educational Association for Berks., Bucks.,
    and Oxon, Ph.D. Thesis, Nuffield College, University of
    Oxford, 1982.

3. For example of course programmes see Appendix 4.

4. For a thorough discussion on this issue see Campbell, D.T.
    and Stanley, J.C., Experimental and Quasi-Experimental
    Designs for Research, Rand McNally, 1966; for a summary
    of the main problems with an uncontrolled design see Moser,
    C.A., and Kalton, G., Survey Methods in Social Investigation,
    Heinemann Education Books, 1977.

5. Cook, T., and Campbell, D., Quasi-Experimentation:
    Design and Analysis, Rand McNally, 1979, P.342.

6. Hunter, W., A Longitudinal Study of Pre-Retirement Education,
    Division of Gerontology, University of Michigan, 1968.

7. Havighurst, R.J., et al., Adjustment to Retirement: A
    Cross-National Study, Van Gorcum, 1972.

8. Strieb, G., and Schneider, C., Retirement in American
    Society Impact and Process, Cornell University Press,
    1971; Glamser, F., The Efficacy of Pre-Retirement
    Preparation, Ph.D., Thesis, Pennsylvania State University,
    1973- Hunter, W. op. cit.

SECTION 2:   <u>Three Case Studies of Pre-Retirement</u>
             <u>Education</u>

    In this section of our report we present three detailed
studies of retirement education. The examples we have
selected are designed to show pre-retirement education
operating in a range of environments, coping with different
types of attitudes towards the idea of preparation and
planning. For those with limited knowledge about this field
we hope that the case studies will illustrate what is
involved in organising and running a course. In addition,
through the medium of the case studies, we hope that the
reader will have a better understanding of later sections
of the report, particularly where we compare the apparent
effects of different types of programmes.

    Finally, these case studies should also illustrate some
of the ways we set about doing the research. For example,
although much of our material is derived from structured
questionnaires, we also visited all the courses studied in
the research, taking verbatim notes during a programme and
observing as closely as possible the reaction of participants.
As a result, we were able to combine insights from both
qualitative and quantitative material when assessing any given
pattern of response.

CHAPTER 4

CASE STUDY NUMBER ONE: THE NATIONAL COAL BOARD

4.   INTRODUCTION

In this chapter we shall examine a three-day course run during February 1980 for a group of 24 miners. The course was organised by the Nottingham Pre-Retirement Council for the South Nottinghamshire Area of the National Coal Board. In a later chapter we shall compare the experiences of the South Nottinghamshire miners with a control group in the North Nottinghamshire Area.

4.1.   Research Method

National Coal Board involvement in PRE is relatively recent (from 1976), although individual counselling on retirement benefits has been established for some time. Out of the NCB's 12 administrative Areas, five are currently engaged in some form of retirement education: three organise courses immediately before retirement, two in the period immediately after leaving work.

Initially, it was hoped to concentrate work in the South Nottinghamshire Area and to organise a randomised trial of the effects of PRE. This was impossible to achieve, however, given the restricted way in which PRE was organised in this area, and the ramifications for local Board practice of any radical change in the allocation of people to courses. In 1980 (the year in which interviews began) 395 people were eligible in the area for voluntary early retirement, and a further 20 were going at normal retirement age. There was provision for three retirement courses per year (with approximately 30 people attending each programme). For each course, every work location was allowed to nominate two people, and there was some attempt to achieve a balance between mine-workers and mine officials.

We tried to achieve some control over this nomination process. The procedure adopted was to send a letter to all the collieries in the South Nottinghamshire Area, asking them to nominate people to attend a pre-retirement course. We requested that preference be given to people going on the early retirement scheme and that they should be planning to leave work around April, 1980. In fact, out of the 27 people who were nominated from the 12 collieries, 14 were retiring in April. Out of this group of 27, one person became ill and was unable to be seen; one person was leaving at the statutory retirement age and was excluded from the survey (he did, however, attend the course). A meeting was arranged with the remaining 25, where the aims of the study were discussed and a request was made for help with the research. The 25 miners all agreed to participate in the survey, and each person was interviewed to assess their attitude towards retirement prior to attending the course. The interviews were repeated four weeks after the course, and a final interview was carried out six to nine months after the individual had retired from work. One of the 25 miners failed to attend the course (because of work commitments), hence the following analysis refers to the 24 miners who attended the programme.

4.2. Sociological Background

One important aspect to consider is the social and occupational factors which may influence the response to PRE. The course we shall be studying is a short (three day) event, located (for most of those interviewed) at the end of a long work career. This career has a number of features worthy of examination. First, length of time spent in a particular occupation may itself be important in influencing attitudes towards retirement (see the work of Simpson et al.)[1]. Secondly, mining work may generate social and communal ties which are carried beyond the work situation. This point has been expressed in the concept of the "occupational community". Salaman identifies this concept as having three character-istics: (1) members see themselves in terms of their occup-ational roles; (2) they share a reference group composed of members of the occupational community; (3) they associate with and make friends with other members and so carry work activities and interests into their non-work lives.[2] The existence of this occupational community may "soften" the impact of retirement, allowing a measure of continuity between the periods of work and retirement. Thirdly, there are important health consequences arising from the work conditions associated with mining. For the older miner, the cumulative impact of any serious injuries and/or the existence of pneumoconiosis, will obviously influence the way retirement is perceived. Moreover, these factors, combined with the miners' position within the class and occupational structure, will also influence judgements about the value of attending a pre-retirement course. These points will be taken up in later sections of this report. At this stage we shall examine the type of retirement course which the 24 miners attended.

South Nottinghamshire run three courses per year, with approximately 30 people attending each course. With some 363 people taking early retirement in 1980, it is obvious that only a small proportion of those eligible were able to attend. The course itself was run by the Nottingham and District Pre-Retirement Council, who organise a number of courses for employers in the Nottingham Area. All the Council's programmes cover the usual themes of money, housing, fitness and leisure. The Council was formed in 1964 and currently run approximately 50 courses each year.

As part of our evaluation of PRE we visited and made detailed observations of the type of course attended by the 24 miners. The decision was made not to attend the course where interviews were being conducted, since it was thought that this might identify the work of research with the organisation of the retirement course. We wished to remain as "neutral" as possible, in the hope that reservations or criticisms about the course might be more easily expressed. In terms of the differences and similarities between the course: the chairman was the same; four out of the speakers were the same; the topics were identical; all speakers came from the same organ-isation. Details of the course are given in Table 4.1.

<u>TABLE 4:1</u>

<u>NCB SOUTH NOTTINGHAMSHIRE AREA: PREPARATION FOR RETIREMENT</u>

	<u>"Looking Forward to Tomorrow"</u>
1st Day:	Introduction by Course Chairman Health in Retirement Fitness in Retirement Unemployment Benefits.
2nd Day:	Money in Retirement Opportunities for Voluntary Service Pensions and Social Security Income Tax Problems
3rd Day:	Enjoying Leisure Security in the Home NCB Pensions and Early Retirement Benefits Course Conclusion/Discussion Session.

4.3. Organisation of the programme

If we include the chairman's introductory talk (which lasted nearly 60 minutes), but exclude the discussion period at the end of the course, the programme consisted of 11 sessions. Six of these could be described as lectures, with emphasis upon a structured presentation followed by a short discussion. The length of talks ranged from 40 to 60 minutes. The presentations fell into one or other of two categories: those offering advice on specific financial, welfare or taxation issues; and those offering assistance on more diffuse areas such as health and leisure. Advice on financial issues was a prominent feature of the course, with separate sessions on unemployment benefit, investments, the state retirement pension, supplementary benefits, taxation and NCB retirement benefits. Three of these sessions adopted a question and answer format.

The speakers from the Department of Employement (D of E) and (Department of Health and Social Security DHSS) were primarily concerned with establishing the conditions for receiving benefits. In these presentations the emphasis was placed upon identifying the rules and procedures which govern receipt of any money. In both cases, the sessions contained a considerable amount of interaction between speaker and audience. Here, for example, is a section from the notes taken on the DHSS contribution:

Speaker reviews conditions for receiving state retirement pension.

Two questions from audience.

Speaker discusses sickness benefits and contributions.

Two questions from audience.

Speaker elaborates on retirement condition; specific types of jobs compatible with being retired; earnings rule.

One question from audience.

Speaker discusses procedure for claiming supplementary benefits.

Outlines invalidity benefit.

Two questions from audience.

By contrast, the sessions on investment and taxation provided considerably less scope for audience-participation. The talk on investments was built around 28 slides illustrating various points about money and retirement. However, the theme of investment was sketched upon a fairly broad canvas, the opening 10 minutes of the talk covering the different uses of money (particularly in the field of leisure). In this talk, the sheer volume of material was a factor inhibiting audience involvement; in the lecture on taxation, the complexity of the

presentation was a more serious problem. The lecture tended to
rely on jargon ("I've already noted that we are on the handrolic
system of coding") and to move from point to point with no guid-
ing theme. Audience participation was minimal (there were four
questions in a 50 minute lecture).

The presentations on health, exercise, voluntary work and
leisure, raise different issues from those discussed above.
Most of these talks ranged over a very broad area, incorporat-
ing a number of social and psychological problems. Whilst this
could often lead to a highly stimulating talk, there was the
occasional problem of insufficient clarity and focus. This was
particularly the case in the lecture on health in retirement.
This presentation covered the following themes: causes of the
increase in life expectancy; psychological consequences of
retirement; marital problems in retirement; sexual activity;
general health advice; diet and nutrition. Inevitably, such
a range of subjects meant that firm advice was lost in a prof-
usion of opinion and argument. By contrast, the lecture on
fitness was clearly structured with an emphasis on audience
involvement (via a demonstration of keep fit exercises). However, the scope of this talk was somewhat restricted both by
the relatively small size of the lecture room, and by the formal
arrangement of chairs and tables.

4.4. Results (Phase 1 - Pre-Course Interview)

The miners received their first interview two weeks before
the course. At this stage, two people had yet to confirm their
date of retirement; the rest were within five months of leaving
work. The majority of the group were aged 60 and were coming
out under the NCB early retirement scheme (the scheme was
introduced in 1977 and the take-up is around 95 per cent of
those eligible). The popularity of early retirement reflects
perceptions both about the impact of work and a view of retirement as a 'reward' for many years of service.

"Because after 46 years, I've had enough and I want to
take advantage of it. I thought a rest would do me
good. One of the lads is down the pit, the other one
will start in the pit soon, it's a family tradition and
I've done my bit. The retirement pension is not bad at
all, and I think I can manage on it. With the pension
lump sum I will be getting I'll be able to pay off the
rest of my HP on furniture".

"To be honest I think I've done enough down the pit -
it's in my mind to return to Sussex. Partly health
reasons - I can't bend my back. I'm on night shifts all
the time, mainly that. I want to go down to Sussex -
all my brothers live there. I've worked six days a week
for years and years and I think I've done enough".

"I've done all my life in the pits. At 60 years, I'm
slowing down, the speed of advance on the coalface has
speeded up so much that we older chaps can't keep up,
it's up to the younger ones now".

Health factors were also important in shaping views about retirement:

".....for the simple reason that I've got a lot of dust on my chest, which won't improve, only get worse, so I thought I had better get out of the dust at the earliest possible date, (and) enjoy retirement while I can. I'm not badly off for money, I've been thrifty and saved, so I thought I'd better enjoy it before it loses more value".

"You've had enough when you've had all those years down (the) pit. They've gone in for this early retirement, which seems to be a good thing. I have dust on my chest, I'm off work at the moment and I am taking antibiotics. My chest is particularly bad in the winter months, so I'm considering whether to work through this summer and pack it in in November, if I'm fit enough".

Finally, in a minority of cases, perceptions of retirement as a "reward" or release from arduous work, were cemented by ideas about new activities to develop in retirement:

"I'm just ready to pack it up, I've had enough – it's about time I let someone younger get on the job. I think it gets harder every week when you get nearer 60. Our work is exceptionally hard, I'd like to do something different – some other type of thing – motor engineering type of thing – I've always been involved on machinery".

"I think I could spend more time at home with the family – spend more time in the greenhouse. The injury like – I've had this injury but this is not the reason I'm retiring. I've got aviaries and a nice garden, fish ponds like. Just that I was asked if I wanted voluntary retirement and the wages were explained and I was satisfied with these and with the injury I felt it would make way for another man if I retired".

These viewpoints can be related to the length of time the group had spent in mining (an average of 36 years). Research by Simpson et al.[3] in the United States, suggests that stability and orderliness of work career may contribute to high involvement in retirement and to minimal feelings of job deprivation. Amongst this group of 25, 17 felt they wouldn't worry about not having a job to do; 13 felt they would not miss any feelings of usefulness or achievement which work may have provided. In a self-completion booklet, individuals were also asked: "Do you think stopping work may make you less satisfied with your life?" and "Do you think stopping work may make you feel your life is not particularly useful?" Nineteen replied "no" to the former question and 22 to the latter. These findings were also corroborated by a number of scales and indices on work and retirement attitudes. The results from these are discussed in a later section of this report.

Fifteen of the miners felt it would either take no time at all or only a few weeks to get used to not working; three felt that it would take more than a few months. Six were intending to look for work in retirement, in most cases within the first year of leaving the pit. In the majority of cases, the need to keep active was the principal reason given for wanting to remain in some form of work:

"To keep myself active and not go get in a lounge-about way. To keep my mind occupied and my body at work - there's nothing better than keeping on the move is there? And to keep from under my wife's feet!"

"I'm a very active man. I do all the work at home, repairs, I also help my family and do their repairs. I think it's just because I can't sit down, you know. It isn't money it's just to keep active. I just can't sit down....achievement is caused by doing work you like to do - making things, decorating. I've got a big workshop".

Bearing in mind that the majority of the group were within a few months of leaving work, the interviews explored the range of thoughts and ideas associated with retirement. Twenty-one were looking forward to retirement; 13 had a clear idea of what sort of life they would experience in retirement, virtually all viewing it in a positive way. Nineteen rejected the idea that they wouldn't know how to occupy their time.

The interview also examined the extent of planning undertaken prior to the course. Fifteen people claimed to have thought seriously about the kind of things they would like to do in retirement. A number of people, for example, were looking forward to greater involvement within their circle of family and friends (particularly grandchildren):

"I love being at home, my wife and I don't fall out with each other. I look forward to being with my niece's children and taking them out in the car, taking them swimming and boating".

"I've got three grandchildren I'll have to look after. I just really want to carry on as I've always done - my wife and I have always done things together and we'll go on the same way".

"Looking after the granddaughter, for a start, we are bringing her up. Doing a lot of things I couldn't do when at work: such as travelling, visiting friends".

Some people were just looking forward to an extended period of leisure time, with opportunities for travelling and for more holidays:

"I'd like to go to various different places - places I've not been to. I'm very fond of country places ... and I like a little bit of social life in the evening. I do to the dancing a couple of nights a week and I like a drink of pop - a pint of beer. What you can do and can't do is controlled by finance isn't it".

"I would like to do bird-watching, and take an interest
in nature. There are a lot of nature walks around
where I live. I'd spend a lot of time on my garden and
allotment. I'm hoping to spend more time with my grand-
son. Me and my wife will maybe travel a little bit more".

"Mostly gardening, also going out in the car to visit
places and friends and an extra holiday if the money
runs to it. I love motoring and will do as much of
that as I can afford".

Finally, in a minority of cases, there were specific
hobbies which people wanted to develop in retirement:

"Model making, I've got a workshop at home. I shall
have my own house and garden to look after. I shall
do more at the Great Central Railway Association,
repairing the locomotives they have there, and mechan-
ical work on the old steam locos. Taking the big dogs
out for walks, I like walking, where I live it's open
country. I shall get more involved with the grandchildren".

"I would like to take an Open University course which
would develop my political thinking and ability. I
would like to take German or a foreign language. Other
than that I've no particular ambition. Bricklaying -
I want to do that better. I want to do joinery and
woodwork. I want to learn more about car maintenance.
I'd like to learn how to keep the car running more
economically and to learn exactly how the car engine
works".

However, a commitment to specific projects or activities
is not the dominant theme of these interviews. We find,
instead, a strong desire to increase involvement in an existing
social network, in a context free from the constraints of everyday work. As one man put it: "I'll be able to go out more
in the evening, to pubs and clubs, without having next day's
work at the back of my mind".

It is when we try to move beyond general statements of
confidence, towards an identification of detailed planning,
that the discussion becomes more complicated. On the one hand,
seven people felt very well prepared and 16 fairly well
prepared for retirement. On the other hand, it is important to
observe that there was considerable variation in the extent to
which planning had taken place. Indeed, in some cases, the
follow-up question ("What sort of things have you done to prepare yourself?") was responded to in a negative form:

"Nothing really. I haven't made any plans yet. I'm
not on the bread line, put it that way, so I've no
worries about money. I've got lots of interests already,
which I will be able to give more time to".

"Nothing really, I just take it as it comes - all my neighbours say they'll not see me sitting around! I always think I can find something to do - we've put up a complete building - brickwork etc. I've always got plenty to do around the house and property".

"Nothing special, really. No, I can't think of anything".

In some instances, the question raised considerable uncertainty in people's minds:

"Well - it's an awkward question that - when I've spoken to the wife and daughter they've said they've got plenty of jobs for me to do - plenty of decorating and gardening. That's the one thing I can think of I've done to prepare myself - I've prepared myself to have a rest first after not taking a holiday when working. There's nothing else at all".

"I'm not very sure what this means (i.e. planning for retirement). I've been active in local politics, that takes a lot of time. Nothing more - just a continuation of my present life-style".

These extracts reveal another important factor inhibiting retirement preparation. This was the view that, in the absence of any major debts, financial planning was unnecessary. The following extracts from interviews illustrate this theme:

"I've always tried to take care of myself health wise - I've not saved a lot of money as I've had to bring five children up. I don't owe anybody 'owt' - I'm not in debt. I have been in debt but I'm not now".

"I've got a nice banking account - a nice pension. I can't think of anything else. We've got our house now - our own property that's about all. We've no debts whatsoever".

"I've saved a bob or two these last few years, so that I can carry on without having to beg for anything. I've bought Premium Bonds in the last few years and invested in the Building Society. I have also bought a stock of clothes, which will see me through the next few years".

In line with these comments, the idea of saving to accumulate a surplus received limited support in this group (a fact which was important in influencing responses to the investment talks on the retirement course). We should be clear, however, about the nature of the problems involved. The questions being posed in this section of the interview were perceived to be rather idealistic by many in the group, i.e. they presumed a life cycle where planning and preparation had been consistent themes. Indeed part of the ideology of retirement planning is that just as one prepares for work (via primary, secondary and tertiary education), so one should prepare for the period after work (through financial planning, etc.). Accompanying this perspective, there is the idea of a progression through a social

and occupational hierarchy, movement within this structure
being "orderly","planned" and "controlled". The "career"
of the older miner, however, suggests a number of different
themes. There was no preparation for mining in the sense of
actively choosing it as a career, instead, the "pull" of the
local labour market and the absence of alternatives provided
the rationale for entering the industry. Thereafter, conting-
encies associated with the national demand for coal, geologic-
al conditions, technological developments and injuries and
accidents at the pit, had the most direct impact on changes
at work. "Choice", in other words, rarely entered the scheme
of things.

We would suggest, from this analysis, that the current
form of retirement planning is out of step with the dominant
class and occupational experience, one which may express
ambivalence about the possibility of controlling the future.
In line with this argument, the group divided equally over
whether it was possible to plan and prepare for retirement.
Amongst those who rejected the idea of planning we find the
following comments:

"Things change from day to day. The value of money
for one thing ...... I've saved money in the past and
what is it worth today?"

"I don't like to plan or you usually get disappointed".

"You have to take it as it comes. Life's too uncertain.
You're here today gone tomorrow ..... you can't plan too
far ahead...."

Where positive answers to the idea of planning were given
(in 12 instances), planning for occupying time (seven mentions)
and financial matters (eight mentions) were the items most
frequently suggested. Seven of the 12 suggested that planning
and preparation should be undertaken over a year before
retirement.

4.4.1. Summary

The evidence from these interviews is that prior to the
course the majority of the miners were looking forward to
their retirement. On the other hand, there is little evidence
of detailed retirement planning and some uncertainty about what
might be undertaken. Nonetheless, the majority of the miners
still felt themselves to be fairly well prepared for leaving
work; financial benefits under the early retirement scheme and
the NCB pension providing a measure of financial security
(18 claimed they would retain up to two-thirds of their earnings
until age 65.)

4.5. Results (Phase II)

Four weeks after the pre-retirement course the miners
were re-interviewed. The aims of this second interview were:
first, to gather immediate views about the value of the course;
secondly, to assess whether there had been any significant

changes in attitudes and knowledge of retirement issues. The
first area we shall examine concerns the reactions of participants to the programme.

It is worth recalling that the majority of the miners
were within five months of their retirement. Not surprisingly,
therefore, 10 felt that the course had come rather late
(Table 4:2). The brevity of the course was also a subject of
criticism (Table 4:3). Fourteen felt that the course was too
short; a similar number considered there was insufficient time
to discuss and exchange ideas (Table 4:4). Eighteen agreed
that certain sessions should have been longer, talks on financial matters being most frequently mentioned. In line with the
strong views about the course length, the 16 who reported on
ways of improving the programme concentrated almost exclusively
on the need to lengthen the course:

"The income tax one - that could have been longer.
I think that everyone on the course would have liked
to ask more questions and to find out how income tax
affects us and things like that. The lady from Social
Security could have been longer. She could have given
us a longer talk and we could have had more discussion
with her - it was cut too short. The whole course was
quick. The Coal Board Pension fellow came and we only
had a quick hour with him and then off he went. It would
have been nice to have had a whole afternoon with him".

'The chap from the NCB in Sheffield who told us about
pre-retirement and pensions should have had a full
morning for his talk, leaving a whole afternoon for
questions and discussion. As it was, there was only
time for three or four questions and he then had to
go. The same thing appertains to the lady from the
Social Security, she should have had far more time.
The chap who spoke on the voluntary services should
also have had far more time to go into details. A
lot more chaps like myself would probably go in for
this type of work if it was explained more fully to
them".

The limited amount of time raised difficulties for people
in their attempts to absorb a mass of new information. A
number of the miners complained of facts being "crammed" into
a very tight schedule:

"All the lectures could have been lengthened a bit,
it seemed a bit rushed, there should have been more
time given to the lecturers to cover the subjects
better and give us more time to take it in. Although
they explained everything well, it was crammed in too
short a space".

"A little longer for the discussions. They have to
cram it all in a short time. Speakers only had an hour
for discussion and the talk and for any questions as
well".

50

TABLE   4:2

"In relation to when you retire,, do you think the course came .....?"	n	%
Too early	–	–
Right time	14	58
Too late	10	42
No response	–	–
	24	100

TABLE   4:3

"Thinking about the length of the course, did you find it ......?"	n	%
Too long	–	–
Right length	10	42
Too short	14	58
No response	–	–
	24	100

TABLE   4:4

"What about the time allowed to discuss and exchange ideas during sessions. Do you think there was ....?	n	%
Too much	1	4
Enough time	9	38
Not enough time	14	58
Don't know	–	–
No response	–	–
	24	100

"The first thing is - not long enough - it should be
longer than it was when we attended. Not one day a
week but a full week because you can't digest all in
one day. I should say one day for one subject ....
There wasn't enough time to ask questions on the
subjects taken".

The need for more detailed discussion was also an
important theme:

"I think more time could be spent on what educational
facilities are available - these were sketchily introduced. I think if you are going to help people more
time could be spent on telling people how to fill in
Inland Revenue returns... more time on that. I would
like to see an Accountant rather than an Inland Revenue
bloke and have more time for questions and discussions.
With 30 of you there's not enough time - they talk and
then you have 10 minutes to 15 minutes for discussion
and that is not long enough. I think that if the Board
are going to develop the pre-retirement aspect they shoud
be prepared to bring people out of the pit for half a
shift to give them a lecture with time for discussion -
that would contact far more people. I think this would
help if there was a discussion after the men had come
off the shift and they had a talk given there and then.
The number of people able to get to the day courses is
limited and that way would get to more people".

We asked the miners which of the sessions they had found
most useful. Out of the 50 items mentioned, there were 11
mentions for state pensions and social security; eight for
fitness in retirement; seven each for safety in the home and
the NCB pensions scheme. The question "which session did
you find least useful?" attracted 16 replies, nine of which
referred to the lecture on income tax.

There were very few replies to questions asking whether
new subjects should be added (three suggestions) or removed
(one suggestion). The low response to these questions reflects
the difficulty of evaluating reactions to pre-retirement courses.
Given that this is their first experience of a course, few
people are likely to carry in their heads distinctions between
"good" and "bad" retirement courses. In general terms, people
are likely to feel that courses are a "good thing" and that
their existence reflects concern on the part of the employer
for their welfare. Moreover, course participants may develop
genuine empathy with the organisers of the programme and may
feel unhappy about criticising their work.

In this research we tried two ways of tapping more critical
views about courses. First, we hoped that a gap of a month
between the ending of the course and the timing of the second
interview would allow the expression of more detailed views.
Secondly, we included questions which were designed to spark
new thoughts and ideas about the programme. For example, we
asked the miners: "Were there any aspects of the course which
surprised you?" There were 12 positive replies to this
question. Four people remarked about the "open and "natural"

way in which issues connected with health and family life had
been discussed. The replies given illustrate the potential of
courses for raising serious issues:

"Oh the nurse...medical side. Normal personal
relations discussed without any embarrassment".

"The medical lady from the hospital....she gave us
information about breast cancer. There was no
embarrassment".

"(The medical lady) I think the lady put it over
very well, she didn't embarrass you with it".

"The woman from the hospital who talked about your
health and the physical side - particularly as regards
your wife. I should have liked to talk with her
personally, to talk about my wife, who is full of
nerves and on tranquillisers".

The last comment illustrates the extent to which courses
can penetrate major areas of concern amongst their participants. Unfortunately, given the way in which programmes are
structured, there is rarely time to explore these issues
via extensive discussion or individual counselling. There
were a number of questions where we tried to examine general
reactions to the course. Had the programme made people aware
of any new problems they might face in retirement? Had it
altered people's views on retirement? Are people intending
to do any specific thing as a result of advice received on
the course? Eighteen reported that the course had made them
aware of problems they had not previously considered (Table
4:5). Thirty-eight items were mentioned, 20 of which fell
into the financial category (state benefits, NCB retirement
benefits, etc.). The only other area to reach double
figures concerned health and fitness.

The type of financial advice considered useful was mainly
concerned with the clarification of rights to state or NCB
benefits:

"Finance, for one thing I now realise that I will be
all right in the first year, but in the second year
I shan't be quite so well off. Because you are on
the dole for the first year and you are not taxed on
that and in the second year you are taxed on everything.
It made me think more about keeping fit. I also learned
quite a bit from the talk on security by the police".

"The amount of tax you would have to pay, and what you
were left with".

"Such as social security, preparation for signing on as
unemployed, it's a big thing, not having signed on
before".

TABLE 4:5

"Has the course made you aware of problems you had not considered before?"		
	n	%
Yes	18	75
No	6	25
No response	–	–
	24	100

TABLE 4:6

"Has the course changed your view of retirement at all?"		
	n	%
Yes, or in some ways	5	21
No	19	79
No response	–	–
	24	100

"Made you think about the national pension, whether you've got enough stamps. Also about the best time of year to retire from the tax point of view. It made you think more about your health when you retire, it made me look at retirement as a different way of life".

Fourteen identified specific things they would do as a result of the course, activities connected with health and fitness being most frequently mentioned:

"Well I shall do more exercise definitely ... swimming and I do quite a bit of dancing. I'll probably do more of that now when I'm retired. I go twice at present which is all for exercise really. I'll probably do more cycling - rather than use the car - that will keep costs down too!"

"For one thing I won't be sitting around. What the Doctor told us made me realise the danger of this. I think I'm going to start going to the swimming baths again, the Doctor said that was the best exercise".

"On the medical side - I've mentioned to the wife about the Clinic (for a breast examination). Not that she's got anything - but just as a check".

The course contained a number of items recommending involvement in a broader range of leisure and voluntary work activities. We asked the miners whether they had thought about doing any new activities as a result of the course. There was one positive reply, a person who was thinking of trying voluntary work.

Finally, in this section, the question was asked: "Has the course changed your view of retirement at all," (Table 4:6). In view of the optimistic views expressed in the Phase I interviews it is perhaps not so surprising that only five people gave a positive reply to this question. The suggestion would seem to be that the miners came to their course with relatively firm and optimistic views about leaving work. The impact of the course was mainly to consolidate rather than change these views in any dramatic way. In the following sections we shall provide a more detailed examination of this finding.

Pre-Retirement Education and Attitude Change

In this section we shall discuss in more detail whether the three day programme attended by the miners had any immediate impact on knowledge and attitudes towards retirement. Table 4:7 gives a list of questions which had also been used in the phase 1 questionnaire. We tested the view that the retirement programme would have a neutral effect both upon retirement attitudes and on knowledge about retirement issues: this was our null hypothesis.

The responses to the questions in Table 4:7 were compared using the McNemar test for significance of changes.[4] This measure is appropriate in situations where the same sample has been questioned on two separate occasions.

55

TABLE 4:7

Phase 1 – Questions repeated at Phase 2

"How long do you think it will take you to get used to not working?" (No time at all; A few weeks; A few months; etc.).

"Do you plan to look for any kind of work after you retire?"

"On the whole, are you looking forward to the time when you will retire?"

"Do you have a clear idea of what life will be like for you in retirement?" (Yes/No/Can't say).

"After retirement, do you think there will be times when you won't know what to do to keep occupied?" (Yes/No/Can't say).

"Taking everything into account, how well prepared do you think you are for retirement? Would you say you are: (Very/Fairly well prepared; Not very well prepared/Not prepared at all; Can"t say)?".

"Some people feel you can plan and prepare for retirement, do you feel this way or not?" (Yes/No/Can't say).

"Do you think leaving work will (Improve your health/ Make your health worse/Not make any difference)?".

"When you think about retirement, do you think of it as (An extended holiday; A new phase of your life; the beginning of old age; A life rather similar to the present; A rejection by society)?".

"As you approach retirement, do any of the following matters worry you? (Retirement income; Your health after you retire. Your relationship with family and friends; The effect of retirement on you personally)".

It should be emphasised that with a small sample size (as in this and the following case studies) conclusions from this measure must be regarded as tentative. It is likely that a sample of (in this instance) 24, will result in the effects of the course being under-stated. However, we shall be able to assess the extent of this when we report on the results from the pooled data in Chapters 7 and 8.

We noted earlier that we are using the McNemar test to examine significant differences between the Phase 1 and Phase 2 interviews. A "significant" difference is one which indicates a real difference between populations. In terms of understanding the strength of differences, Rowntree has provided the following note:

"The bigger the difference, the more confidently we can reject the null hypothesis (that there is no real difference between the means of the populations from which the samples are drawn). To be significant at the one per cent level (one chance in 100 of so large a difference), the difference must be bigger than if it were significant only at the five per cent level (five chances in 100). So we'd reject the null hypothesis more confidently with a difference significant at the one per cent level".[5]

To indicate the strength of any statistical difference between our groups we shall use the following terms: extremely significant (0.1 per cent); highly significant (at one per cent); significant (at five per cent).

For these case study reports we shall also use a 10 per cent level of significance, given that our statistical measure may be under-stating the effect of course.

The McNemar test was run on all of the questions listed above, and none of the computed values reached the 10 per cent level of significance. It was not possible, therefore, to reject the null hypothesis and we can conclude (with the reservations concerning sample size noted earlier) that the course appears to have made no impact on the items we have examined.

The study also contained a number of scales and indices. We used two statistical measures (the t-test and the Wilcoxon matched pairs signed-rank test) to explore the significance of changes over Phase 1 and Phase 2. We included in the questionnaire two measures examining attitudes and commitment to work. The inclusion of these items reflects a view in the retirement literature that a high commitment to work is a factor inhibiting retirement adjustment. Indeed, one of the justifications for a retirement course is seen to be its capacity to direct people to a broader range of interests beyond those provided by work. In the Phase 1 interviews scoring on both of these scales tended towards the lower range, indicating negative attitudes to work. Changes in scores over the two interviews were not statistically significant. The commitment to work scale showed only small changes between Phase 1 and Phase 2. There was an increase (from seven to 12 people) in those agreeing with the

TABLE 4:8

Resistance to Retirement Scale: Comparison of Phases 1-2 Responses

	PHASE 1 RESPONSE			PHASE 2 RESPONSE		
	Strongly Agree/ Agree	Not Sure	Strongly Disagree/ Disagree	Strongly Agree/ Agree	Not Sure	Strongly Disagree/ Disagree
People should not be made to retire solely because of their age.	14 58%	5 21%	5 21%	16 67%	4 17%	4 17%
I am looking forward to the time off that retirement will bring.	22 92%	1 4%	1 4%	21 88%	1 4%	2 8%
If it were up to me alone, I would keep on working as long as possible.	5 21%	1 4%	18 75%	6 25%	2 8%	16 67%
I think things will go well for me in retirement.	22 92%	2 8%	— —	23 96%	1 4%	— —
Retirement is mostly good for a person.	19 79%	4 17%	1 4%	20 83%	3 13%	1 4%

TABLE 4 : 9

Knowledge Scale: Comparisons of Phase 1-2 Responses						
T = TRUE F = FALSE	PHASE 1 RESPONSE			PHASE 2 RESPONSE		
	Correct	Incorrect	Don't Know	Correct	Incorrect	Don't Know
A state retirement pension is always free of tax. F	10 42%	7 29%	7 29%	10 42%	11 46%	3 13%
Medical prescriptions are free to men over 65 and women over 60. T	21 87%	1 4%	2 8%	20 83%	3 13%	1 4%
People may receive a supplementary pension if their income is below a certain level. T	21 87%	- -	3 13%	21 88%	2 8%	1 4%
People may receive rent or rate rebates only if they receive a supplementary pension. F	2 8%	15 63%	7 29%	10 42%	12 50%	2 8%
There is a scheme in existence to provide free or cheap legal advice for people who need it. T	20 83%	1 4%	3 13%	24 100%	- -	- -
After 65, people get an age allowance entitling them to a greater amount of tax free income. T	11 46%	3 13%	10 42%	14 58%	4 17%	6 25%
It is possible for people to obtain an attendance allowance when they need constant care at home. T	19 79%	1 4%	4 17%	22 92%	- -	2 8%

statement "I have sometimes regretted being in the kind of work I am now in"; and a decrease (from 11 to seven) in those agreeing with the statement. "The work I do is one of the most satisfying parts of my life". In the attitudes to work scale we also find only small changes, the two exceptions being an increase (from nine to thirteen people) in those definitely disagreeing with the question: "Do you think you will miss any feelings of usefulness or achievement which work may have provided?"; and a decrease (from eight to three people) amongst those in definite agreement with this statement.

A self-completed "resistance to retirement" scale was also used in both phases. This scale contained five statements designed to assess the acceptability of retirement to the individual. The scale had a range of 5-25, with a high score indicating a low resistance to retirement. The mean score for the group in Phase 1 was 18.4 and in Phase 2 18.3. Once again, there were very small fluctuations in scores over the two phases. Both results indicate a high degree of optimism about retirement (Table 4:8). In Phase 1, 22 people thought that things would go well for them in retirement (23 in Phase 2); nineteen that retirement was mostly good for a person (20 in Phase 2); and 22 were looking forward to the time off that retirement would bring (21 in Phase 2).

The self-completion booklet contained seven factual questions designed to test the individual's knowledge about social security and related issues. With a maximum score of seven, mean scores showed a significant improvement over the two interviews - from 4.3 to 5.2. Table 4:9 gives the results of scores on individual items. The number of people giving a correct response to the statement: "A state retirement pension is always free of tax" remained unchanged over both interviews - a disappointing result given the preponderance of talks on financial matters. The difficulties with the talk on income tax is reflected in the finding that 10 either didn't know or gave the incorrect answer to the statement: "After 65, people get an age allowance entitling them to a greater amount of tax free income". By contrast there was an improvement in correct replies to the statement: "People may receive rent or rate rebates only if they receive a supplementary pension". Over the two interviews, correct scores increased from two to 10.

Finally, in the self-completed booklet we included a quiz entitled "Facts of Ageing". This was originally developed by Palmore in America, and an anglicised version was used in the Keele survey.[6] The scale had 13 factual statements about older people and respondents had to indicate whether the statements were true or false (see Table 4:10). The quiz consisted of five statements about the social demography of old age (2,3,9,11,13); seven statements referring to views about older people and older workers (4,5,6,7,8,9,10,12); and one general statement about health and physical activity. Responses to the statements about older people and older workers reflect some of the constraints inherent in mining work. For example, at Phase 1 interview only five (21 per cent) identified as false (the correct answer) the statement: "Most older workers cannot work as effectively as younger workers".[11] Moreover, 16 (67%) on Phase 1 and 14 (58%)

TABLE 4:10

Facts About Ageing Scale: Comparison of Phases 1-2 Responses

Item	PHASE 1 RESPONSE			PHASE 2 RESPONSE		
T = TRUE F = FALSE	Correct	Incorrect	No response	Correct	Incorrect	No response
For people in their 60's and 70's regular exercise can restore physical activity and reduce heart rate and blood pressure. T	21 88%	3 12%	- -	22 92%	2 8%	- -
At least 1 in 10 of peopled past 65 live in long stay institutions (ie homes for the aged, geriatric hospitals). F	11 46%	12 50%	1 4%	11 46%	13 54%	- -
Nearly three quarters of people aged 65 or more in England and Wales live in a household without a car. T	16 67%	7 29%	1 4%	16 67%	8 33%	- -
Most older workers cannot work as effectively as younger workers. F	5 21%	19 79%	- -	10 42%	14 58%	- -
The majority of older people are healthy enough to carry out their normal activities. T	17 71%	7 29%	- -	19 79%	5 21%	- -
Most older people are set in their ways and are unable to change. F	8 33%	16 67%	- -	10 42%	14 58%	- -
Old people usually take longer to learn something new. T	16 67%	8 33%	- -	20 83%	4 17%	- -
It is almost impossible for most old people to learn new things. F	18 75%	6 25%	- -	17 71%	7 29%	- -
One third of old people live alone. T	13 54%	10 42%	1 4%	14 58%	10 42%	- -
In general most old people are pretty much alike. F	12 50%	12 50%	- -	12 50%	12 50%	- -
People aged 60 and over make up 20% of Great Britain's total population. T	17 71%	7 29%	- -	21 88%	3 12%	- -
When a person retires his health usually gets worse. F	15 63%	9 37%	- -	17 71%	7 29%	- -
A majority of pensioners in Great Britain live in households below, at, or just above the official povery line. T	12 50%	12 50%	- -	15 63%	9 37%	- -

on Phase 2 identified as true (the incorrect answer) the
statement: "Older people are set in their ways and are unable
to change". The group divided equally in both Phases over the
statement: "In general most older people are pretty much alike".

As can be seen in Table 4:10 there was an increase in
correct answers in Phase II for most items. The Wilcoxon and
t-test were used to test the null hypothesis that individuals
were just as likely to switch from correct to incorrect
responses over the two Phases, as vice versa. The results
indicate that there was a signficant increase in correct replies.
However, it is possible that this result was unrelated to the course and
may have arisen as a natural consequence of getting closer to
retirement. Our Phase 3 interview should provide further
information on whether the course had stimulated greater awareness of social and psychological aspects of ageing.

4.5.1. Summary (Phase 2 interviews)

The second interviews with the miners attempted to gather
their immediate reactions to the course and to examine its
 impact on their knowledge and attitudes. It is clear that
there was some dissatisfaction at the brevity of the programme
and criticism of particular sessions. On the other hand, the
majority of the miners could identify problems of which the
course had made them aware and most could identify items of
information which they had personally found useful; in addition,
14 identified specific things they would do as a result of the
course, activities connected with health and fitness being most
frequently mentioned.

Finally, we tried to measure the impact of the course on
attitudes towards retirement and knowledge about retirement
issues. On all of our scales and indices the miners produced
scores indicating very positive views about retirement; in
this area at least, the course was given very little scope for
changing participants' views.

In a seven-item test on knowledge, although there was a
major improvement in their ability to differentiate between
rent/rate rebates and supplementary pension, the results on
taxation and retirement pensions and age allowances were
somewhat disappointing. Finally, there were indications for
increased awareness - as a result of the course - about the
social and psychological aspect of growing old. It remains
to be seen, however, whether this will be sustained over a
period of months rather than weeks.

4.6. Results (Phase 3 interviews)

Eleven months after their first interview (10.5 months
following the pre-retirement course) the miners were seen for
a third and final time. At this point the miners had been
retired for an average of just over seven months. (One person
had continued at work and he is excluded from the analysis
below). The first section of the questionnaire contained a
number of questions designed to explore the process of withdrawal from the work place: for example, was the day of ret-

irement marked by any special event? Had people maintained contact with the colliery? How did people recall the early days of retirement?

For most people the event of retirement was marked by a ceremony or party of some kind (usually organised by their workmates). Sixteen recalled spending the initial period of retirement either engaged in domestic tasks or just pottering about the house. Many of the miners - after an average of 36 years in the industry - reported a simple desire to relax and enjoy a new sense of freedom:

"I did nothing, just stayed at home and took it easy".

"Just nothing, just relaxed at home and did nothing at all".

"I just spent them lazing about and enjoying sleeping in".

In line with these comments 18 reported feeling happy when they first retired; five had mixed feelings; none reported feeling unhappy. Twenty-one had been back to their workplace since retirement. We find both social (to see workmates) and financial (to pay for concessionary coal allowances) factors behind the large numbers of people returning to their colliery. On the other hand, very few people had maintained formal social ties with their workplace. Of the 10 people reporting a club or association for retired members at their pit, only three had taken part in any of its activities

At the Phase 1 and Phase 2 interviews the miners had appeared relatively optimistic about the prospect of retire-ment. What were their views and experiences seven months after leaving work? Most in this group had taken early retirement, and only one person reported that they now wished they had stayed on working longer. Eleven had got used to not working in "no time at all"; three took "a few weeks"; five took a "few months"; four were "still not adjusted to retirement".

The area in which the miners lived presented few opport-unities for part-time work and this, together with tax disadvant-ages and the impact of any earnings on Board benefits, meant that very few had considered paid work in retirement. At the time of the interview two men were doing part-time work (one as a chiropodist, the other as a barman). There is one person for whom information in this area was not recorded. Of the remaining 20 in the sample none reported having looked for paid work since their retirement; one person reported that he intended to look within the next few months. Eighteen reported no worries about not having a job; the same number reported that they didn't miss any feelings of usefulness or achievement which may have been gained through work. Thirteen, however, said they missed being with other people at work.

In the self-completed booklet we asked the 20 who were not working, the following two questions: "Do you think stopping work altogether has made you less satisfied with your life?"; "Alternatively, do you think stopping work has made you feel that

your life is not particulary useful?" Only two agreed with
the former question, and one with the latter. Replies to these
questions suggest that leaving work had presented few problems
for this group. This could, of course, have been predicted from
the Phase 1 interviews, hence the influence of the retirement
programme has probably been marginal. However, there is also
the question of whether the course had influenced new activities
for retirement. As we indicated in our description of the
programme, the various sessions provided a range of advice for
greater involvement in voluntary work, adult education and new
hobbies. Ten months after the course, how much of this advice
had been followed?

Only a limited response was made to the advice on voluntary work. Of the 20 people not doing any kind of paid work,
only four were doing voluntary work, and two were doing this
before the course. In the sample as a whole, one person had
attended an adult education class since their retirement; of
the remaining 22, only one person had actually thought about
attending classes. Two had taken up new hobbies and interests
since leaving work. If we examine the results from the three
interviews, although 15 of the 23 claimed in Phase 1 that they
had thought seriously about the kind of things they would like
to do after leaving work, there is little evidence that this
was maintained in the transition and early period of retirement.
There is also little evidence that the retirement course
stimulated new thinking about leisure activities.

One of the reasons for the limited response to the material
on leisure may be that the conceptualisation of retirement (at
this stage at least) emphasised more the sense of freedom from
work. By contrast, the course had developed a focus of retirement as a time for new social and leisure activities. Evidence
for tension can be found in replies given to a number of questions. Thus, although 21 identified retirement as "a new phase
of life", 14 also felt it to be like an "extended holiday".
When asked what aspects of retirement they had found particularly
pleasureable, the same number reported enjoying the experience
of freedom which seemed to accompany retirement:

"I don't have to put the alarm clock on in the morning,
I can go out when I want for a walk, I read a lot, I've
been reading about the old coal fields and the old
farming ways. Also I play a bit of snooker and won the
Club Championship since I retired. Also me and my son won
the dual competition, we were very thrilled about that".

"Being able to do as you like, and to be your own boss
for a change. Not having to get up at ungodly hours to
go to work".

"You don't have to get up at a certain time in the morning,
you're not clock-watching all the time. The whole day's
your own".

"Doing things in my own time, not having to find time for
them between periods of work. I really enjoy getting out
in the fresh air and going for long walks".

The advantages of living without a routine or regular timetable were commented upon by virtually all of the miners. Few reports actively disliking retirement. Three had found it difficult to keep occupied in retirement, all of these reporting that it was an "occasional" problem. Although this data would suggest only limited difficulties appearing in the transition to retirement, disenchantment in the long-term is an obvious possibility. In this context, we need to examine in greater detail the capacity of the retirement programme to provide help for the miner: What evidence is there to suggest he had been influenced by the ideas and advice which had been offered?

4.6.2. The Impact of the Course

In this section we shall consider what action - if any - the miners took as a result of attending the course. Ten months had elapsed since the ending of the programme and the final interview, there should be signs, therefore, of some response to the various sessions. Indeed, we would argue that it is unlikely that the course would stimulate extensive activity beyond this period; the influence of the programme should be at its peak, we would argue, in the period between our second and third interviews. What is the evidence provided by our data? We asked a series of questions to see if people could recall receiving advice on particular areas (e.g. finance). We then asked: "What have you done as a result of receiving this advice?" (Table 4:11). All of the group remembered having talks on the area of finance; only two, however, had actually done anything as a result of the advice:

"The speaker on social security suggested we should make an appointment at the social security office. I did this before I retired, and found them very helpful in explaining the position to me".

"One of the talks said that you should get your house put in order as regards repairs and not wait 'til you are 70 to do it. I thought a lot about this and got several repairs done to the house".

Everyone in the group remembered receiving talks on health and fitness, and there was strong evidence that the latter in particular had had considerable influence. Thirteen claimed to be taking action as a result of advice in this area, suggestions for regular exercise being the most popular advice.

"I now do more swimming, and dancing and try to keep active physically".

"Not sitting about for too long in one position, and taking exercise. I've paid particular attention to this, and I do as much exercise as I can".

"I do some of the exercises she told us about, also plenty of walks".

TABLE 4:11

"Have you done anything as a result of advice on any of the following topics...?				
TOPIC	YES		NO	
	n	%	n	%
Finance	2	9	21	91%
Health/diet	13	57	10	43
Leisure	–	–	23	100
Employment/ Voluntary work	–	–	23	100

"I do regular exercises and cut down on eating as I have a weight problem. As a result I feel a lot better for it".

The popularity of the talk on exercises can be attributed to two main factors: (a) there was considerable interest in the idea of regular exercise (some men, for example, acknowledged the problems of becoming "overweight" or "out of condition" without the routine of work); (b) the course was perceived as "useful" because it presented a series of clearly-defined objectives.

On the subject of leisure, only 16 actually remembered covering this topic, none having done anything as a result of the talk. Twenty-two recalled the talk on employment and voluntary work; none had taken any action. Eighteen could recall other subjects being given on the course, but there was little evidence to suggest that any specific action had been taken as a result of advice received. Overall, nine of the miners had taken no action as a result of the course; 13 had undertaken one action; one had taken more than one action.

More detailed comments on the course came in reply to the following question: "From your initial experience of retirement, can you suggest any ways in which the pre-retirement course could be improved?" Sixteen gave suggestions for improving the course: having a longer course (nine mentions) and improving financial advice (seven mentions) being the main recommendations. The concern with length echoes the findings from the Phase 2 interviews:

"I think probably two days a week and more time to have lectures - a longer time to talk to the lecturers and for them to talk to us. The items covered should have lasted longer - the pensions bloke from Sheffield could have another couple of hours really. He didn't explain things thoroughly enough, there wasn't time to talk longer. He was in a hurry you know. More about the money and your pension and what they could do to help you. Explaining how you get the money - I had all these Giro things coming and I didn't understand about how to go on about the Giro. I didn't understand how it worked. No I can't think - I was very lucky to get on the course really wasn't I?"

"More time should be given to each subject, the course could have been extended to at least 10 days. As it was, it was so concentrated that you tended to forget a lot of it".

"It should be extended, they should have at least six days instead of three. They seemed to have to rush everything to get it into three days".

"It should be longer, it should be 4-5 days. In three days, there's too much concentrated together, there's too much to take in".

TABLE 4:12

PHASE 1

"How long do you think it will take you to get used to not working? Do you think it will be ... (No time at all; A few weeks; A few months; or more than a few months; Can't say; Will be continuing in employment)?"

"Have you taken up any new leisure activities?"

"After retirement, do you think there will be times when you won't know what to do to keep occupied?"

"When you think about retirement, do you think of it as ... (An extended holiday; A new phase of your life; The beginning of old age; A life rather similar to the present; A rejection by society?)"

"Taking everything into account, how well prepared do you think you are for retirement. Would you say you are ... (Very well prepared; Fairly well prepared; Not very well prepared; or Not prepared at all; Can't say?)"

"Some people feel you can plan and prepare for retirement. Do you feel this way, or not? (Yes; No; Can't say?)"

"As you approach retirement, do any of the following matters worry you? (Retirement income; Your health after you retire; Income tax in retirement; Your housing after you retire; Your relationships with family or friends; The effect of retirement on you personally?)"

PHASE 3

"It takes some people a little while to get used to not working full-time. About how long would you say it took you to become used to not working? Would you say it was ... (No time at all; A few weeks; A few months;   Still not adjusted to retirement ; Never stopped/continued in full-time employment ; Other, specify?")

"Have you taken up any new hobbies or interests since you retired?"

"Have you found times since your retirement when it has been difficult to keep occupied?"

"When you think about your retirement, do you think of it as ... (An extended holiday; A new phase of your life; The beginning of old age; A life rather similar to when you were working; A rejection by society?)"

"Taking everything into account, how well prepared do you think you were for retirement? Would you say you were ... (Very well prepared; Fairly well prepared; Not very well prepared; or Not prepared at all; Can't say?)"

"Some people feel you can plan and prepare for retirement. Do you feel this way, or not? (Yes; No; Can't say?)"

"Now that you are retired, do any of the following matters worry you? (Your income in retirement; Income tax; Your health; Your housing; Your relationship with family or friends; The effect of retirement on you personally?)"

In the area of financial advice there was particular criticism of the lecture on tax:

"I thought the chap from the Income Tax Office told us nothing that we didn't know already, I think an Accountant would have been more helpful, you want to get all the tax advantages you can".

"I feel that a talk from the Inland Revenue is not useful at all. A talk on this subject from an Accountant to tell you what sort of allowances you can claim for would be of far more benefit".

"The talk about our retirement income should have been longer, there was a bit too much to take in at one go. The talk about income tax was a farce, the chap did his best, but he wasn't very helpful, as everybody's tax is different".

Finally, a number of people mentioned the need for changing the timing of the course:

"The course itself was very good, but I think it should have been six months before retirement. So that you have plenty of time to think over what was said, and make enquiries about points you're not sure about".

"It should be about six months before retiring, to give you plenty of time to think about it. Nothing else".

The findings revealed so far fail to indicate any major changes in retirement plans as a result of the course. It is still possible, however, that our group of miners experienced a less stressful transition period as a result of the advice. Is there any evidence to support this?

4.6.3. Attitude Change Over the Transition

When assessing attitude change in the last months at work and the first months of retirement, we found considerable stability amongst the miners. The McNemar test was used to examine the extent of change from the pre-course interview and the final interview. Table 4:12 indicates the questions used in this analysis.

Two questions reached a 10 per cent level of significance: fewer people at Phase 3 were worrying about their health and about income. The "resistance to retirement" scale showed a move towards greater optimism (Table 4;13). This was significant at 10 per cent. The underlying stability in feelings of life satisfaction is reflected in Table 4.14-4:16. The "Facts about Ageing" measure did not yield significant differences over the two phases, suggesting that any post-course improvement may have been lost.

4.6.4. Summary

Our findings would suggest that in certain areas (notably diet and exercise) the retirement programme appears to have

Resistance to Retirement Scale: Comparison of Phase 1-3 Responses

	PHASE 1 RESPONSE			PHASE 3 RESPONSE		
	Strongly Agree/ Agree	Not Sure	Strongly Disagree/ Disagree	Strongly Agree/ Agree	Not Sure	Strongly Disagree/ Disagree
People should not be made to retire solely because of their age.	13 57%	5 22%	5 22%	16 70%	1 4%	6 26%
I enjoy the time that retirement allows.	22 96%	–	1 4%	23 100%	–	–
If it were up to me alone, I would keep on working as long as possible.	4 17%	1 4%	18 78%	1 4%	3 13%	19 83%
I think things will go well for me in retirement.	21 91%	2 9%	–	23 100%	–	–
Retirement is mostly good for a person.	19 83%	3 13%	1 4%	23 100%	–	–

Satisfaction with Life

TABLE 4:14

"On the whole, how satisfied would you say you are with your life today?"				
	Phase 1 Response n	%	Phase 3 Response n	%
Very satisfied	14	61	16	70
Fairly satisfied	8	35	7	30
Not very satisfied	1	4	–	–
Not satisfied at all	–	–	–	–
No response	–	–	–	–
	23	100	23	100

TABLE 4:15

"Do you ever find yourself feeling "blue" or depressed?"				
	Phase 1 Response n	%	Phase 3 Response n	%
Often	–	–	–	–
Sometimes	5	22	2	9
Hardly ever	18	78	21	91
No response	–	–	–	–
	23	100	23	100

TABLE 4:16

"In general, how would you say you feel most of the time, in good spirits or in low spirits?"				
	Phase 1 Response n	%	Phase 3 Response n	%
I am usually in good spirits.	22	96	21	91
I am in good spirits some of the time and in low spirits some of the time.	1	4	2	9
I am usually in low spirits.	–	–	–	–
No response	–	–	–	–
	23	100	23	100

made some impact. However, its influence upon other areas
(notably, retirement attitudes and action in the area of
finance and leisure activities) is less easy to discern. It
should be noted, however, that the miners came to the course
with relatively optimistic views about retirement, and thus
the margin for change - in this area at least - was relatively
slight. We shall now discuss the implications of our findings
for the organisation of the retirement programme.

4.7. Discussion

In the previous section we reported upon interviews of
miners in the period of transition to retirement. In this
section we shall first draw a profile of the miners in retirement and then consider its implications for PRE.

The main picture to emerge is a situation where withdrawal
from work takes place within a close-knit network of relationships and activities. Amongst our group, five still had at
least one child at home; of the thirteen whose children had all
left home, 10 lived within 10 minutes of their nearest son or
daughter (as measured by their usual method of transport).
All 13 had seen their children within the week prior to the
interview. Seventeen had grandchildren, eight having four or
more. Apart from sons or daughters, 18 had seen a relative
within the week prior to the interview.

These contacts were supplemented by a network of friendships beyond the family. Virtually all of the miners reported
having friends in their neighbourhood. A minority (eight
people) had begun to make new friends in their retirement.
Most reported having a "confidant" with whom they could discuss
issues of personal concern or worry.

In terms of activities, consolidation of an existing
pattern was again the dominant theme. Most people reported
an increase in time spent on activities around the home. The
freedom to enjoy evenings in pubs and clubs without the
pressure of shift work was emphasised. Increased time spent on
activities such as snooker, watching football, going on walks,
having more holidays, was also mentioned.

How does this profile relate to the subject-matter and
organisation of the course? The programme attended by the
miners had three broad components: (a) living in retirement
(e.g. leisure activities, voluntary work); (b) health and
fitness; (c) financial advice. We shall now analyse the relationship of each component to the above profile.

4.7.1. Living in Retirement

There was little evidence - either in the Phase 2 or
Phase 3 interviews - that this component had made any significant impact. Indeed, in the case of the talks on leisure,
quite apart from the seven who couldn't remember having had a
session, nobody did anything as a result of the talk. Of course,
it may be argued that people are more likely to respond to this
lecture further into their retirement; moreover, it may have
played a role in boosting the individual's confidence and morale.

On the first point, the group of people who couldn't even remember the talk tends to suggest that it had a limited impact. There is a stronger case to be made for the second point, although this is probably more applicable to the course as a whole rather than individual items.

In terms of the other talks in this section, the session on "security in the home" was treated with interest, but there was no evidence to suggest that it had stimulated any particular activities. The same can also be said of the session on voluntary work.

There are two important issues to consider in the light of this analysis. If the objectives of the course are mainly to boost the individual's confidence in the transition to retirement, then the existence of these lectures can be justified. If, on the other hand, the objective is to achieve more fundamental changes in attitudes and expectations, then we would question the timing of the Nottingham course. Moreover, if this objective is taken seriously, then major issues will need to be faced by course organiser, employers and trade unions.

Returning to our profile of the miners, we find a group who had entered a period of stability in terms of family life and leisure activities. In this respect, suggestions for more involvement in adult education classes, broadening the individual's range of hobbies, encouraging participation in voluntary work, were out of step with the individual's overall development. This argument can be supported by research findings on the activities of older men and women. Castles and Guillemard, for example, in a French study, found that people in retirement tend to continue the same kind of interests they had enjoyed previously.[7] Such findings have also been confirmed in Britain by Abrams.[8] The implication of this research is that attempts at re-structuring work and family life are doomed to failure if they are begun when individuals are about to enter retirement. The conclusions from these studies need to be taken seriously by course organisers. Unless they are willing to depart from the type of programmes described in this report they should not expect the inclusion of general advice on leisure and related subjects to have any serious impact on the individual's retirement. It may contribute to the building of a good atmosphere inside a group, beyond this their inclusion in their present form seems very difficult to justify.

4.7.2. The Health and Fitness Component

In terms of activities undertaken as a result of the course this was easily the most successful component. This was partly because it touched a genuine concern that exercise - without the routine of work - might become restricted; partly also because the talk dealing with fitness was clearly focused, giving a positive and therapeutic approach to growing old. This session provided a useful case study confirming that where objectives are clearly set and where the content of the talk meets a need within the audience, important changes in behaviour and attitudes can be made.

4.7.3. The Financial Component

Although there was considerable appreciation of most of the sessions, some areas did come in for criticism (in particular the session on income tax). The significance of this is, we think, fairly clear. Thus most of the miners are unlikely to be eligible for supplementary benefits and may have to pay income tax whilst in receipt of NCB early retirement benefits. In the context of the retirement programme, therefore, where the course was relatively strong (e.g. information on state benefits) the information presented may have had no immediate relevance for the group. On the other hand, the area where it was weak (e.g. taxation) was seen as highly topical.

We would suggest that much of the material on state benefits could be successfully conveyed through well produced hand-outs. Time was spent, for example, explaining the process of claiming and the conditions for receiving benefits. This could probably be done more successfully if the verbal presentation was replaced by leaflets and booklets. The distribution, at the end of the course, of Age Concern's "Your Rights" handbook is a step in the right direction. By reducing the verbal presentation in this area more time could be allocated to examining the different components of the individual's retirement income. Given the number of items involved, it might be helpful to group together all the speakers on financial matters for a day (or more) of questions and answers together with individual counselling. We found evidence from our interviews that people were often confused about the relationship between different kinds of state benefits and benefits from the NCB (in particular, whether receipt of one benefit automatically led to withdrawal of money from other sources). This confusion was not helped by the organisation of the course, with the spreading of talks on financial matters throughout the three weeks: the effect of this led to an unnecessary fragmentation and lack of coherence in discussions on retirement income.

Although most of the components in the financial section can be justified, the talk on investments does raise some interesting issues. There is very little evidence from our interviews that any action had been taken as a result of the talk. Although we would concede that the closeness of the miners to their retirement produced a major constraint on this topic, other factors operated to reduce its effectiveness. The talk itself consisted of a "shopping list" of various ways of increasing one's savings (e.g. government bonds, building society accounts). The various items were presented in rapid succession, with the pro's and con's of each quickly summarised. With many in the group being unused to discussions of this type, and with no hand-outs distributed in advance of the session, the effectiveness of any recommendations was bound to be somewhat limited. A strong case could be made, we would suggest, for re-structuring this item on a question and answer basis, with more opportunity for personal discussion. There also needs to be an improvement in the range of leaflets and printed matter given to the group.

The Organisation of the Course: Some General Comments

Criticism about the length of the miners' programme was an important theme at the Phase 2 and Phase 3 interviews. Many expressed concern at the way in which material was crammed into a short space of time and there were complaints about the difficulty of following highly concentrated lectures.

The problems arising from the shortage of time were compounded by two factors. First, no attempt was made - either at the beginning of the course, or at the beginning of each lecture - to identify the main concerns of the group. As a result it is likely that time was wasted in covering issues which the participants did not see as relevant. Questions which were considered important often had to be fitted into a short space following a 40 minute lecture. Secondly, speakers failed to use the willingness of the group to initiate and maintain discussions. Arguably, the lecture-form was inappropriate to a group whose experience of learning had been through discussion and debate with friends and workmates. By using the conventional lecture the course played to the "weaknesses" rather than the "strengths" of the participants. Instead of using their confidence and ability to ask questions, the programme adopted a format where questions and discussion were secondary.

The limitations of the lecture model were reinforced by the venue chosen for the course (a single room in a building in the centre of Nottingham). Although a central location had a number of organisational advantages, 30 people placed in a relatively small seminar room provided a rather restricted forum. It wasn't possible, for example, to sub-divide the group for periods of discussion and counselling. The availability of other rooms would, we feel, have added greater depth and scope to the course.

One final recommendation concerns course length. The course we evaluated is run on a three week/one day per week basis. Criticism about the length of the programme could, we think, be met by running the course over consecutive days. This would reduce the fragmentation of issues discussed earlier; would help the build-up and exchange of new ideas; finally, it would increase group solidarity and discussion.

CHAPTER 4

FOOTNOTES AND REFERENCES

1. Simpson, I.H., et al., <u>Social Aspects of Aging</u>, Duke University Press, 1966.

2. Salaman, G., <u>Community and Occupation: An Exploration of Work/Leisure Relationships, Cambridge Papers in Sociology</u>, Cambridge University Press, 1974.

3. Simpson, I.H., et al., <u>op. cit.</u>

4. For an explanation of this statistic see the glossary in Appendix 1.

5. Rowntree, D., <u>Statistics without Tears</u>, Pelican Books 1981, p.118

6. Palmore, E., 'Facts on Ageing: a short quiz', <u>The Gerontologist</u>, 17, 4, 315 - 20, 1977.

7. Cited in Rapoport, R., and Rapoport, R., with Strelitz, Z. <u>Leisure and the Family Life Cycle</u>, RKP, 1975.

8. Abrams, M., 'Education and the Elderly'. <u>The Alice Foley Annual Memorial Lecture</u>, W.E.A., Bolton, 1980.

CHAPTER 5

CASE STUDY NUMBER TWO: THE SCOTTISH RETIREMENT COUNCIL

5.   Introduction

In this second case study we shall examine the work of an
established provider of retirement education, the Scottish
Retirement Council. The Council have the longest experience of
any organisation in terms of running courses and an evaluation
of their work has formed a key part of our research. It was
also thought that the Council would provide a comparison with
the younger Bristol Retirement Council, which is discussed in
a later section of this report.

5.1. Research Methods

In evaluating the work of the Retirement Council we faced
a number of difficulties: first, because of its distance from
Keele (most of the interviews were done by members of the
Project Team); secondly, because of the geographical spread
of the people attending courses (although we concentrated on
courses run in the Glasgow area, many people came from
companies and towns outside the city). To overcome some of
the problems involved in contacting potential respondents, we
concentrated on one particular venue (Langside College), taking
three programmes for men which started in the first part of 1980.
A total of 78 people had been enrolled (principally through
their companies).

Our basic procedure was to select for a personal interview
only those working for companies in the Glasgow area. To cut
down travelling time we arranged the Phase 1 interviews at the
individual's place of work (this did, however, create groups
with whom it was difficult to arrange interviews, e.g. night
shift workers, people on locations outside their work base and
personal applicants to courses). Our tactic for all these
individuals (together with those working for companies outside
Glasgow) was to send a postal questionnaire to assess whether
our interview group was distinctive in any way (results from the
postal group are discussed at various points in the report).
Sampling details are set out in Appendix 2.

5.2. The Development of the Scottish Retirement Council

The Council (first known as Glasgow Retirement Council)
was formed in 1958. A year later it mounted its first experimental course (at Langside College). The first annual report
identified the purpose of the course as follows:

"The purpose of the courses was to persuade men,
while still at work, to think about and plan for
their years of retirement; to provide them with
information and guidance which would enable them
better to plan for their future and to introduce to
them hobbies and interests to absorb their attention
during years of enforced leisure. It was intended
that, in these courses, those who were over-anxious

and fearful of the prospect of retirement would
find reassurance and that those who, in ignorance,
might be optimistic and in danger of disillusionment
and morale breaking disappointment should find sensible
advance warning of the problems to be met in retirement".[1]

The reference to "enforced leisure" is a reminder about
the historical context in which the courses emerged. This
was a period where workers were being urged to delay their
retirement, given a national context of (a) labour shortages;
(b) poor economic growth; (c) an ageing population. Thus the
work potential of the elderly was the subject of considerable
debate and scientific investigation throughout the 1950s. At
a government level, there was the National Advisory Committee
on the Employment of Older Men and Women (formed in 1952). At
a more academic level, numerous projects emerged to look at
questions such as retraining older workers, their accident rate
in industry and their ability to learn new skills. In general
terms, most of the projects were optimistic about the value
of older workers to industry. Moreover, they contributed to
a wider debate that work had therapeutic value to individuals
and that to deny its availability - via compulsory retirement -
was morally wrong. Optimistic findings from the work of
researchers were convenient for those expressing concern about
the economic effects of retirement. Of additional help, were
a range of medical and sociological studies suggesting that
retirement was detrimental to the health of older men: anxiety, suicide and premature death being listed among its consequences.

The Glasgow group's full title (The Glasgow Council for
Preparation for Occupational Activities on Retirement) itself
reflects this work-orientated environment. It was, without
question, an atmosphere which was to dominate the early part of
the Council's work. The problems which were seen to beset
people once they moved away from a work role were summarised in
the following list of points, given in the Seventh Annual
Report (1965-66):

"There are certain basic questions to which every man
and woman must, sooner or later, find his or her own
answers if the retirement years are to be really worth
living - and the sooner, the better."

First   When I retire and income falls from earnings to
        pension, how am I to maintain a proper measure
        of the standard of living I have been building
        up for myself over the years?

Second When the pressures of work are off, which have
        kept me physically and mentally on my toes until
        this time how shall I keep myself physically fit
        and mentally alert?

Third   When I am separated from those who have been my
        companions of every day at work, who are to be
        my companions and where will I find them?

Fourth   When the challenges of work which have given
          purpose to my life day by day are gone, what
          new interests, challenges, and purposes must
          I devise for myself?

Fifth   When I cease to fulfil the working role which
          has given me a sense of belonging, of being needed
          and of being useful, what part can I now play as
          an active contributing member of society?[2]

5.2.1. The Growth of Courses

·   Within the political and sociological context sketched
above the Council's work has expanded at a prodigious rate
(see Table 5:1). As we shall observe later in this report,
the expansion outlined in Table 5:1 may have caused problems
for the Council, particularly as it continued to rely upon
voluntary chairmen and lecturers. The burden of administering
(by 1980-81) nearly 60 courses per year inevitably brought re-
percussions for the quality of programmes. Moreover, the
Council had now to adapt to a quite different environment,
where attitudes both to retirement and to older workers were
undergoing radical change. Normal age retirees were developing a more positive view about the benefits of leaving work.
There was also the development of high unemployment and earlier retirement, areas to which the Council responded with
varying degrees of success. According to the Twenty-Second
Annual Report (1980-81):

"Although the Council's work has continued steadily
throughout the past year it is not surprising that
the state of the economy has affected it in a number
of ways. The increasing rise in early retirement and
in redundancy has had its influence on the men and
women attending our courses. The two groups are quite
different in their attitudes to Preparation for Retirement. Those taking early retirement, usually as
volunteers, are happy to attend, albeit rather ahead of
schedule, and the numbers sent to us by many organisations
have risen considerably. On the other hand, those being
made redundant (in many cases of identical   age groups)
have been extremely reluctant to attend and their numbers
have fallen. This is very noticeable among men, whose
numbers fell by over a hundred last year. It also follows
quite naturally that many companies and organisations,
having dispensed with their older employees, are unlikely
to have many people retiring over the next two or three
years and some fall in numbers may be expected for this
reason. Last year the Council held 59 courses in the
Strathclyde Region, the total number of students falling
slightly to 1,176".[3]

These changes form the essential background to this report.
Before examining their implications we shall analyse the type
of courses run by the Council and present our findings on interviews with participants.

TABLE 5:1

Courses provided for men and women

by the Scottish Retirement Council

(1959-1981).

	Number of Courses			Number of Participants		
	Men	Women	Total	Men	Women	Total
1959/60	3	–	3	43	--	43
1960/61	5	1	6	64	7	71
1961/62	7	3	10	95	39	134
1962/63	7	3	10	109	42	151
1963/64	10	5	15	135	52	187
1964/65	10	5	15	183	67	250
1965/66	10	5	15	193	62	255
1966/67	10	4	14	189	43	232
1967/68	15	4	19	247	52	299
1968/69	15	5	20	279	79	358
1969/70	15	5	20	313	107	420
1970/71	21	5	26	376	104	480
1971/72	22	10	32	388	126	514
1972/73	23	10	33	451	159	610
1973/74	26	10	36	591	176	767
1974/75	29	10	39	587	167	754
1975/76	35	10	45	739	206	945
1976/77	35	11	46	764	247	1,011
1977/78	40	15	55	857	265	1,122
1978/79	43	15	58	907	276	1,183
1979/80	42	15	57	917	357	1,274
1980/81	43	16	59	805	371	1,176
	466	167	633	9,232	3,004	12,236

Note: Separate courses are provided for men and women.

Source: The Scottish Retirement Council,Twenty-Second Annual Report,1980-81,p.4.

5.3. The Structure and Content of the Council's Courses

In Table 5:2 we have set out a selection of courses run at Langside College over a 20 year period. The early courses emphasise cultural and leisure needs in retirement, in contrast to later courses where financial issues form a larger component of the course. Another important change is that whilst the early courses had four out of the seven days allowing some time for group discussion, this element is removed entirely in the later programmes. Moreover, in the early days of the Council's work there was an evening introductory meeting for course members and lecturers. This was subsequently dropped (presumably due to administrative problems with an increasing number of courses) and an introductory session was put at the beginning of Day 1.

Despite the increased portion of time allotted to financial issues, the Glasgow Course - more than any others we have studied - makes a concerted attempt to influence recreational and cultural habits: approximately 10 hours on any one course being devoted to this area (in the early 1960s the figure may have been 13 hours, with emphasis on cultural as opposed to recreational pursuits). An important element in the analysis below will be to assess the medium-term response to this advice (evidence from some of our other courses suggests this is one of the less satisfactory parts of pre-retirement education).

We noted earlier the reduced amount of time allotted for discussion. This aspect was brought out when we attended sessions of courses run by the Council. It was not possible (because of the time factor) to attend a complete course; instead, we visited the second and final days of a course (for men) at Langside College and the opening day of a course (also for men) at Clydebank Technical College. A total of 10 different sessions were observed over the three days, seven of which conformed to a lecture-model (the length of each talk ranging from 42 to 82 minutes). The influence of the lecture-model was reinforced by the organisation of the course (desks arranged in traditional college fashion; attendance register taken at the beginning of each day).

The opening day of the Clydebank course began with a 59 minute introductory talk on the development of retirement. An important theme of the talk was its attempt to combat myths associating retirement with mental deterioration. The session also examined the question of voluntary work and part-time work in retirement.

The rest of the day was devoted to sessions from two speakers from the local DHSS office. The first talk lasted 42 minutes with a limited number of questions at the end. As with DHSS presentations observed on other courses, the standard of the talk was poor, with explanations of particular details about state pensions often highly confusing. The atmosphere wasn't helped by admission from the speaker to the audience that "he was the worst speaker on the course". The afternoon presentation from the DHSS lasted 40 minutes, with 20 minutes for questions and discussions. This still left the course with 50 minutes of spare time, only a limited amount of which was used for discussion.

TABLE 5:2

SCOTTISH RETIREMENT COUNCIL

DAY RELEASE COURSES FOR OLDER WORKERS (MEN)

PREPARATION FOR RETIREMENT

	DAY 1	DAY 2	DAY 3	DAY 4	DAY 5	DAY 6	DAY 7
1961-62	Introductory Meeting of members and lecturers Retirement and Money Discussion Crafts and Hobbies	Retirement and Physical Health Discussion Appreciation of Drama	Retirement and Mental Health Appreciation of Literature Gardening	Visits of Observation Foreshall Hospital, Geriatric Unit and Old People's Home Merrylee Lodge, Corporation Modern Purpose-built Home for Old People Appreciation of Art Kelvingrove Museum and Art Galleries	Retirement and Social Living Film Discussion Appreciation of Music	Retirement and Leisure – Further Ed. Provision Visit: Crafts & Hobbies Centre for Retired Persons at Penilee Books and Libraries Angling for Pleasure	The Consolations and Opportunities of Age Film Group Discussion Appraisal of Course
1968-69	Introductory Meeting Money Matters Eat Well and Keep Well Interests Out-of-Doors	Keeping Physically Fit Balancing the Budget Part-time Employment Opportunities	Keeping Mentally Alert Visit: David Cargill Club Books and Libraries	Visits of Observation Meet at Foreshall Hospital, Geriatric Unit and Old People's Home, Corporation Homes for the Elderly Safety in the Home Gardening	Aspects of Social Living Opportunities for Social Service Appreciation of Art: Kelvingrove Museum and Art Galleries	A Life of Leisure – Opportunities in Adult Education The Theatre and Television Visit: Crafts and Hobbies Centre for Retired Persons, Penilee, Crafts and Hobbies	The Bonus Years: Challenge and Opportunity Group Discussion Appraisal of Course
1973-74	Introductory Meeting Money Matters Books and Libraries Interests Out-of-Doors	Keeping Physically Fit Balancing the Budget Leisure Interests: Students' Forum	Keeping Mentally Alert Eat Well and Keep Well Retired Employees' Associations	Visits of Observation: Meet at Langside Geriatric Unit, Merrylee Lodge and Scott House, Corporation Homes for the Elderly Safety in the Home Gardening	Aspects of Social Living Opportunities for Social Service Visits: Crafts and Hobbies Centre for Retired Persons, Penilee Arts and Crafts	A Life of Leisure – Opportunities in Adult Education The Theatre and Television Appreciation of Art: Kelvingrove Museum and Art Galleries	The Bonus Years: Challenge and Opportunity The Theatre and Television Group Discussion Appraisal of Course
1977-78	Introduction to Course Money Matters: Pensions Money Matters: Supplementary Pensions Interests Out-of-Doors	Keeping Mentally Alert Income Tax Consumer Problems	Keeping Physically Fit (1) Keeping Physically Fit (2) Eat Well and Keep Well Security in the Home	Visit: Langside Geriatric Unit/University Geriatric Unit, Southern General Hospital, Merrylee Lodge and Scott House/Strathmore House Books and Libraries Gardening	Holidays for the Retired Visit: David Cargill Club/Dixon Halls Day Centre Visit: Penilee Centre Arts and Crafts	Opportunities in Adult Education Opportunities for Social Service Appreciation of Art: Kelvingrove Museum and Art Galleries	Aspects of Social Living Balancing the Budget The Bonus Years/Group Discussion Appraisal of Course
1981-82	Introduction to Course Money Matters: Pensions Money Matters: Supplementary Pensions Painting and Decorating	Mental Health Visit: Penilee Centre At Home with Electricity	Keeping Physically Fit Books and Libraries Eat Well and Keep Well Interests Out of Doors	Holidays for the Retired Opportunities in Adult Education Income Tax Gardening	Security in the Home Balancing the Budget Appreciation of Art: Kelvingrove Museum and Art Galleries	A Life of Leisure – Opportunities in Adult Education The Theatre and Television Group Discussion Appraisal of Course	First Aid Visit: David Cargill Club/Dixon Halls Day Centre Enjoy Your Retirement Appraisal of Course

The second day of the Langside course began with a 56 minute lecture on physical health, with a brief (four minute) period for discussion. The talk provided an overview of health issues, e.g. definition of health, health in Scotland, value of exercise, nutrition, problems relating to excess weight, dental health, effects of smoking, alcohol, nervous stress and causes of heart disease. This ambitious list of subjects raises complex issues about the type of health education retirement courses can handle. At this stage we shall simply make the point that from our observations, more detailed coverage (with more discussion) of a narrower range of subjects may have contributed to a more effective session.

The second lecture was a detailed examination of the dangers arising from electricity in the home. Despite its length (the talk lasted for 82 minutes) the session aroused evident interest amongst the group. There was opportunity for question and discussion throughout the session and the interest of the group seemed to be sustained.

The afternoon began with a 65 minute session on cookery, with a demonstration of various recipes from a sheet distributed at the beginning of the class. In some of the interviews conducted in Glasgow we encountered criticism of some of the recipes used (for example, that they were too expensive); however, this didn't appear to be viewed as a problem in this particular session.

The day concluded with a talk from a representative of Glasgow Parks department. This was built around a large number of slides illustrating parks in the Glasgow area. The session lasted for 47 minutes with a 10 minute period for discussion at the end. This type of session illustrates the Council's concern with educating people about leisure and recreational opportunities. However, the objectives of this particular talk were unclear. It may have stimulated interest for those keen on municipal parks; whether it needs to occupy 60 minutes of a retirement programme must be questioned.

The final day of the Langside course began with a 57 minute session on first aid. The rest of the morning comprised a visit to a centre for retired people in Glasgow. In the afternoon there was a final session exploring the benefits of retirement - given by somebody who had been retired for 15 years. The theme of the talk was the need to maintain activities through part-time and voluntary work and hobbies.

5.3.1. Concluding Observations

Two related issues emerge from our visit to the courses at Glasgow. First, on both courses there was only a limited amount of chairing during each session. This was an undoubted weakness of the programmes, given the indifferent quality of some of the speakers (particularly those dealing with the state pension and supplementary benefit). Secondly, in the sessions we attended the period allowed for discussion was relatively short. Even where time was available for an extensive period of group discussion, passive chairing gave this little encouragement.

The issue raised by both the above points is whether the reduction in hours allotted for discussion (Table 5:2) reflects tensions or inadequacies in the way courses have traditionally been chaired. From the examples we observed it is clear that the chairmen saw their role simply as that of introducing speakers and resolving administrative problems; in few instances did they intervene to clarify points of ambiguity or facilitate points of discussion.

Before taking our analysis further, however, we shall discuss the results of our survey with men who attended three courses at Langside College during 1980. We begin our anlysis with a description of the 29 men who were personally interviewed two weeks before their retirement programme.

5.4. Survey Results (Pre-Course Interview)

The Glasgow group were homogeneous in respect of age (21 were aged 64) but divided on the basis of their occupational background (14 were manual workers: 15 non-manual). The split reflects Council policy of providing a mixture of social and occupational backgrounds for their programmes. The range of occupations of those interviewed was fairly wide and included clerical workers, machinists, labourers and engineers.

Most of the group were close to their retirement (21 were six months or less away from leaving work). Twenty-three were leaving because of a fixed retirement age. In contrast to many of our other groups, only a minority of the latter would have stayed at work if given the opportunity. There was uncertainty, however, about whether work of any kind was to be sought in retirement. Five thought they would definitely look for work, but the rest either didn't know or could only say they would "probably" look for work. Although only six felt they would be sorry if they didn't get a job, a larger number (19) were concerned about missing being with other people at work.

This concern with the loss of workmates did not appear to produce pessimism about retirement itself. Twenty-six were looking forward to it; twenty had a clear idea of their future life, the majority viewing it in a positive way. Eleven people did feel that there might be problems keeping occupied, most however, thought this would happen only occasionally.

If our group seem fairly optimistic about retirement, can this be attributed to any conscious planning and preparation? Although a majority of those interviewed said that they felt "well prepared" for retirement, there was no indication of any extensive activity in respect of planning. For example, although most people were six months or less away from retirement, 11 claimed "hardly ever" to think about it with just five thinking about it "often". Nineteen had yet to work out the income they would receive in retirement. Moreover, 14 felt that planning for retirement was unrealistic. The following replies were representative of this group.

"I will just take it as it comes. It might not turn out as you prepared and then you would have wasted your time". (Progress Chaser, age 64).

"Just accept whatever comes along".
(Electrician, age 64).

"You've just got to wait and see what happens".
(Painter, age 64).

"Don't really need to - everyday activities I do
will be enough to keep me going".
(Clerk, age 63).

Only a small number of specific worries concerned our group
at this stage. Six were worried about income and four about
income tax. It is worth noting, however, that seven people
claimed to be worrying about the effects of retirement upon them
personally; 14 could think of something they would dislike about
retirement, with boredom and reduced income being prominent
among the list of concerns.

5.4.1. Concluding Comments on Phase 1

The interviews with 29 men, two weeks before their retirement course, found a group with positive attitudes towards
retirement, but divided on the question of planning and preparation. The group was also undecided about whether they would
return to work after retirement.

Four weeks after the course at Langside, the men were re-
interviewed to assess their immediate response to the programme
and to explore any change in attitudes towards retirement. We
shall now discuss the results of this interview.

5.5. Survey Results (Post-Course Interview)

In the first part of this section we shall examine comments
made by respondents about their course. In the second part, we
shall examine any changes in attitudes and knowledge about retirement issues brought about by the programme. Material will
be provided from both our interview and postal groups to indicate points of comparison.

The structure of the course seemed to have met the expectations of most of those we interviewed. The majority felt that
the course had come at the right time (Table 5:3); there was
satisfaction with the length of the course (Table5:4); and with
the time allowed for discussion (although there was some
dissension on this point from our postal group - see Table 5.5.).
None could identify a session which they had found too long,
although some talks could have been longer (Tables 5:6 and 5:7),
particularly those on gardening and painting and decorating.

Amongst the items considered "most useful", information
about pensions, income tax and gardening received most support.
In terms of "least useful" items the spread of topics was quite
broad, with the visit to the geriatric unit being most often
mentioned (eight times). From other questions we asked, however,
it was clear that this talk had aroused considerable ill-feeling
(in the interview group, 18 out of 29 felt that the visit should
be stopped); amongst the postal group the figure was 21 out of 35).

"In relation to when you retire, do you think the course came ....?				
RESPONSE	Interview n	Group %	Postal n	Group %
Too early	3	10	3	9
Right time	20	69	23	66
Too late	5	17	9	20
No response	1	3	–	–
	29	100	35	100

TABLE 5:4

"Thinking about the length of the course, did you find it ....?"				
RESPONSE	Interview n	Group %	Postal n	Group %
Too long	3	10	2	6
Right length	24	83	28	80
Too short	2	7	5	14
No response	–	–	–	–
	29	100	35	100

TABLE 5:5

"What about the time allowed to discuss and exchange ideas during sessions. Do you think there was ....?"				
RESPONSE	Interview n	Group %	Postal n	Group %
Too much time	1	3	–	–
Enough Time	19	66	20	57
Not enough time	8	28	13	37
Don't know	1	3	1	3
No response	–	–	1	3
	29	100	35	100

TABLE 5:6

RESPONSE	Interview n	Group %	Postal n	Group %
"Did you find any of the sessions too long?"				
Yes	7	24	6	17
No	22	76	28	80
Don't Know	-	-	1	3
No response	-	-	-	-
	29	100	35	100

TABLE 5:7

RESPONSE	Interview n	Group %	Postal n	Group %
"Do you think any of the sessions should have been longer?"				
Yes	16	55	20	57
No	13	45	14	40
Don't know	-	-	1	3
No response	-	-	-	-
	29	100	35	100

Comments on this topic also appeared in response to the question about whether improvements could be made to the course (19 of the interview group and 18 of the postal group mentioned some area for improvement). Concern about the visit to the geriatric unit was voiced in the following way:

"I didn't like the visit to the geriatric home, it was no help to people looking forward to retirement. You feel you were intruding, going around.... It's just not beneficial".
(Cost Accountant, Age 61).

"Visit to the geriatric unit was too much like: 'this is your future'. I didn't like that at all. I am looking forward to retirement, not looking for geriatric homes".
(Shop Manager, age 64).

"We were taken down to an old people's home but we left there quite depressed - I would have left that out. A simple explanation of facilities would have been better".
(Project Assistant, age 60).

This visit has now been dropped from the programme and from the comments of our respondents there would appear little justification for its return. However, it is of some concern that similar criticisms were voiced in Whittington's research on the Glasgow courses in the mid-sixties.[4] If her results were not communicated to the Council then this was certainly unfortunate; if, on the other hand, they were known, it would seem that there was an unnecessarily lengthy delay before the visit was abandoned.

Criticism about the quality of lecturing was mentioned by 10 people in our interview group. In common with some of our other courses, the sessions with speakers from the DHSS came in for strongest criticism.

"The lecturer (from the DHSS) talked down to you ... she seemed to forget that we are all grown-up people. Quite a few of us objected to it. The majority of the class didn't care for her".
(Shop Manager, age 64).

"The talk from DHSS was a bit weak .... left a little to be desired. Intention was good - but it didn't come off. Good topic but not dealt with very well".
(Training Assistant, age 63).

"Supplementary pension person was very bad, she was too concerned with whether you were going to rob them".
(Labourer, age 64).

"I didn't like the social security lecturer - she was very crude. If you've worked all your life they penalise you. They investigate all your finances. She almost seemed to be blaming us for working all our lives. She wasn't a very good lecturer".
(Painter, age 64).

It is important to separate two elements in these comments. First, concern at the quality of the lecture (clarity of presentation, ability to answer questions etc.); secondly, criticism about the role of the DHSS as a source of financial help. Some of our respondents seemed to feel that the DHSS were more concerned with concealing rather than revealing information about benefits. This last problem raises complex issues about the way in which state welfare is perceived and the specific role of the DHSS in the distribution of benefits. Presenting the issues in this way suggests the problems with this session will not be met simply through replacing "bad" with "good" lecturers; that deeper questions connected with images of welfare must be tackled; and that to achieve a more satisfactory response to this question may require the involvement of agencies independent of the DHSS. We also explored whether the courses had enlightened people either about specific problems or changed general attitudes towards retirement. Only a minority (Table 5:8) claimed that the course had made them aware of problems they had not considered before; most had retained the view of retirement they had had prior to the course (Table 5:9). More positively, a larger number could identify lines of action they would take as a result of the course (14 with the interview group; 28 with the postal group).

Finally, amongst the interview group, there was evidence that the sessions on "leisure and recreation" had made some impact (Table 5:10). Whether this will be sustained over a longer period will be assessed in our third interview. So far we have analysed some immediate comments and reactions to the course. Can we identify other changes from questions repeated over the two Phases?

5.5.1. Pre-Retirement Education and Attitude Change

Table 5:11 lists a number of questions which were repeated over the Phase 1 and Phase 2 interviews. The responses at Phase 1 and Phase 2 were compared for each question using the McNemar Test of significance of changes. There were only two questions where the results reached at least the 10% level of significance. These were questions concerning whether the group had worked out their income and how well prepared they felt for retirement. The McNemar Test showed an extremely significant change on the former question.

At Phase 1 only 10 had worked out their income; by Phase 2 this had increased to 24. Attitudes towards preparation for retirement showed a more modest change (significant at 10 per cent).

Comparisons between Phase 1 and Phase 2 also revealed on one of our measures a weakening in attachment to work. The attitude to work scale has a range of 4-20, a high score indicating a positive view of work. Scores for the 27 who received this measure over both phases declined from 11.3 (Phase 1) to 8.7 (Phase 2). Both the t-test and the Wilcoxon matched pairs signed-ranks test indicate this as highly significant. By contrast, the commitment to work scale, with a range of 7-21

TABLE 5:8

"Has the course made you aware of problems you had not considered before?"				
RESPONSE	Interview n	Group %	Interview n	Group %
Yes	9	31	6	17
No	19	66	29	83
No response	1	3	–	–
	29	100	35	100

TABLE 5:9

"Has the course changed your view of retirement at all?				
RESPONSE	Interview n	Group %	Interview n	Group %
Yes or in some ways	8	28	8	23
No	21	72	25	71
No response	–	–	2	6
	29	100	35	100

TABLE 5:10

"(Apart from returning to work) have the sorts of things you have thought about doing in retirement changed since you attended the pre-retirement course?"				
RESPONSE	Interview n	Group %	Interview n	Group %
Yes	9	31	6	17
No	19	66	24	69
Don't know	–	–	4	11
No response	1	3	1	3
	29	100	35	100

Table 5:11

Phase 1 - 2   Repeated Questions

"How long do you think it will take you to get used to not working? (No time at all; A few weeks; A few months; or More than a few months; Can't say; Will be continuing in employment)".

"Do you plan to look for any kind of work after you retire?" (Yes; No; Not yet decided).

"When you think about retirement, do you think of it as .... (An extended holiday; A new phase of your life; The beginning of old age; A life rather similar to the present; A rejection by society)?".

"On the whole, are you looking forward to the time when you will retire?".

"Do you have a clear idea of what life will be like for you in retirement?".

"After retirement do you think there will be times when you won't know what to do to keep occupied?".

"Taking everything into account, how well prepared do you think you are for retirement. Would you say you are... (Very well prepared; Fairly well prepared; Not very well prepared; or Not prepared at all)?".

"In the run up to your retirement have you......... (Talked over retirement with people outside work; Worked out your income in retirement; Taken up any new leisure time activities)?".

"Have you been worrying at all about your retirement?"

"Some people feel you can plan and prepare for retirement. Do you feel this way, or not?".

"As you approach retirement, do any of the following matters worry you: (Retirement income; Your health after you retire; Income tax in retirement; Your housing after you retire; Your relationship with family or friends; The effect of retirement on you personally)?".

(a high score indicating a high work commitment), made no significant movement over the Phases (12.4 at Phase 1 and 13.4 at Phase 2). The latter contains a list of general attitudes to work (e.g. "To me my work is just a way of making money"; I have sometimes regretted being in the kind of work I am now in"; "Some of my main interests and pleasures are connected with my work") and it is possible that these were more resistant to change than the more specific questions asked in the attitude to work scale.

Another measure we used was designed to examine "resistance to retirement". The responses over the two phases are illustrated in Table 5:12. This measure can be converted into a scale with a range of 5-25, high scores indicating low resistance to retirement. There was no movement over the two Phases (17.3 at Phase 1 and 17.2 at Phase 2) with the Phase 1 score indicating positive views towards retirement even before the course.

The study also contained a number of factual items designed to test the individual's knowledge concerning social security and related issues. With a maximum score of seven, mean scores increased over the two interviews from 4.8 to 5.2 (non-significant). Table 5:13 gives the results of scores on individual items. One-third of the group over both interviews gave an incorrect reply to the question on the state retirement pension. Uncertainty continued to be expressed in Phase 2 about the relationship between rent and rate rebates and the supplementary pension. There was, however, an increase in the number indicating knowledge about the age allowance.

Finally the self-completion booklet contained a quiz assessing people's knowledge about physical and social aspects of growing old. The measure had 12 factual statements about older people and respondents had to indicate whether the statements were true or false. The quiz consisted of four statements about the social demography of old age (2, 9, 11, 13); seven statements referring to views about older people and older workers (4, 5, 6, 7, 8, 10, 12) and one general statement about health and physical activity. Table 5:14 illustrates the responses of the group over Phase 1 and Phase 2. Unlike our other groups a number of people were unable to answer "true" or "false" to the 12 statements and, as a result, we have not tested for any significant changes on mean scores.

Comparing frequencies, however, we note stability in key areas (e.g. over three-quarters say "older people are set in their ways and unable to change" over both interviews, the group is also evenly divided in both interviews over whether "older workers can work as effectively as younger workers").

5.5.2. Summary of Results at Phase 2

The results of Phase 2 suggest conflicting responses being made to the course. On the one hand we find more people claiming to have calculated their income in retirement and to feel better prepared for the event. Conversely, the course had had a limited impact on the group's knowledge of a selected number of retirement issues and had left undisturbed general attitudes to retirement (although these were fairly positive even before the course).

TABLE 5 :12

Resistance to Retirement Scale: Comparison of Phases 1-2 Responses

	PHASE 1 RESPONSE			PHASE 2 RESPONSE *		
	Strongly Agree/ Agree	Not Sure	Strongly Disagree/ Disagree	Strongly Agree/ Agree	Not Sure	Strongly Disagree/ Disagree
People should not be made to retire solely because of their age.	18 62%	1 3%	10 34%	17 61%	1 3%	10 36%
I am looking forward to the time off that retirement will bring.	22 76%	5 17%	2 7%	22 79%	2 7%	4 14%
If it were up to me alone, I would keep on working as long as possible.	8 28%	1 3%	20 69%	8 29%	2 7%	18 64%
I think things will go well for me in retirement.	23 79%	6 21%	- -	23 82%	4 14%	1 4%
Retirement is mostly good for a person.	15 52%	10 34%	4 14%	19 68%	6 21%	3 11%

* Information not collected for one individual at Phase 2.

TABLE 5:13

Knowledge Scale: Comparisons of Phase 1-2 Responses						
T = TRUE F = FALSE	PHASE 1 RESPONSE			PHASE 2 RESPONSE *		
	Correct	Incorrect	Don't Know	Correct	Incorrect	Don't Know
A state retirement pension is always free of tax. F	14 48%	10 35%	5 17%	18 64%	10 36%	–
Medical prescriptions are free to men over 65 and women over 60. T	27 93%	1 3%	1 3%	26 93%	1 4%	1 4%
People may receive a supplementary pension if their income is below a certain level. T	27 93%	1 3%	1 3%	25 89%	1 4%	2 7%
People may receive rent or rate rebates only if they receive a supplementary pension. F	15 52%	11 38%	3 10%	16 57%	7 25%	5 18%
There is a scheme in existence to provide free or cheap legal advice for people who need it. T	25 86%	4 14%	– –	27 96%	–	1 4%
After 65, people get an age allowance entitling them to a greater amount of tax free income. T	16 55%	3 10%	10 35%	23 82%	3 11%	2 7%
It is possible for people to obtain an attendance allowance when they need constant care at home. T	20 69%	9 31%	– –	23 82%	5 18%	–

* Information not collected for one individual at Phase 2.

94

TABLE 5:14

Facts About Ageing Scale: Comparison of Phases 1-2 Responses

T = TRUE
F = FALSE

Item	T/F	PHASE 1 RESPONSE Correct	Incorrect	No response	PHASE 2 RESPONSE * Correct	Incorrect	No response
For people in their 60's and 70's regular exercise can restore physical activity and reduce heart rate and blood pressure.	T	23 79%	5 17%	1 3%	22 79%	6 21%	– –
At least 1 in 10 of peopled past 65 live in long stay institutions (ie homes for the aged, geriatric hospitals).	F	14 48%	12 41%	3 10%	18 64%	10 36%	– –
Nearly three quarters of people aged 65 or more in England and Wales live in a household withouta car.	T	This question was not given to the Glasgow group.					
Most older workers cannot work as effectively as younger workers.	F	14 48%	14 48%	1 3%	14 50%	14 50%	– –
The majority of older people are healthy enough to carry out their normal activities.	T	25 86%	2 7%	2 7%	27 96%	1 4%	– –
Most older people are set in their ways and are unable to change.	F	9 31%	18 62%	2 7%	9 32%	19 68%	– –
Old people usually take longer to learn something new.	T	23 79%	5 17%	1 3%	23 82%	5 18%	– –
It is almost impossible for most old people to learn new things.	F	20 69%	6 21%	3 10%	23 82%	5 18%	– –
One third of old people live alone.	T	18 62%	4 14%	7 24%	8 29%	19 68%	1 3%
In general most old people are pretty much alike.	F	21 72%	5 17%	3 10%	22 79%	6 21%	–
People aged 60 and over make up 20% of Great Britain's total population.	F	23 79%	3 10%	3 10%	21 75%	7 25%	–
When a person retires his health usually gets worse	F	19 66%	6 21%	4 14%	21 75%	7 25%	–
A majority of pensioners in Great Britain live in households below, at, or just above the official poverty line.	T	18 62%	8 28%	3 10%	19 68%	8 29%	1 3%

*Information was not collected from one individual.

5.6. Survey Results Phase 3 (Post-Course Interview)

Nearly a year after their pre-retirement courses the Glasgow group were interviewed for a third and final time. At this point they had been retired for an average of nearly nine months. We managed to contact 23 out of the original 29. Of the remaining six, two were deceased; one we were unable to contact; three refused to be interviewed for a third time. Another questionnaire was sent to our postal group, 21 out of the original 35 supplying us with information about their retirement. This information is included in the discussion below.

5.6.1. The Transition to Retirement

The majority of those we interviewed reported having a retirement ceremony (usually organised by their workmates). Fourteen had been back to their company since their retirement. At the time of the third interview only a small proportion of either our postal or interview groups were actually working. Those in the latter group were asked a series of questions to assess their attitude to being without a job. Sixteen were not worried about not having a job to do and 15 did not think they missed any feelings of usefulness which work may have provided. However, as might have been predicted from our Phase 1 interviews, 11 did report missing the friendships of people at work.

Despite missing workmates, both our interview and postal group had made fairly rapid adjustment to leaving work (Table 5:15). Many of those we interviewed commented upon the "holiday atmosphere" which characterised the early days of retirement:

"I celebrated. We had drinks. We went out and bought clothes which we needed - both myself and my wife".
(Joiner, age 64).

"Things to do in the house - my wife was still working. Did the shopping which I'd never done before. The first month seemed to go really quickly. I was embarrassed when I was in the shops - but not now - I've learned to cook and watch the prices. It's been an education".
(Clerk, age 64).

However, we should also note a minority who reported difficulties after the "holiday feeling" had subsided:

"I got up early and went around doing things.....had a walk, looked at the Job Centre. But after that I got a bit bored. I was looking forward to my holidays at the beginning. Now I've nothing to look forward to".
(Plumber, age 64).

"I used to go along to the Bowling Green. Of course it was mid summer when I retired. Now things are much more difficult. You're just relaxing at that period of time - trying to get used to it".
(Maintenance Foreman, age 64).

TABLE 5:15

"It takes some people a little while to get used to not working full-time. About how long would you say it took you to become used to not working? Would you say it was ....?"				
RESPONSE	Interview Group n / %		Postal Group n / %	
No time at all	11	48	9	43
A few weeks	2	9	4	19
or a Few months	5	22	5	24
(Stil not adjusted to retirement)	2	9	1	5
(Never stopped/continued in full-time employment)	-	-	1	5
Other	1	4	1	5
No information	2	9	-	-
	23	100	21	100

"Went on holiday immediately to Belgium - which was probably a mistake - when you usually come back from holiday you're looking forward to going back to work - but I had nothing. I felt dreadful - I should have left it for a couple of months before going on holiday". (Labourer, age 64).

These last comments raise questions about how far new leisure activities (particularly those which may have been suggested by the course) had provided support in the critical first year of retirement. A minority in both the postal and interview groups claimed to have developed new activities. In the interview group, 11 claimed to have thought about leisure activities in advance of leaving work; a further eight reported that there were things that they would like to do but hadn't yet done (these included travelling and further education classes). How far this interest in leisure had been stimulated by the course is difficult to determine. We did ask both of our groups whether they had taken any action as a result of advice given on leisure in the retirement programme: four of the interview group said they had done, together with eight of the postal group. Despite these fairly modest results it is possible that the course may have had an indirect effect on attitudes e.g. giving people greater confidence about their ability to handle time in retirement. On the other hand, we find the interview group evenly divided over whether they had found it difficult to keep occupied in retirement (10 claimed to be having difficulties); a result suggesting that it is possible to over-estimate the impact of the course on the leisure area. Some of the problems of occupying time emerged when we asked people whether there was anything they disliked about retirement. Five mentioned problems of isolation and missing people; three commented upon financial difficulties:

"The bad weather gets me down. I dislike being stuck in the house. I like to travel". (Maintenance Foreman, age 64).

"Boredom...there is too much time on your hands". (Clerk, age 64).

"Having to cut standards - you have to count every penny. Sometimes when I get up in the morning I wonder what I'm going to do - I've got nothing to look forward to". (Plumber, age 64).

"Miss the company" (Maintenance Worker, age 64).

"Miss my friends at work". (Electrician, age 64).

"It's the loneliness - you don't mix with people so much". (Labourer, age 64).

"The loss of companionship of business associates". (Cashier, age 64).

On the other hand only one person in the group could find
nothing pleasurable about retirement, the sense of freedom and
relaxation being the key items:

> "Having more time to do things in my own time - you
> can plan ahead better. Socially I'm better off - I
> can plan ahead. My relationship with my family and
> friends is better since I retired".
> (Clerk, age 64).

> "Having more time to do the things I want to do,
> gardening and seeing my family more. We have gone
> on a couple of Saga holidays to Durham and the Isle
> of Wight. We take advantage of the pensioners' bus
> pass and the concessionary train fares and often go
> off for the day. We're also going to bowling and
> swimming which is free for pensioners".
> (Costing Clerk, age 64).

> "Not having to go to work.....not getting up.....not
> having to face a job".
> (Lathe Operator, age 64).

In most cases, home-centred activities formed the central
focus of activities: with 13 doing more gardening; 14 more
housework; 10 watching more TV; 14 more reading. This pattern
of activity would suggest that if there had been an influence
on the part of the reitrement programme it had been along fairly
conventional lines: there was no evidence to suggest that the
course had encouraged the group to think about a broader and
more extensive range of leisure activities.

5.6.3. The Impact of the Course

We tried to assess whether the group had responded to areas
of advice given on the courses. In both our groups the financial
sessions had generated some response (Table 5:16) with 11 of the
interview group claiming to have taken some action (mainly investing in Granny Bonds or sorting out supplementary benefit).
Nine of the interview group claimed to have taken action in the
health area with regular walks and cutting down on food being
the main items. Advice on employment had been taken by relatively few. Two people in the interview group reported taking
action as a result of advice received on other sections of the
programme.

A number of interpretations can be made of these results.
A positive interpretation would be that with 17 out of 23 in
the interview group claiming to have taken some form of action,
the course had achieved a considerable degree of success. Yet
one should also note that in 12 instances action had been
confined to one area alone (usually finance), suggesting that
the response to the course had been highly selective. The
suggestion is that certain items of information were extracted
(e.g. amount of state pension; effects of the earnings rule),
with other sections of the course being ignored (particularly
those dealing with the social psychology of retirement, leisure
and voluntary work). However, even accepting this interpretation, the range of reactions to the programme was still fairly
wide.

TABLE 5:16

"Have you done anything as a result of advice on any of the following topics ....?"						
TOPIC	Interview Group			Postal Group		
	Yes	No	No response	Yes	No	No response
Finance	11 48%	12 52%	-- --	8 38%	12 57%	1 5%
Health/Diet	9 39%	14 61%	– --	7 33%	14 67%	– –
Leisure	4 17%	19 83%	-- --	8 38%	13 62%	– –
Employment/ Voluntary work	3 13%	19 83%	1 4%	4 19%	16 76%	1 5%

TABLE   5:17

PHASE 1	PHASE 3
"How long do you think it will take you to get used to not working? Do you think it will be ....(No time at all; A few weeks; A few months; or, More than a few months: Can't say; Will be continuing in employment)?"	"It takes some people a little while to get used to not working full-time. About how long would you say it took you to become used to not working? Would you say it was .... (No time at all; A few weeks, etc.)?"
.Have you taken up any new leisure activities?"	"Have you taken up any new hobbies or interests since you retired?"
"After retirement, do you think there will be times when you won't know what to do to keep occupied?"	"Have you found times since your retirement when it has been difficult to keep occupied?"
"When you think about retirement, do you think of it as ......(An extended holiday; A new phase of your life; The beginning of old age; A life rather similar to the present; A rejection by society)?"	"When you think about retirement, do you think of it as ...... (An extended holiday; A new phase of your life; The beginning of old age; A life rather similar to when you were working; A rejection by society)?"
"Taking everything into account, how well prepared to you think you are for retirement. Would you say you are .....(Very well prepared; Fairly well prepared; Not very well prepared; or, Not prepared at all; Can't say)?"	"Taking everything into account, how well prepared to you think you were for retirement? Would you say you were .... (Very well prepared; Fairly well prepared; Not very well prepared; or Not prepared at all; Can't say)?"
"Some people feel you can plan and prepare for retirement. Do you feel this way, or not? (Yes; No; Can't say)?"	"Some people feel you can plan and prepare for retirement. Do you feel this way, or not? (Yes; No; Can't say)?"
"As you approach retirement, do any of the following matters worry you? (Retirement income; Your health after you retire; Income tax in retirement; Your housing after you retire; Your relationship with family or friends; The effect of retirement on you personally)?"	"Now that you are retired, do any of the following matters worry you? (Your income in retirement; Income tax; Your health; Your housing; Your relationship with family or friends; The effect of retirement on you personally)?"

At one extreme there was a group clearly resistant to
what the course was trying to achieve

"It was very boring at times, sitting around all the
time...a lot of them (i.e. other people on the course)
were falling asleep....it was particularly bad on the
last day when one of the 'big shots' came and told us
what to do and what not to do. A lot of the course
didn't apply to me anyway because my wife is working
and won't qualify for social security".
(Clerk, age 64).

"They started telling us about courses at University -
in French and German - people around here would find
you ridiculous (if you went to them). To be honest our
attitude towards the course was 'well that's one day
less at work....only four days to go'. It's working
class people who go on these courses and there is a
feeling 'well at least it's a day off work'. The course
hasn't been a lot of good to me. Most of us went along
and listened to the lecturers and said 'well that was
quite an interesting lecture but it won't affect my
retirement very much'. They lectured at you, they should
ask you first what your problems are".
(Progress Chaser, age 64).

These statements do not completely reject the course but
they do indicate reactions to a method of approach which appears
to be lecturing to the working man about how we should order his
life in the period after work. Conversely, there was another
group genuinely appreciative - as evidenced in the comment
below - of the attention given to them:

"I was pleasantly surprised at how comprehensive it was...
I couldn't improve on it. Seeing people in a similar
situation to yourself was very helpful. The course made
you feel that there were people concerned about you - that
made you feel good".
(Lathe Operator, age 64).

In the middle, however, are those who have no strong
reaction either way to the programme and whose attitudes are
neither challenged nor changed in any fundamental way. Indeed,
it is striking that when we look at attitude change between
Phase 1 (the pre-course interview) and Phase 3 (the final
interview) there is general stability in responses to key
questions. (See Table 5:17). The only change was a move towards
taking up new leisure activities (significant at five per cent),
although the course may have had only an indirect influence on
this area. The sense of stability is reinforced when we examine
Tables 5:18 to 5:21 and assess the responses to questions both
about retirement and about attitudes towards life in general
before and after retirement. In both these areas there is
either very little change over the transitional phase or a movement towards greater optimism.

The argument, then, which begins to emerge is for general
attitudes being left unaffected by the course. In line with
this there is little substantial movement in people seeking a

TABLES 5:18 - 5:20

On the whole, how satisfied would you say you are with your way of life?	Phase 1 Response		Phase 3 Response	
	n	%	n	%
Very satisifed	9	39	9	39
Fairly satisfied	13	57	11	48
Not very satisifed	1	4	-	-
Not satisifed at all	-	-	-	-
No response	-	-	3	13
	23	100	23	100

Do you ever find yourself feeling "blue" or depressed?	Phase 1 Response		Phase 3 Response	
	n	%	n	%
Often	-	-	-	-
Sometimes	10	43	4	17
Hardly Ever	13	57	16	70
No response	-	-	3	13
	23	100	23	100

In general, how would you say you feel most of the time, in good spirits or in low spirits?	Phase 1 Response		Phase 3 Response	
	n	%	n	%
I am usually in good spirits	18	78	16	70
I am in good spirits some of the time and in low spirits some of the time	5	22	4	17
I am usually in low spirits	-	-	-	-
No response	-	-	3	13
	23	100	23	100

TABLE 5:21

Resistance to Retirement Scale: Comparison of Phases 1-3 Responses

	PHASE 1 RESPONSE			PHASE 3 RESPONSE *		
	Strongly Agree/ Agree	Not Sure	Strongly Disagree/ Disagree	Strongly Agree/ Agree	Not Sure	Strongly Disagree/ Disagree
People should not be made to retire solely because of their age.	14 61%	—	9 39%	12 60%	—	8 40%
I enjoy the time off that retirement allows.	18 78%	3 13%	2 9%	17 85%	3 15%	—
If it were up to me alone, I would keep on working as long as possible.	6 26%	1 4%	16 70%	5 25%	2 10%	13 65%
I think things will go well for me in retirement.	19 83%	4 17%	—	17 85%	2 10%	1 5%
Retirement is mostly good for a person.	11 48%	8 35%	4 17%	12 60%	6 30%	2 10%

* Three people were not asked this question at Phase 3.

change of direction to their lives in responses to the
programme. Where the course does appear to have an influence
is in some practical areas, for example, in helping people to
calculate post-retirement income; in providing advice on tax
and investments. Beyond this,its impact on more substantive
areas is relatively slight.

5.7. Discussion

   To understand the situation facing the Scottish Retirement
Council we need to go back to its origins in the 1950s. In
this period, as we suggested earlier, there was concern about
the traumatic effects of retirement and about the inability of
people to use leisure constructively. This was undoubtedly
mirrored in many of the survey reports of the day (Townsend
being a classic example).[2] The problem for the Council has been
one of adjusting to a situation where retirement is meeting with
greater acceptance. Unfortunately, this change has yet to be
acknowledged in many of the leaflets distributed by the Council.
For example, in a discussion on psychological problems of retirement we learn the following:

   "......retirement prevents the further satisfaction
   of the needs that were previously satisfied at work.
   More than that, it does so suddenly. It is a shock,
   a crisis which demands that we reorganise our lives
   to meet it. This kind of change of gear becomes much
   harder for us as we get older and more used to a
   fixed habitual routine of life. The shock of retirement affects our lives. It demands a sudden alter-
   ation in our habits of spending money, it often
   separates us from many of or most of our friends, it
   may involve going to live in a different area or even
   a different town and it very often deprives us of a
   great number of our usual enjoyments".

   For some individuals this description may be accurate, but
as a general description it is no longer acceptable. Certainly,
it presents a far too depressing picture to be of very much use
on most pre-retirement courses. Attitudes towards retirement
are, however, only one dimension of changes to which the Council
must now adjust. Two other aspects of equal importance are
greater variation in financial provision (particularly with the
spread of occupational pensions); variation in retirement ages
(is separate provision required for early voluntary retirees?
Involuntary retirees? Redundant older workers?). These changes -
as the Council's latest Annual Report itself recognises - raise
quite fundamental policy issues. From our analysis of the
interviews, however, it is clear that only limited change has
been implemented. Financial advice to meet the diversity of
needs on any course is still very limited; health advice remains
pitched at such a broad level that it is difficult for individuals
to adopt specific courses of action; much of the leisure advice
still assumes a group liable to be undermined through "enforced
leisure".

   The obvious response to those criticisms would be that:
"given that we are running 60 courses a year it is virtually

impossible to keep abreast of the sociological changes described".
That, of course, is precisely the Council's problem; namely the
conflict between providing educational courses (with all the
administrative burden that implies) <u>and</u> attempting to innovate
and develop experimental retirement programmes. In the concluding analysis of the report we shall offer some suggestions
as to how these problems might be resolved.

CHAPTER 5

FOOTNOTES AND REFERENCES

1. The Glasgow Retirement Council, First Annual Report, 1960, pp. 8-9.

2. The Glasgow Retirement Council, Seventh Annual Report, 1966, p.4.

3. The Scottish Retirement Council, Twenty-Second Annual Report, 1981, p.7.

4. Whittington,D. A Study of the effectiveness of day release courses in 'Preparation for Retirement' organised by Glasgow as reflected in participants' reactions. M.Ed. Thesis. University of Glasgow, 1967.

5. Townsend, P. The Family Life of Old People, Penguin Books 1957.

CHAPTER 6

CASE STUDY NUMBER THREE: SHELL INTERNATIONAL

6.   INTRODUCTION

In this third evaluation report we consider one of the most
ambitious of the courses analysed in our survey. The organisation concerned is Shell International, a multi-national oil
company who have been running a six-day pre-retirement programme
since 1976. As we shall see below, the course contains many
features which commentators on pre-retirement education (PRE)
recommend to those organising courses. Moreover, unlike many
of the courses we studied, external pressures had not forced any
major compromise with key features of the course, the structure
of the programme remaining fairly settled since its introduction.

6.1. Research Methods

The company divide their courses into two groups according
to income. For this research we decided to concentrate upon
the lower income group (salaries below £10,000). We approached
all the individuals attending the three junior level courses
organised in 1980. The responses were as follows:

February Course

15 eligible employees: 10 agreed to participate

April Course

12 eligible employees: 10 agreed to participate

November Course

12 eligible employees: 9 agreed to participate

Out of the 29 who received an initial interview, one person
became seriously ill and was unable to be interviewed again; one
refused to be interviewed for a second time.

6.2. The Organisation of Pre-Retirement Education

Prior to the introduction of a pre-retirement course,
there was provision for a two hour session with each employee
on financial aspects of retirement. This was augmented by a
short talk on health and a review of the amenities available
to pensioners within the organisation. Because of what were
seen as rapid changes in pension legislation and the economic
environment underpinning retirement, a programme was devised
covering a range of subjects to be discussed over a six day
period.

At the start of the evaluation, eight courses were run each
year. Course size is limited to around 25 people i.e. 15 staff
and 10 partners. Participants are normally 12-18 months away
from retirement, with most being in their mid-to late-fifties
i.e. 50-55 years for staff with overseas service; 58-60 for UK
regionals. Two levels of courses are provided: one for junior
staff (incomes below £10,000); the other for senior staff
(incomes £10,000 plus). A large proportion of the latter will

have been stationed abroad for most of their working life.

6.3. The Pre-Retirement Programme

In this section we present a description of the type of course attended by our respondents. The course observed was for those at junior level and with one exception had identical content and structure to the courses attended by those we interviewed. The distinctive feature of two of the latter courses was a talk on bereavement, this was later dropped from the programme and was not included in the course described below. Details of the course are given in Table 6:1.

Considerable attention is given to facilitating group discussion during the programme. Participants are seated at tables arranged in a large square; name cards placed around the tables encourage the use of first names. The first day is devoted to exploring immediate feelings towards leaving work, with an examination of current research on attitudes concerning work and retirement. These opening sessions are seen as a deliberate attempt to "loosen-up" the group and to get people familiar with the personal biographies and attitudes of other group members.

From this general exploration of retirement the course proceeds in the following week to a discussion of individual topics (interspersed by discussion groups). Below we describe three of the six days, concentrating on the sessions devoted to finance and health.

6.3.1. Financial Advice

Apart from the three sessions on the company pension, unemployment benefits and national insurance, the course provides a further day and a half for a discussion on personal finances. These sessions encourage considerable participation by the group, usually after an opening presentation from the specialist speaker. The opening session of the financial talk attempted an overview of the impact of retirement on personal income, the merits of commutation, the effects of inflation and the value of annuities. The second session detailed the main sources of investment with an evaluation of their advantages and disadvantages. This period lasted for two hours and attempted a fairly ambitious coverage of financial issues. For those who may have only limited expertise in this area (and they probably represented about half the group) the weight of detail in this session may have been fairly daunting. There was some confirmation of this in the afternoon discussion period, where a minority expressed confusion about the range of possibilities on offer. The positive side to the discussion about this problem is that, in contrast to many courses, people did feel confident enough to openly express matters of concern. In this example there was a constructive debate about what the course was trying to achieve and what the limits were to pre-retirement education. One way of making the description of investments less abstract, would be to rearrange the financial talks. On the fourth day there was a valuable session examining different case studies of people about to retire. These were particularly well-handled and a variety of situations were presented. It would be

TABLE 6:1

SHELL INTERNATIONAL: PREPARATION FOR RETIREMENT COURSE

1st Day:	Retirement perspective (discussion on the nature of retirement, review of research projects, case studies).
2nd Day:	The Company Pension. Unemployment and related benefits National Insurance Employment prospects and opportunities.
3rd Day:	Financial presentation Part I: The Investment Scene; where to go for advice.
4th Day:	Part II: Case Studies Medical Matters (Part I): A General Practitioner's View of Retirement.
5th Day:	Voluntary Work Company facilities for pensioners Private Health Schemes Medical Matters (Part II): A Positive View of Health and Retirement.
6th Day:	Adult Education Psychological aspects of retirement Small group discussion Course Assessment.

more appropriate, however, to have a discussion on these
case studies (preferably in small groups) on the preceeding
day. Each group could then bring a range of questions out of
which the various investment possibilities would arise. This
might allow the different options to appear more distinctive
than is the case at present.

The section on Wills which concluded the morning
session of the fourth day was well-structured and aroused
considerable interest (only a minority in the group claimed
to have made a Will).

6.3.2. Health Advice

The afternoon was comprised of the first of the two sessions
devoted to health in retirement. This session was given by a
GP and was divided into two parts: the first dealing with general health; the second, on various aspects of the participants'
relationship with his or her doctor. In the afternoon of the
fifth day there was a talk from a company doctor on more detailed aspects of health, including: diet, exercise, smoking, heart
disease, blood pressure, and alcohol. Including tea breaks, the
two sessions lasted for nearly four hours.

There seems little doubt that the case for a presentation
from a GP is very strong, particularly in a context where
employees will have received considerable medical support from
the company during their working life. However, there may be
a case for a more flexible approach to the four hour contact
time, allowing for more comment and involvement from the group.
There was a reliance in these sessions on a formal presentation
or quasi-lecture, a feature at odds with the participatory element in other areas of the course.

In addition to the above talks there was a session on
private health schemes and a discussion on the effects of
retirement on scheme membership. This session was fairly brief
(lasting under 30 minutes) and didn't have sufficient time to
properly explore the value either of private health care in
retirement or the merits of different schemes. If this session
is retained it needs to be supplemented by material such as
the "Which?" guide to private health care.

Finally, both the medical sessions make some attempt at
providing a positive approach to health in retirement. This is
reinforced by the session on adult education on the last day of
the course, where various myths about the ageing process are
challenged. This part of the programme also looks at the
questions of learning in later life and the opportunities for
acquiring new skills and abilities.

6.4. Survey Results (Phase 1)

At the time of the first interview, our sample was on
average 10.3 months away from retirement. Eight had six months
or less to go; 19 had a year or more. This was a long-service
group, 21 out of the 27 having been employed with the company
for 20 or more years. The majority were white-collar workers,
all of whom were in their fifties. The sample was divided between

13 males and 14 females. All of the group were retiring at 60 or earlier (four were taking early retirement). There were nine single people in the group together with one divorcee and one widower.

Seventeen gave compulsory retirement as the main reason for their leaving work, and 10 of these would have elected to remain with the company if they had been given the opportunity. Everyone in the sample was asked whether they would look for work after retirement: nearly half thought this might be the case; virtually all claiming they would look within the first year of their retirement.

Only six people were actually worried about not having a job to do, but 20 did feel they would definitely (12) or probably (eight) miss being with people at work. The friendship element was an important factor behind the reasons people gave for wanting to work in retirement:

"It is largely because of the loss of companionship of people that I want to do something. I need something to occupy me for a few years".
(Female, Secretary, age 59).

"I will be moving to a house at Eastbourne and I think this is the best way to meet new people and make friends".
(Female, Administrative Assistant, age 53).

"Can't stagnate, I don't want to lose the company of people throughout the day. I am on my own at home so I want to get out and meet people".
(Male, Telephone Technician, age 58)

Despite this concern about the loss of work-based friendships, considerable optimism was expressed about retirement. Although it was nearly a year away, a majority thought about it often. Twenty were looking forward to it, although only 11 had a clear idea of the changes which it might bring. Only seven thought they might have problems keeping occupied after leaving work. This optimism was reflected in the images people associated with retirement. For example, only two identified it as the "beginning of old age" and none viewed it as a "rejection by society".

There was considerable evidence that the idea of planning and preparation was seen as a realistic objective. Eighteen felt themselves to be very (four) or fairly (14) well prepared for retirement, with a majority suggesting that preparation should be started a year or more before retirement. Financial planning and mental preparation ("conditioning oneself to a complete change of life", as one respondent put it) were the areas to which most attention had been directed. Eighteen claimed to have thought seriously about the kind of things they would like to do in retirement. Amongst the comments we find:

"To become involved in social work of some kind - 'Citizens Advice Bureau', for example".
(Female, Administrative Assistant, Age 53).

"I have time to try and write which I have always wanted
to do....but never had peace and quiet....".
(Male, Salaries Clerk, age 58).

"I am starting on a world tour next November. I am
very keen on producing my own fruit and flowers; following tennis tournaments over the South Coast; music -
records and concerts; reading, cookery, decorating, needle-
work and all the things I have never had enough time for.
I also want to take up an Adult Education course. I shall
do keep fit classes each week".
(Female, Secretary, age 58).

"I would very much like to take up floral arrangements
and would like to join a keep fit class and I am fond
of ballroom dancing".
(Female, Copy Typist, age 58).

There is evidence to suggest, therefore, that even before
the course a majority of the group had committed themselves
to some form of retirement planning. It may be that - through
the years - our respondents had developed a life-style where
the idea of planning played an important role (in relation
to their occupational careers, their family and their personal finances). This was assisted by an organisational framework
which was committed to career and retirement planning. This
environment undoubtedly contributed to the optimism with which
retirement was viewed. A majority could think of something they
would like about retirement, greater freedom being the main item
(22 mentions).

"Free from the discipline of doing something at the
same time everyday".
(Female, Secretary, age 59).

"Leisure time...being able to do things as I want
and when I want. Play tennis and watch cricket;
spend more time with my father".
(Male, Administrative Assistant, age 59).

"Being with my family. Being able to go out and
about more. Without the grind of the rat race".
(Male, Salaries Clerk, age 59).

"Time to do the things I want to do. Being free
from daily commitments".
(Female, Supervisor, age 53).

Eight people did feel they would find something to dislike
about retirement, the friendship element again being crucial:

"I shall miss my friends, the biggest problem will
be missing people at work".
(Female, Secretary, age 54).

"Loneliness. Always working with a group, you've got
to adjust to being on your own".
(Female, Administrative Assistant, age 55).

"I shall miss the companionship of colleagues".
(Male, Marketing, age 59).

"Being lonely".
(Female, Administrative Assistant, age 50).

"Being at home all day - every day - might be nobody
there to talk to....everybody is at work".
(Female, Typist, age 58).

"I suppose if not able to occupy myself - boredom
I think! I shall miss all my friends and contacts
(in the company) - perhaps one could develop more
relationships nearer home".
(Male, Personnel Officer, age 58).

6.4.1. Summary

Although the pre-course interviews did find evidence for
some wishing to remain at work, considerable optimism was expressed towards retirement. Most important of all, the idea of
planning for retirement received support from the majority of
those interviewed,with long-term preparation being viewed as
a realistic objective.

6.5 Survey Results (Phase 2)

We shall first discuss our findings on the reactions of
participants to the course and then assess whether there
has been any significant change in respect of attitudes towards
retirement and knowledge about retirement issues. A majority
of the group were satisfied with the timing of the course in
relation to their retirement, although 10 did feel that it had
come too late (Table 6:2). There was clear support for the
length of the course (Table 6:3), although 16 felt there was
insufficient time to discuss and exchange ideas during the
sessions (Table 6:4). In terms of the length of individual
sessions, 10 felt that the presentation on investments could
have been longer; six felt the need for a longer talk on taxation.

We asked people to identify particular topics which they
had found "most useful". Advice on investments was the dominant
item, receiving 20 mentions; the maximum received by any other
topic was five mentions (for national insurance). In terms of
"least useful" items, the talk on bereavement received nine
mentions (six people thought that the talk should have been
omitted from the course). Since only two out of the three courses
we studied received the talk on bereavement, these results suggest
a fairly high level of resistance to this topic (or, to be accurate, with the way in which it was presented). There was a feeling
amongst some of our respondents that the talk should have been
less about the emotional impact of bereavement and more about its
practical consequences:

"Shorten course on bereavement and combine it with the
medical course - it went on for much too long and was
too 'heavy'. Need an explanation in simple language
as to what a husband and wife should do in first instance
if they woke up to find their partner had died in their
sleep".
(Male, Operations Assistant, age 57).

TABLE 6:2

"In relation to when you retire, do you think the course came ....?"		
Response	n	%
Too early	1	4
Right time	16	59
Too late	10	37
No response	–	–
	27	100

TABLE 6:3

"Thinking about the length of the course, did you find it ......?"		
Response	n	%
Too long	3	11
Right length	22	82
Too short	2	7
No response	–	–
	27	100

TABLE 6:4

"What about the time allowed to discuss and exchange ideas during sessions. Do you think there was ....?"		
Response	n	%
Too much time	–	–
Enough time	10	37
Not enough time	16	59
Don't know	1	4
No response	–	–
	27	100

Since the survey the talk on bereavement has been dropped and the programme now includes a session on making a Will. Judging from our results this would appear to have been a positive move.

Very few people could identify new subjects to add to the course, although 19 mentioned areas which could be improved. Apart from the item on bereavement, there were 10 suggestions for improving the financial presentation. A number of people mentioned the need for more time to be allowed for discussion. Two people felt that a course five years before retirement would be worthwhile - one which concentrated exclusively on the financial side. There was a minority view that the course was of less relevance for those on lower incomes:

"Mainly for people who had a lot of years service - 30 years or more and a lot of money to invest, these are the ones who need more time to talk about investment. But doesn't cover people who haven't had many years service and who don't have that much pension and we need more help really as we won't have so much money and still have to manage all the bills".
(Male, Telephone Technician, age 58).

"I thought when they produced two financial whiz kids they seemed to concentrate on the higher income brackets. Talked about investing £40,000. Many of us have never seen this sort of money - there were different classes".
(Female, Copy Typist, age 58).

The tension arising from a mixed group is also implicit in the following comment:

"Although I fully appreciate the difficulties involved and possibly the impracticality of it, it would obviously be of mutual benefit if all members were of equal standing with the same mutual problems. One in our course was from overseas staff - lots did not apply to him. Some were in a lower category with different problems".
(Male, Marketing, age 59).

We mentioned earlier that eight in the group were single people and there were two comments that the course gave insufficient attention to their particular needs:

"I was the only single lady on the course and I feel it would have been a good idea if it could have been so arranged that there were some other single ladies on it at the same time. The problems we face and some aspects of our retirement are totally different to those of the married people".
(Female, Secretary, age 54).

"Course should be more directed to the problems of single people - too much given to married couples. If one wanted information regarding the position of the single person one had to ask for it. It would have been helpful to have the aims and objectives of each session given in advance of the course, so that one could have prepared any questions in advance also.
(Male, Purchasing Supervisor, age 59).

Table 6:5

```
┌─────────────────────────────────────────────────┐
│         Phase 1 - 2 Repeated Questions            │
├─────────────────────────────────────────────────┤
│                                                   │
│ "How long do you think it will take you to get used to │
│ not working? (No time at all;  A few weeks;  A few │
│ months;  or More than a few months;  Can't say;  Will │
│ be continuing in employment)".                    │
│                                                   │
│ "Do you plan to look for any kind of work after you │
│ retire?"  (Yes; No; Not yet decided).             │
│                                                   │
│ "When you think about retirement, do you think of it │
│ as .... (An extended holiday;  A new phase of your │
│ life;  The beginning of old age;  A life rather sim- │
│ ilar to the present;  A rejection by society)?". │
│                                                   │
│ "On the whole, are you looking forward to the time │
│ when you will retire?".                           │
│                                                   │
│ "Do you have a clear idea of what life will be like │
│ for you in retirement?".                          │
│                                                   │
│ "After retirement do you think there will be times │
│ when you won't know what to do to keep occupied?". │
│                                                   │
│ "Taking everything into account, how well prepared │
│ do you think you are for retirement.   Would you say │
│ you are ... (Very well prepared;  Fairly well prep- │
│ ared;  Not very well prepared;  or Not prepared at │
│ all)?".                                           │
│                                                   │
│ "In the run up to your retirement have you ....... │
│ (Talked over retirement with people outside work; │
│ Worked out your income in retirement;  Taken up any │
│ new leisure time activities)?".                   │
│                                                   │
│ "Have you been worrying at all about your retirement?". │
│                                                   │
│ "Some people feel you can plan and prepare for    │
│ retirement.   Do you feel this way, or not?".     │
│                                                   │
│ "As you approach retirement, do any of the following │
│ matters worry you: (Retirement income; Your health │
│ after you retire;  Income tax in retirement;  Your │
│ housing after you retire;  Your relationship with │
│ family or friends:  The effect of retirement on you │
│ personally)?".                                    │
│                                                   │
└─────────────────────────────────────────────────┘
```

We tried to explore how far the course had promoted thoughts about taking specific courses of action or led to a re-evaluation of retirement itself. Nineteen identified specific things they would do as a result of the course, the area of finance (15 mentions) being the most popular item. (No other subject reached beyond three mentions). The following replies were typical of many:

"Look into and act on the question of mutual life insurance so our position over our house is covered in the event of the death of one of us. Will also make sure that my sister and I talk over and act on any matters relating to our finances. The course has reinforced my view that this must not be put off any longer".
(Female, Administrative Assistant, age 53).

"Go to the consultant for advice on investment and not invest myself".
(Female, Accounts Supervisor, age 53).

"Made me feel less confident - I thought I had it 'all buttoned up' but the course made me think again and more carefully about certain aspects of retirement. Nevertheless, I am quite happy with the decision to retire, but I shall now make more effort to get things done. I shall write to the social security department".
(Female, Administrative Assistant, age 55).

"Will go into the question of investment a lot more deeply".
(Male, Architect, age 58).

Twelve mentioned problems which the course had made them aware of, financial questions again being the key item (nine mentions). At a more general level, however, only six mentioned that the course had changed their view of retirement.

The programme contained a number of items recommending involvement in a broader range of leisure, educational and voluntary activities. In the second interview we asked people whether they had thought about doing any new activities as a result of the course. There were just five positive replies.

6.5.1. Pre-Retirement Education and Attitude Change

We shall now discuss in more detail whether the course had actually influenced attitudes towards retirement. Table 6.5. gives a list of questions repeated at Phase 1 and Phase 2. The responses were compared for each question using the McNemar test of significance of changes. In the context of the retirement programme our null hypothesis is that the course will have a neutral effect both upon retirement attitudes and on knowledge about retirement issues. The test was run on all the above questions, none of the computed values reaching the ten per cent level of significance. It was not possible, therefore, to reject the null hypothesis. In fact, there was remarkable consistency in the replies given over the two phases. This point is illustrated in the Tables 6:6-6:8.

TABLE 6:6

" After retirement, do you think there will be times when you won't know what to do to keep occupied?"				
Response	Phase I Response		Phase 2 Response	
	n	%	n	%
Yes	7	26	8	30
No	19	70	19	70
Can't say	1	4	–	–
	27	100	27	100

TABLE 6:7

"Taking everything into account, how well prepared do you think you are for retirement. Would you say you are ...."				
Response	Phase I Response		Phase 2 Response	
	n	%	n	%
Very well prepared	4	15	7	26
Fairly well prepared	14	52	15	56
Not very well prepared	5	18	3	11
Not prepared at all	3	11	1	4
Can't say	1	4	1	4
	27	100	27	100

TABLE 6:8

"Some people feel you can plan and prepare for retirement. Do you feel this way, or not?"				
Response	Phase I Response		Phase 2 Response	
	n	%	n	%
Yes	17	63	17	63
No	10	37	8	30
Can't say	–	–	2	7
	27	100	27	100

The consistency of these replies reinforces our earlier argument that people came to the course with fairly committed views about retirement. They were, in many areas, optimistic about their future life, the role of the course helping to confirm the validity of an existing set of attitudes. This argument is given some support in the scales and indices used in the study, for example, the questionnaire contained a five item measure designed to examine resistance to retirement. Scoring was in the range 5-25, a high score indicating low resistance to retirement (Table 6:9). The group had a fairly high score in the initial interview (17.3), one which remained virtually unchanged at Phase 2 (17.5). If we examine replies to these measures some interesting points emerge.

The evidence appears to be that people are able to separate the imposition of retirement (something to be criticised) from the event itself. Indeed, there are many features of retirement which are seen as highly attractive. Given this outlook, the response individuals make to the course becomes rather selective. People do not (or very rarely) attend to relieve general anxieties about leaving work; rather, they go to secure information and clarification on specific topics. From the comments made about individual items it is clear that the financial presentation was seen to be a crucial area, with the remaining subjects generating varying degrees of interest but nothing very tangible in respect of affecting plans for retirement. This shouldn't, however, be taken as a justification for building the course exclusively around financial issues. First, many of the other subjects will have increased the individual's confidence about their retirement. Secondly, it may be that action in the non-financial areas comes at a later stage, if this is the case we should find some evidence in our final interview. Thirdly, with early retirement and younger retirees, the leisure, educational and health areas may come to be perceived with equal importance as those concerned with finance.

6.6. Survey Results (Phase 3)

Eighteen months after their retirement programmes and eight months into their retirement, a third interview was completed. From our original group of 27, one person had died and six had yet to reach compulsory retirement age. The discussion below thus refers to the 20 whom we were able to interview at Phase 3, with comparisons - where relevant - to their attitudes at Phase 1.

6.6.1. The Transition to Retirement

Seventeen reported a leaving party before their retirement and unlike our other groups this had usually been organised by the company. Eighteen had returned to the company since their retirement, mainly to see friends, attend retirement parties or to attend social functions:

"Why did you go back to the organisation?"

"To have lunch with friends and attend farewell parties and meetings of the social club".
(Male, Administrative Assistant, age 57).

TABLE 6 : 9

Resistance to Retirement Scale: Comparison of Phase 1-2 Responses

	PHASE 1 RESPONSE			PHASE 2 RESPONSE		
	Strongly Agree/ Agree	Not Sure	Strongly Disagree/ Disagree	Strongly Agree/ Agree	Not Sure	Strongly Disagree/ Disagree
People should not be made to retire solely because of their age.	20 74%	6 22%	1 4%	21 78%	3 11%	3 11%
I am looking for- ward to the time off that retirement will bring.	24 89%	3 11%	– –	23 85%	4 15%	– –
If it were up to me alone, I would keep on working as long as possible.	3 11%	5 19%	19 70%	4 15%	1 4%	22 81%
I think things will go well for me in retirement.	20 74%	6 22%	1 4%	23 85%	4 15%	– –
Retirement is mostly good for a person.	14 52%	10 37%	3 11%	13 48%	13 48%	1 4%

"I have been back to do a bit of shopping and to visit
my friends. To have lunch with them and talk to them".
(Female, Secretary, age 58).

"For other retirement parties and I've been back for
a couple of meals and also to use the shop. I still
bank down there so when I go down I visit my office
and see my friends".
(Female, Secretary, age 59).

"I was invited back to lunch and to a long service dinner
and to the 25 years club".
(Female, Administrative Assistant, age 50).

Eight were working either full- or part-time, in five
instances with the company itself. Three individuals were actually
working full-time, albeit for very different reasons:

"What is the most important reason for your wanting
to work in retirement?"

"I don't want to work but the company was in a spot and
I felt I had to do it for them. The new computer
programmes will not be ready until next year and then
I shall feel able to go. In all honesty I must admit
that the extra salary and the effect on my pension is
very nice but it would not have been enough on its own
to make me stay on".
(Male, Salaries Clerk, age 59).

"The challenge of proving to myself, family and friends
whether I can make it financially in the big world without the protection and security provided by the company".
(Male, Job Evaluator, age 58).

"I didn't actually want to but the DOE said they would
not pay me unemployment benefit unless I was available
for work and as I had not budgeted to have to pay my
own stamp for the next five years until I am 60 I was
forced to get some sort of employment which would enable
me to safeguard my retirement pension".
(Female, Secretary, age 54).

Outside of full- or part-time work, six reported taking
on new hobbies in this early period of retirement. However,
12 reported interests or hobbies which they wanted to do but
hadn't yet taken up, these including: voluntary work, arts and
crafts, sports and travelling. Even without these activities,
only one person claimed to be having difficulties keeping
occupied. Eight months into retirement, the majority felt that
retirement had worked out very much as they had expected.
Sixteen claimed they had been fairly or very well prepared for
retirement. As in our Phase 1 interviews, most individuals
continued to be fairly committed to the idea of planning, with
long term planning (two years plus) meeting with considerable
support.

In this Phase 3 interview we asked people to identify any aspects of retirement they had found pleasurable or anything which they had disliked. Everyone we saw identified something pleasurable about retirement, the experience of greater freedom being the most popular item.

Five people mentioned aspects of retirement they had disliked and in one instance there had been fairly major problems of adjustment:

"At first everything was lovely, going out having freedom, but after a while I got bored and got another job, which I don't like at all. In comparison with the job I retired from it is like having a holiday. I'm leaving the one I have now. I don't like the loneliness. I went out to look for people, I have a car which helps. I go out if I'm unhappy or bored. I would dislike it more if I didn't have a car, loneliness is very important in my life if I wasn't able to meet people and go out then that would be part of the dislikes.....I miss my workmates very much".
(Female, Administrative Assistant, age 50).

6.6.2. The Impact of the Course

With some 18 months having passed since their course, we were particularly interested in whether people had taken action as a result of advice they had received and in their general comments about the programme. From the comments made at Phase 2 (four weeks after the course) we were anticipating some activity in the area of finance. In fact, seven reported some form of activity (Table 6:10), although others remarked that the course had made them more aware of financial matters. Amongst the group of seven, advice on commutation was seen as the most helpful area.

Recommendations on health (four mentions) and leisure (no action taken) met with less response, although they may have had an indirect influence upon the group. Seven, however, responded to suggestions on employment and voluntary work.

As a general response to the course - in the areas mentioned above - 13 out of the 20 who were interviewed, claimed - 18 months after the course - to have taken some action. Bearing in mind, however, that 15 had either done nothing at all or had responded to just one area of advice, the response to the course had been fairly specific.

We also asked people - given their initial experience of retirement - whether they could think of any areas for improvement on the programmes. Many commented, in fact, that they felt that the course had been excellent and generally well organised. There were suggestions for a refresher course just before retirement, a point which was also brought out in response to the question:

"In relation to when you retire, do you think the course was too early, too late or about the right time?"

Eleven registered concern at the timing of the course, including seven who felt that it had come too early.

TABLE 6:10

"Have you done anything as a result of advice on any of the following topics ....?"				
Topic	Yes		No	
	n	%	n	%
Finance	7	35	13	65
Health/Diet	4	20	16	80
Leisure	-	-	20	100
Employment/Voluntary Work	7	35	13	65

Criticism continued to be voiced about the session on bereavement and there was support for more basic information on the financial side:

> "I felt that the lecture on health was too long -
> that is the sort of thing that one can talk over
> with one's doctor. The financial talk was excellent -
> but I think that it should also include a more basic
> lecture for those who are not quite used to financial
> matters ......

> ....a little more information again for those not too
> well educated, on the Social Security subjects and
> just how to go about getting help. Otherwise it was
> excellent".
> (Male, Salaries Clerk, age 59).

> "The finance talk needs to be altered a little to give
> more help to those who do not have much capital or
> pension - it was difficult to understand for those of
> us who were not as well educated as some. I only under-
> stand it because I had had it all explained to me three
> years earlier when my husband died and I had to deal with
> investing his money".
> (Female, Photo-Copier Operator and Printer, age 58).

> "I think they could have covered more of the actual
> mechanism of getting a DHSS pension. They did cover
> the business of getting a job - I think Shell could
> have covered it a lot more. I think there was too
> much talk aimed at those with a lot of money. It got
> too much".
> (Female, Secretary, age 59).

6.6.3. Attitude Change in the Transition to Retirement

With the group now eight months into retirement we were interested in seeing if there had been any changes in attitudes towards retirement since the Phase 1 interview and whether pre-retirement education had played a negative or positive role in this process. Tables 6:11-6:17 illustrate some of the changes over this 18 month period. Very little movement had in fact occurred over the 18 months. It seems clear that people had entered the final phase of work with fairly settled and positive views about retirement, views which were to remain static over the transitional period. What implications does this have for the organisation of the pre-retirement course?

6.7. Discussion

An obvious point is that although attitude change is a fairly marginal element in people's experience of the course, the programme does meet a need for help in areas such as finance and employment. In terms of content, in fact, we met very little criticism about how the course was handled. However, there were problems, as we have indicated, with the timing of the course, and this is an area where improvement could be made. At present, people received the course 18 months prior to their retirement.

TABLE 6:11

"How well prepared do you think you are/were for retirement?"				
Response	Phase 1 Response		Phase 3 Response	
	n	%	n	%
Very/fairly well prepared	14	70	16	80
Not very well/Not prepared at all	6	30	4	20
Can't say/No response	–	–	–	–
	20	100	20	100

TABLE 6:12

"Some people feel you can plan and prepare for retirement, do you feel this way or not?"				
Response	Phase 1 Response		Phase 3 Response	
	n	%	n	%
Yes	13	65	14	70
No	7	35	6	30
Can't Say/No response	–	–	–	–
	20	100	20	100

TABLE 6:13

"After retirement, do you think there will be times/Have there been times in retirement when it will be/has been difficult to keep occupied?"				
Response	Phase 1 Response		Phase 3 Response	
	n	%	n	%
Yes	5	25	1	5
No	14	70	18	90
Can't say/No response	1	5	1	5
	20	100	20	100

TABLE 6:14

"When you think about retirement, do you think of it as .... the beginning of old age?"				
Response	Phase 1 Response		Phase 3 Response	
	n	%	n	%
Yes	2	10	2	10
No	18	90	16	80
Can't say/No information	–	–	2	10
	20	100	20	100

TABLE 6:15

"When you think about retirement, do you think of it as .... a rejection by society?"				
Response	Phase 1 Response		Phase 3 Response	
	n	%	n	%
Yes	–	–	1	5
No	20	100	18	90
Can't say/No information	–	--	1	5
	20	100	20	100

TABLE 6:16

"On the whole, how satisfied are you with your way of life today?"				
Response	Phase 1 Response		Phase 3 Response	
	n	%	n	%
Very satisfied	5	25	6	30
Fairly satisfied	13	65	13	65
Not very satisfied	2	10	–	–
No Response	–	–	1	5
	20	100	20	100

TABLE 6:17

"Do you ever find yourself feeling "blue" or depressed?				
Response	Phase 1 Response		Phase 3 Response	
	n	%	n	%
Often	–	–	–	–
Sometimes	8	40	6	30
Hardly ever	12	60	13	65
No Response	–	--	1	5
	20	100	20	100

This period was presumably taken as a compromise between having a course very close to retirement or having one some years before leaving work.

Unfortunately, there are definite problems with this arrangement. On the one hand, it is far enough away from retirement to create problems regarding the accuracies of the material for the individual's retirement. On the other hand, the programme is sufficiently close to retirement to make the changing of general attitudes highly unlikely (even the financial advice may be difficult to implement within this period). These problems are, in some instances, being made more acute with the increasing number of people taking early retirement, a factor which will reduce the period between the course and eventual retirement. It is worth recalling that the original group of 27 were, at the time of their programme, just 10 months away from retirement. If trends towards early retirement continue such a figure is unlikely to be exceptional.

One alternative to the dilemma we have stated is to divide the course into two blocks of three or four days, organising one course for people between the ages of 45-50 (although this would not be called preparation for retirement) and another for when they are in their last six months at work (this would be called a pre-retirement course). The former would be concerned with attitudes towards mid-life change, long-term financial planning and health in mid-life.

The latter would provide information vital for the transition. It would not be concerned with changing attitudes but merely with providing knowledge. The pre-retirement course described in this report tried to do both these things. This may have been possible when there was greater homogeneity in retirement ages. However, with more variation in this area (together with the other changes affecting policies towards retirement), this model may become less effective.

SECTION 3

In this section we attempt a detailed account of the impact of retirement education. This is done both on a comparative basis and through pooling all the individuals interviewed for our research. Thus, our description tries: first, to examine whether retirement education has <u>any</u> impact; secondly, whether some courses are more effective than others.

TABLE 7:1
COURSES STUDIED

	B.A.	BRISTOL	EMI	MARS	NCB	SHELL	GLASGOW	JAGUAR
Length of course	2 Days	2 Days	2 Days	2 Days	3 Days	6 Days	7 Days	8 Days
Course Organiser	B.A.	Bristol Ret'nt Council	Legal & Gen-eral	Mars	Notts Pre-Ret'nt Council	Shell	Scottish Ret'nt Council	Jaguar
How close to ret-irement?	Final Year	Mostly Final Year	Final Year	3 Years	Mostly Final Year	1 Year – 18 mnth.	Mostly Final Year.	Final Year.
Grades of workers	All Grades	All Grades	All Grades	All Grades	All Grades	Junior or Senior	All Grades	All Grades
Sex	Men + Women	Men + Women	Men + Women	Men + Women	Men	Men + Women	Men	Men + Women

* Excluding partners where invited.

CHAPTER 7

IMMEDIATE POST-COURSE CHANGES

7. Introduction

In this chapter we shall describe the social characteristics of individuals attending the eight programmes included in our survey. We shall also study the immediate impact of the course, drawing upon data from our Phase 2 interview. Table 7:1 summarises the main characteristics of the courses studied (for further information on these the reader is referred to Chapter 3).

7.1. The Phase 1 Interview: A Comparison of the Eight Groups

Our interview two weeks prior to each course provides us with basic information on the comparability of the eight groups. To indicate the strength of any statistical differences between them we shall use the following terms: extremely significant (at 0.1 per cent), highly significant (at 1 per cent) and significant (at 5 per cent). In the majority of cases we shall use a chi-squared statistic for testing differences between independent samples.

Using the Registrar General's classification of occupations, the differences between the groups were extremely significant (Table 7:2). The two extremes were represented by the miners (manual) and Shell (almost entirely non-manual). Both the Retirement Councils have a policy of encouraging a mixture of social and occupational groups, a feature most clearly represented by the case of the Scottish Council. However, it is worth noting that unskilled workers are under-represented on all our courses, social class three (manual and non-manual) being the dominant group. Only two of our courses had a near equal number of women to men participants (Table 7:3), and the preponderance of men in our sample should be kept in mind when reading this report. Although the majority of people in the eight groups were married, one of the groups (Shell) included nine single people. The groups varied in terms of their mean retirement age (Table 7:4). The youngest was Shell International (57.8 years) and the oldest, Jaguar (64.3 years).

When we examined the length of time before retirement, differences between the groups were found to be extremely significant (Table 7:5). Two of the courses had a majority with less than three months to go before leaving work (National Coal Board and Bristol Retirement Council). Shell and Mars had approximately two-thirds of their participants nine months or more from retirement. Obviously, at these extremes, the aims and objectives of the course must vary. For those whose retirement is imminent, the course should become a means of acquiring knowledge about basic factual items (e.g. the state pension, supplementary benefits). For those further away from retirement, discussions about financial investments and retirement attitudes may take on a deeper meaning.

TABLE 7.2

SOCIAL CLASS								
Social Class	NCB EXPERI-MENTAL	MARS	BRISTOL	JAGUAR	B.A.	EMI EXPERI-MENTAL	GLASGOW	SHELL
Non-Manual	– –	3 10%	10 35%	5 36%	16 40%	12 50%	15 52%	25 93%
Manual	24 100%	27 90%	19 65%	9 64%	24 60%	12 50%	14 48%	2 7%
TOTAL	24	30	29	14	40	24	29	27

$x^2 = 61.7$ d.f.= 7   0.1% significant

TABLE 7.3

GENDER								
Gender	NCB EXPERI-MENTAL	MARS	BRISTOL	JAGUAR	B.A.	EMI EXPERI-MENTAL	GLASGOW	SHELL
Male	24 100%	26 87%	20 69%	13 93%	33 83%	15 63%	29 100%	13 48%
Female	– –	4 13%	9 31%	1 7%	7 17%	9 37%	– –	14 52%
TOTAL	24	30	29	14	40	24	29	27

$x^2 = 39.2$ d.f. = 7   0.1% significant

TABLE 7.4

MEAN RETIREMENT AGE (YEARS)							
NCB EXPERI-MENTAL	MARS	BRISTOL	JAGUAR	B.A.	EMI EXPERI-MENTAL	GLASGOW	SHELL
60.3	62.4	61.0	64.3	63.4	63.2	64.0	57.8

TABLE 7:5

Length of time before Retirement

Time Before Retirement	NCB EXPERI-MENTAL	MARS	BRISTOL	JAGUAR	B.A.	EMI EXPERI-MENTAL	GLASGOW	SHELL
Less than 3 months	16	3	15	–	6	9	11	4
	67%	10%	52%	–	15%	38%	38%	15%
3 - 9 months	6	5	13	14	24	11	14	7
	25%	17%	45%	100%	60%	46%	48%	26%
More than 9 months	2	16	–	–	10	4	2	16
	8%	53%	–	–	25%	17%	7%	59%
TOTAL	24	24 *	28 *	14	40	24	27 *	27

x^2 = 95.7   d.f. = 14   0.1% significant

(* The remaining individuals in these groups had not received confirmation of their retirement dates).

TABLE 7:6

"Do you plan to look for any kind of work after you retire?"							
Response	NCB EXPERI-MENTAL	MARS	BRISTOL	JAGUAR	B.A.	GLASGOW	SHELL
Yes	6	11	18	5	23	6	13
	25%	37%	62%	36%	58%	21%	48%
No/Not Yet Decided	18	19	11	9	17	23	14
	75%	63%	38%	64%	42%	79%	52%
TOTAL	24	30	29	14	40	29	27

x^2 = 17.9   d.f. = 6   1% significant

NOTE: EMI has been excluded from this table, since the question was not asked at Phase 2.

A fixed retirement age was the main factor in the decision to leave work for six out of the eight groups. The clear exception to this trend was the miners, the bulk of whom were taking early retirement.

There was a highly significant difference in participants' views over whether work would be sought in retirement (Table 7:6). Financial disincentives together with health problems reduced the number of miners looking for work. The Bristol group contained a number of people retiring early on a small company pension, a feature which increased their need for employment.

Only small proportions in each group felt they would actually worry about not having a job, although the problem of missing friends and, to a lesser extent, missing feelings of usefulness or achievement did seem to pre-occupy many (there were no statistical differences amongst our groups on these items). We tried to assess how long individuals thought adjustment to retirement would take (Table 7:7). Although the differences between the groups were not statistically significant, we should note that variation between Glasgow and British Airways (58 per cent of the former visualising immediate adjustment, compared to 26 per cent of the latter).

The groups varied significantly over whether they were looking forward to retirement (Table 7:8). Most positive were Glasgow (with just three negative replies). More ambivalent were British Airways and Bristol Retirement Council. These were also the groups expressing the highest level of concern about financial issues, and this was probably a factor influencing this result. Most of our groups were evenly divided over whether they had a clear idea of their future life in retirement. Age and social class may have influenced some of the responses. The Shell group were the most ambivalent on this question. This group is also the youngest of those we interviewed and it may be that the length of time they were expecting to face in retirement produced an element of uncertainty. By contrast, EMI had the second highest number of non-manual workers and was one of the closest to retirement, both these aspects may have contributed to a positive response to this question. There was some concern in all of our groups about keeping occupied in retirement, although a majority of those we interviewed claimed to have done some thinking about what they would like to do in retirement.

7.1.1. Attitudes towards planning and preparation

We tried to explore various aspects of planning and preparation for retirement. Although the majority of the groups felt well-prepared even before their programmes (Table 7:9) some reservations were expressed by individuals at British Airways (where a majority felt they were either not very well-prepared or not prepared at all). Virtually all the groups were evenly divided over whether planning was possible. The Shell group made the most positive response to this question, a feature reflecting both support for planning within the organisation and the greater resources of a predominantly white collar group. However, the overall impression from our sample

TABLE 7:7

"How long do you think it will take you to get used to not working?"							
Response	NCB EXPERI-MENTAL	MARS	BRISTOL	JAGUAR	B.A.	GLASGOW	SHELL
No time at all	7 29%	10 40%	9 36%	5 39%	9 26%	11 58%	11 46%
Few weeks	8 33%	2 8%	2 8%	4 31%	11 31%	3 16%	5 21%
Few months Plus	9 38%	13 52%	14 56%	4 31%	15 43%	5 26%	8 33%
TOTAL	24	25	25	13	35	19	24

$x^2 = 16.5$ d.f. = 12   Non-significant

TABLE 7.8

"On the whole, are you looking forward to the time when you will retire?"							
Response	NCB EXPERI-MENTAL	MARS	BRISTOL	JAGUAR	B.A.	GLASGOW	SHELL
Yes	21 88%	19 63%	16 55%	10 71%	23 58%	26 90%	20 74%
No/Mixed/Don't Know	3 12%	11 37%	13 45%	4 29%	17 42%	3 10%	7 26%
TOTAL	24	30	29	14	40	29	27

$x^2 = 15.7$ d.f. = 6   5% Significant

TABLE 7:9

Response	NCB EXPERI-MENTAL	MARS	BRISTOL	JAGUAR	B.A.	EMI EXPERI-MENTAL	GLASGOW	SHELL
"How well prepared do you think you are for retirement?"								
Very/Fairly Well Prepared	23 96%	24 86%	22 82%	10 83%	19 49%	18 78%	18 67%	18 69%
Not very Well Prepared/Not Prepared At All	1 4%	4 14%	5 18%	2 17%	20 51%	5 22%	9 33%	8 31%
TOTAL	24	28	27	12	39	23	27	26

x^2 = 23.4 $\qquad$ d.f.=7 $\qquad$ 1% Significant

TABLE 7:10

Response	NCB EXPERI-MENTAL	MARS	BRISTOL	JAGUAR	B.A.	EMI EXPERI-MENTAL	GLASGOW	SHELL
Control over Life Events								
I have Control-led the Events in my Life.	11 46%	9 30%	6 22%	3 21%	7 18%	6 27%	7 24%	6 22%
My Life has been Shaped by the Events.	13 54%	21 70%	21 78%	11 79%	31 82%	16 73%	22 76%	21 78%
TOTAL	24	30	27	14	38	22	29	27

x^2 = 6.9 $\qquad$ d.f.= 7 $\qquad$ Non-significant

TABLE 7:11

Response	NCB EXPERI-MENTAL	MARS	BRISTOL	JAGUAR	B.A.	GLASGOW	SHELL
"Do you think of retirement as an extended holiday?"							
Yes	11 46%	11 37%	9 31%	8 57%	17 42%	15 52%	4 15%
No	13 54%	19 63%	20 69%	6 43%	23 58%	14 48%	23 85%
TOTAL	24	30	29	14	40	29	27

x^2 = 12.1 $\qquad$ d.f.= 6 $\qquad$ Non-significant

was of a group with a low commitment to long term planning
(only 48 people of <u>all</u> those we interviewed gave 18 months or
more before retirement as the time to start preparation). This
was perhaps linked with a view - characteristic of many we
interviewed - that life was too uncertain to plan in any detail.
To gather information on this point, we asked people to choose
between the following statements: "I have controlled the events
in my life", or "My life has been shaped by the events which
have happened" (Table 7:10). A clear majority in each group
identified with the latter. This is a finding which, although
not wholly surprising, does have important implications for pre-
retirement education, suggesting that the idea of <u>long-term</u> planning may meet with some resistance - at least amongst the present
generation of retirees.

We also examined whether our groups varied on general
images held about retirement. Most of the groups were evenly
divided on whether they saw retirement as an 'extended holiday'
(the exception being the predominantly white collar Shell group -
Table 7:11). The most interesting result came when we asked
people whether they saw retirement 'as the beginning of old age'.
There were significant differences between our groups, those
with the highest proportion of manual workers were the most
likely to see retirement in this way (Table 7:12). There were
highly significant differences between the groups on whether they
saw retirement as a 'life rather similar to the present'. The
manual worker groups, however, predicted a greater amount of
change. (Table 7:13).

There were significant differences between our groups on
whether they had any health problems, with white collar workers
reporting fewer problems than the blue collar groups. However,
only small proportions on each of the courses were actually
worrying about their health and a considerable number felt that
retirement would actually improve it. (Table 7:14).

The groups varied widely in their present income level
(Table 7:15), with Jaguar and Shell groups representing the two
extremes.

7.2. <u>The Phase II Interview.</u>

Four weeks after their course, we returned to all of those
we had interviewed. The purpose of this second interview was to
gather information on two main areas: first, the views of
participants about the course: had they found it too long?
Too short? Was there sufficient time for discussion? Secondly,
had there been changes on some of the key questions relating to
expectations about retirement and attitudes towards retirement
preparation.

Although for some we interviewed, the course was coming
within three months of their retirement, this did not appear to
increase dissatisfaction with the timing of the programme
(Table 7:16). However, there were highly significant differences
between the groups on whether they thought their course had been
of the right length (Table 7:17); the data indicates that the
<u>longest courses</u> received the <u>least</u> amount of criticism on this
question.

138

TABLE 7:12

	"Do you think of retirement as the beginning of old age?"						
Response	NCB EXPERI- MENTAL	MARS	BRISTOL	JAGUAR	B.A.	GLASGOW	SHELL
Yes	11 46%	11 37%	9 31%	6 43%	11 28%	5 17%	2 7%
No	13 54%	19 63%	20 69%	8 57%	29 72%	24 83%	25 93%
TOTAL	24	30	29	14	40	29	27

x^2 = 13.7   d.f.=6   5% Significant

TABLE 7:13

	"Do you see retirement as a life rather similar to the present?"						
Response	NCB EXPERI- MENTAL	MARS	BRISTOL	JAGUAR	B.A.	GLASGOW	SHELL
Yes	17 71%	14 47%	12 41%	7 50%	18 45%	5 17%	6 22%
No	7 29%	16 53%	17 59%	7 50%	22 55%	24 83%	21 78%
TOTAL	24	30	29	14	40	29	27

x^2 = 20.7   d.f.= 7   1% Significant

TABLE 7:14

	"Do you think retirement will affect your health?"							
Response	NCB EXPERI- MENTAL	MARS	BRISTOL	JAGUAR	B.A.	EMI EXPERI- MENTAL	GLASGOW	SHELL
Improve	15 63%	16 53%	16 55%	6 43%	16 40%	11 48%	9 31%	13 50%
No differ- ence/ get Worse.	9 38%	14 47%	13 45%	8 57%	24 60%	12 52%	20 69%	13 50%
TOTAL	24	30	29	14	40	23	29	26

x^2 = 7.5   d.f. = 7   Non-significant

TABLE 7:15

Proportion of Groups Earning less than £5,200 (at Spring 1980)							
NCB EXPERI-MENTAL	MARS	BRISTOL	JAGUAR	B.A.	EMI EXPERI-MENTAL	GLASGOW	SHELL
75%	53%	72%	100%	38%	65%	86%	19%

TABLE 7:16

"In relation to when you retire, do you think the course came ....?"							
Response	NCB EXPERI-MENTAL	MARS	BRISTOL	JAGUAR	B.A.	EMI EXPERI-MENTAL	GLASGOW	SHELL
Too early	–	5	5	–	3	–	3	1
	–	17%	17%	–	8%	–	11%	4%
Right time DK	14	18	17	11	27	16	20	16
	58%	60%	59%	79%	68%	70 %	71%	59%
Too late	10	7	7	3	10	7	5	10
	42%	23%	24%	21%	25%	30%	18%	37%
TOTAL	24	30	29	14	40	23	28	27

x^2 = 17.4   d.f. = 14   Non-significant

TABLE 7:17

"Thinking about the length of the course, did you find it ....?"							
Response	MARS	BRISTOL	EMI EXPERI-MENTAL	B.A.	NCB EXPERI-MENTAL	SHELL	GLASGOW	JAGUAR
Days	2	2	2	2	3	6	7	8
Too short	10	6	5	9	14	2	2	1
	33%	21%	21%	22%	58%	7%	7%	7%
Right length /Too long	20	23	19	31	10	25	27	13
	67%	79%	79%	78%	42%	93%	93%	93%
TOTAL	30	29	24	40	24	27	29	14

x^2 = 29.2   d.f. = 7   1% significant

TABLE 7:18

"What about the time allowed for discussion?""Was there ....?"								
Response	MARS	BRISTOL	EMI EXPERI- MENTAL	B.A.	NCB EXPERI- MENTAL	SHELL	GLASGOW	JAGUAR
Days	2	2	2	2	3	6	7	8
Enough/Too Much	20	20	15	31	10	10	20	12
	67%	69%	68%	78%	42%	37%	69%	86%
Insufficient/ DK.	10	9	7	9	14	17	9	2
	33%	31%	32%	22%	58%	63%	31%	14%
TOTAL	30	29	22	40	24	27	29	14

x^2 = 20.7   d.f. = 7   1% significant

TABLE 7:19

"Has the course made you aware of any problems which you had not considered before?"								
Response	NCB EXPERI- MENTAL	MARS	BRISTOL	JAGUAR	B.A.	EMI EXPERI- MENTAL	GLASGOW	SHELL
Yes	18	6	13	6	18	9	9	12
	75%	20%	45%	43%	45%	38%	32%	44%
No	6	24	16	8	22	15	19	15
	25%	80%	55%	57%	55%	63%	68%	56%
TOTAL	24	30	29	14	40	24	28	27

x^2 = 18.3   d.f. = 7   5% significant

There were highly significant differences on whether the programmes allowed sufficient time for discussion (Table 7:18). Course length appeared to be one factor influencing this finding. However, we should also note that one of the longest courses (Shell) had the highest number expressing reservations on this area. It may be that despite the length, the amount of information presented was such that individuals felt there was still insufficient time for discussion. It may also reflect the high expectations of this particular group and a positive evaluation of the benefits of group discussion. There were significant differences over whether the courses had increased awareness about retirement problems (Table 7:19). In six out of the eight courses - despite variations in occupational back-grounds and type of course - similar responses were given to this question (with most people saying that the programme had not made them aware of new problems). It is worth noting, however, the two extremes either side of this result. Only 25 per cent of the miners felt they hadn't become aware of new problems, in comparison with 80 per cent of those from Mars. Neither course structure nor content are likely to have been the key variables influencing this result. It is possible that the miners were faced with more retirement problems; however, it is more likely that the result is an effect of the timing of the respective programmes. Of the groups we interviewed, the miners were closest to their date of retirement - two-thirds were leaving work within three months. Mars, on the other hand, were furthest away - two-thirds were retiring nine months or more after the course. Thus, the NCB programme could raise numerous practical issues which had a direct bearing on the immediate future of the miners. There were also various problems connected with early retirement which the programme could discuss. The Mars course, on the other hand , was pitched at a more abstract level. This factor, together with its distance from retirement, appeared to reduce its impact. This shouldn't be taken as an argument for placing courses immediately before the individual leaves work. Instead, such a finding supports the view that courses organised some distance before retirement need to have different methods and techniques from conventional courses if they are to have any impact.

Although the courses varied in their content, we tried - by grouping certain topics - to assess the popularity of different pre-retirement themes. Of the three main areas - finance, health and leisure - the first was perceived as the 'most useful' on virtually all the courses which we studied. When we look at the type of financial advice which people found helpful, general information and information about state benefits were seen as the key areas (Table 7:20) . Only one of our groups mentioned that the advice received on investment had been 'useful'; not surprisingly this was also the group with the most financial resources (Shell). In terms of items which had been found least useful the financial area was again important, with criticism of presentations on supplementary benefits and income tax featuring amongst two of our groups (the miners and British Airways - see Tables 7:21 and 7:22).

TABLE 7:20

"Financial Items Considered Most Useful"								
Item	NCB EXPERI- MENTAL	MARS	BRISTOL	JAGUAR	B.A.	EMI EXPERI- MENTAL	GLASGOW	SHELL
GENERAL FINANCE	2	9	7	4	21	12	–	–
	9%	82%	58%	80%	55%	50%	–	–
BUDGETING	–	2	–	–	–	–	2	–
	–	18%	–	–	–	–	6%	–
PENSIONS	7	–	–	–	6	4	12	2
	32%	–	–	–	16%	17%	33%	6%
STATE BENEFITS	11	–	5	1	9	8	11	4
	50%	–	42%	20%	24%	33%	31%	12%
INCOME TAX	2	–	–	–	2	–	11	2
	9%	–	–	–	5%	–	31%	6%
NATIONAL INSURANCE	–	–	–	–	–	–	–	5
	–	–	–	–	–	–	–	15%
INVESTMENT	N/A	–	–	–	–	–	–	20
		–	–	–	–	–	–	61%
TOTAL *	22	11	12	5	38	24	36	33

* Numbers in column refers to the total numbers of items mentioned per group.

TABLE 7:21

Items found "least useful"							
Item	NCB EXPERI-MENTAL	MARS	BRISTOL	JAGUAR	B.A.	EMI EXPERI-MENTAL	GLASGOW	SHELL
FINANCE	9 56%	5 28%	9 33%	2 15%	18 53%	3 18%	8 21%	8 25%
HEALTH	- -	2 11%	4 15%	3 23%	3 9%	2 12%	6 16%	5 16%
LEISURE	4 25%	4 22%	4 15%	2 15%	10 29%	8 47%	11 29%	2 6%
OTHER	3 19%	7 39%	10 37%	6 46%	3 9%	4 24%	13 34%	17 53%
TOTAL	16	18	27	13	34	17	38	32

TABLE 7:22

Financial Items found "least useful"							
Item	NCB EXPERI-MENTAL	MARS	BRISTOL	JAGUAR	B.A.	EMI EXPERI-MENTAL	GLASGOW	SHELL
GENERAL FINANCE	- -	4	4	- -	1	- -	- -	- -
BUDGETING	- -	1	- -	- -	- -	- -	1	- -
PENSIONS	- -	- -	5	- -	- -	- -	2	- -
STATE BENEFITS	- -	- -	- -	2	16	3	5	2
INCOME TAX	9 -	- -	- -	-	1	-	- -	- -
NATIONAL INSURANCE		- -	- -	-		- -	- -	2
INVESTMENT	- -	- -	- -	- -	- -	- -	- -	4
TOTAL *	9	5	9	2	18	3	8	8

* Numbers in this column refers to the total number of items mentioned per group.

We asked individuals in each of our groups whether their course had <u>changed</u> their view of retirement. The results produced a striking degree of consensus (Table 7:23), notwith-standing enormous variations amongst our groups and in the structure and content of the programmes attended. These findings suggest that the overwhelming majority of individuals come to their course with a fairly definite view of retirement (positive or negative) one which is modified only slightly (if at all) by participation on a course (this would appear to confirm the results from American research discussed in Chapter 3).

Finally, in this section, there were extremely significant differences between the groups in terms of whether they intended to do anything as a result of the course (Table 7:24). As Table 7:25 suggests, the financial advice given on the Shell course appears to have exerted a dominant influence on this group. For the others, however, despite the popularity of the sessions on finance, other areas appear equally important. However, we should also note that four of the groups had quite high proportions (between 50 per cent and 70 per cent) saying that they <u>would not</u> do anything specific as a result of the retirement programme.

7.2.1. <u>Expectations about retirement and attitudes to retirement preparation</u>

As at Phase 1 there were no significant differences between the groups in terms of how long people thought it would take to get used to not working. We find considerable stability over the two phases in the category a "Few months or more' with five groups having between 40 per cent to 50 per cent of their respondents in this category. Although our groups differed significantly on whether they were looking for work (the miners and Jaguar being least enthusiastic - see Table 7:26) fewer people were interested in taking a job than at the first inter-view (Table 7:6). This result may have been influenced by information on the earnings rule together with the impact of the courses in stressing positive features of retirement. We tried to assess whether the difference between the groups reflected changes which had occurred between the first and second inter-view, or whether they were a product of differences existing at the pre-course interview. Our approach to this problem was to use a chi-quared test on the numbers from each group who, between Phase 1 and Phase 2, had either given the same answer or switched from positive to negative or vice versa.

Our result was <u>non-significant</u>, indicating that the phase 2 results were a reflection, more of the differences between groups evident at the Phase 1 interviews, than of the courses themselves.

As with the first interview, there were no significant differences at Phase 2 on whether people had a clear idea of retirement. There is some evidence to suggest a positive move over the two phases and a majority in each of our groups expressed a clear idea of their future life. However, the two groups who were most negative on this measure at Phase 1 retained this position at Phase 2 (Shell and British Airways).

TABLE 7:23

Response	NCB EXPERI-MENTAL	MARS	BRISTOL	JAGUAR	B.A.	EMI EXPERI-MENTAL	GLASGOW	SHELL
"Has the course changed your view of retirement?"								
Yes	5 21%	6 20%	8 28%	4 29%	11 28%	3 13%	8 28%	6 22%
No	19 79%	24 80%	21 72%	10 71%	29 73%	21 88%	21 72%	21 78%
TOTAL	24	30	29	14	40	24	29	27

$x^2 = 3.0$ d.f. = 7   Non-significant

TABLE 7:24

Response	NCB EXPERI-MENTAL	MARS	BRISTOL	JAGUAR	B.A.	EMI EXPERI-MENTAL	GLASGOW	SHELL
"Will you do anything specific as a result of advice received on the course?"								
No	8 33%	21 70%	11 38%	3 21%	24 60%	12 50%	15 56%	8 30%
Yes	16 67%	9 30%	18 62%	11 79%	16 40%	12 50%	12 44%	19 70%
TOTAL	24	30	29	14	40	24	27	27

$x^2 = 19.6$ d.f. = 7   1% significant

TABLE 7:25

Proposed Action as a Result of Advice received on PRE Programme								
Proposed Action	NCB EXPERI-MENTAL	MARS	BRISTOL	JAGUAR	B.A.	EMI EXPERI-MENTAL	GLASGOW	SHELL
No. Interviewed.	24	30	29	14	40	24	27	27
FINANCE	3 12%	5 17%	4 14%	4 29%	8 20%	2 8%	5 18%	15 55%
HEALTH/ FITNESS/ DIET	10 42%	1 3%	5 17%	3 21%	– –	2 8%	3 11%	1 4%
HOUSING	– –	2 7%	3 10%	2 14%	6 15%	1 4%	– –	– –
EMPLOYMENT	3 12%	– –	1 3%	– –	3 7%	– –	– –	3 11%
PERSONAL RELATION-SHIPS	– –	– –	6 21%	– –	– –	– –	– –	1 4%
LEISURE	– –	4 13%	2 7%	3 21%	2 5%	1 4%	4 15%	– –
SAFETY IN THE HOME	– –	– –	3 10%	2 14%	– –	– –	1 4%	– –
VOLUNTARY WORK	2 8%	– –	– –	1 7%	1 2%	– –	2 7%	2 7%
OTHER	– –	– –	3 10%	– –	1 2%	2 8%	2 7%	– –

NOTE: Percentages are expressed as a proportion of respondents in each group.

TABLE 7:26

Response	NCB EXPERI-MENTAL	MARS	BRISTOL	JAGUAR	B.A.	GLASGOW	SHELL
Yes	2	10	12	1	16	10	10
	8%	33%	41%	7%	40%	36%	37%
No/DK	22	20	17	13	24	18	17
	92%	67%	59%	93%	60%	64%	63%
TOTAL	24	30	29	14	40	28	27

"Do you plan to look for any kind of work after you retire?"

x^2 = 13.1   d.f. = 6   5% significant

TABLE 7:27

Response	NCB EXPERI-MENTAL	MARS	BRISTOL	JAGUAR	B.A.	GLASGOW	SHELL
Yes	11	20	9	9	15	16	7
	46%	67%	31%	64%	38%	55%	26%
No	13	10	20	5	25	13	20
	54%	33%	69%	36%	63%	45%	74%
TOTAL	24	30	29	14	40	29	27

"When you think about retirement, do you think of it as an extended holiday?"

x^2 = 16.2   d.f. = 6   5% significant

Each individual was asked whether the things they had
thought about doing in retirement had changed since the course.
Although there was a significant difference between the groups
on this measure, the proportion in any group recording a positive
response was very small. Attitudes towards planning for
retirement were examined through two main questions. The first
asked individuals for a subjective assessment of their level
of preparation for retirement. At Phase 2 (unlike at Phase 1)
there were no significant differences on this measure with very
high degrees of optimism being expressed by each group. For
the majority, this was a continuation of responses at Phase 1.
The British Airways group, however, had moved considerably on
this question, with the number of feeling not well prepared or
not prepared at all falling from 51 per cent at Phase 1 to 20
per cent at Phase 2. There was slightly more conviction expressed
by each group about the possibility of being able to plan,
although a sizeable minority continued to show reservations.

There was no movement at all on the question of whether
people would miss colleagues at work, with substantial majorities
in each group considering that they would. Worries about missing
the sense of usefulness provided by work were also present,
though at a lower level than at Phase 1.

Unlike at Phase 1, the groups differed significantly over
whether they saw retirement as an extended holiday (Table 7:27),
the two extremes were Mars (67 per cent) and Shell (20 per cent).
These differences may be related to contrasting images of retirement, one focusing on this period as providing the opportunity
for rest and leisure; the other, recognising the opportunity for
more active involvement in community life. Such differences may
reflect a basic divergence in perspectives about retirement and
unless personal resources of finance and health are favourable,
it may be difficult to influence beliefs within the context of
a short course. The question of whether people saw retirement
as a 'life similar to the present' also brought out extremely
significant differences: non-manual groups foresee greater change
than manual worker groups (Table 7:28).

More positively, there were no significant differences in
responses to the question: 'Do you see retirement as the beginning
of old age?' Only small proportions in each group gave an
affirmative answer, with the extremes represented by Shell
(4 per cent) and Bristol (31 per cent).

There were no significant differences on whether people were
looking forward to retirement and there was evidence for increased
optimism since the first interview. The exception to this trend
was the Bristol group, 41 per cent of whom expressed ambivalence
towards retirement. We know that this course had a group of
individuals faced with some major financial problems in retirement
and our data would suggest that many of these difficulties had
still to be resolved.

As at Phase 1, relatively small numbers claimed to be worrying
generally about retirement, its effect on their health or impact
on personal relationships. However, a concern with income and
income tax continued to be expressed by the groups who had
registered concern at the first interview. (Bristol and British
Airways).

149

TABLE 7:28

Response	NCB EXPERI- MENTAL	MARS	BRISTOL	JAGUAR	B.A.	GLASGOW	SHELL
Yes	21 88%	19 63%	13 45%	6 43%	21 53%	8 28%	8 30%
No	3 13%	11 37%	16 55%	8 57%	19 48%	21 72%	19 70%
TOTAL	24	30	29	14	40	29	27

"When you think about retirement, do you think of it as a life rather similar to the present?"

$x^2 = 26.6$ d.f. = 6   0.1 significant

150

7.2.2. Summary of the Phase 1 and Phase 2 interviews

As we proceed with our analysis, patterns in the data will emerge more clearly. However, at this point we might observe two things: first, there is an indication from the data that participation on courses is encouraging more positive feelings about retirement (we shall report further information on this point in the next section). Secondly, and less positively, we have found that on a number of questions where a particular group expressed negative views at Phase 1 (e.g. about income or about the problems of keeping occupied) participation on the course had done little to disturb such views. There may, of course, be certain types of problems which are difficult to resolve within the framework of what are in the majority of cases relatively short courses. This is a point we shall consider in a later section of this chapter.

7.3. The impact of the course on all participants

Because of the similarities between the various groups, we decided to pool together all the individuals who attended our eight courses. This will allow us to identify any important characteristics of our participants and explore in greater detail reactions to pre-retirement education.

People brought a variety of expectations about retirement education to their courses. In some cases, the course was part of a broader framework of pre-and post-retirement support. In other instances, it occurred in isolation, the retirement party itself being one of the main institutional acknowledgements of a change in role and status. There were also contrasts in the motives which people brought to their course. All of the programmes we evaluated took place in work time, so the 'choice' was between attending a course (with no loss of earnings) and continuing to work. In virtually all of our organisations there were some who decided not to attend. Perhaps because the course was seen as 'above their heads' or 'only for those with money' or even because 'no-one can tell me anything about retirement'. There may also be some who were extremely worried about the prospect of leaving work but who felt unable to share their concern within the context of a fairly large group.

At this stage, however, we are concerned with the participants in retirement education: the people who decide that a course is a 'good idea', provides 'a few days off' or can resolve a specific worry or query. So who were the participants on our programmes? Two-thirds were drawn from social class three (26 per cent non-manual; 40 per cent manual). Unskilled workers were clearly under-represented in our sample (there were just eight), a feature which probably reflects the situation on PRE courses nationally. This was a long service group, two-thirds of the sample having worked in excess of 20 years for their company.

The mean age of the group at the time of the first interview was 60.9 years. The majority were within a year of leaving work. Forty-four per cent were retiring at the age of 60 or below; 41 per cent at age 65. Two-thirds were leaving work because of a fixed retirement age and a sizeable proportion of this group would have preferred to have remained at work if it had been possible.

Out of the 193 who were given a full interview at both
phases (i.e. excluding EMI) 43 per cent thought they might
look for work (in the majority of cases, within the first year
of retirement). Not everyone, however, was thinking of paid
work, and when we asked what type of employment people would
like to have, voluntary work emerged as the most popular item
(mentioned by 28 people). In this Phase 1 interview we were
particularly interested in examining general attitudes towards
work and retirement. We have already seen that a large
percentage of our group were thinking of returning to work.
However, only ten people thought they would worry about not
having a job. By contrast, a concern with missing friendships
formed in the workplace was clearly an issue for many we interviewed (68 per cent); 37 per cent also thought that they might
miss the sense of usefulness or achievement gained through
work.

For the majority we interviewed, retirement was just a few
months away. At this stage, 45 per cent of those we interviewed
found themselves thinking about retirement 'often'; 26 per cent
admitted, however, that it 'hardly ever' entered their thoughts.
We also found contrasts in the length of time which people thought
it would take them to adjust to retirement, 32 per cent reporting
'no time at all'; a slightly larger and more pessimistic group
considered it might take a 'few months or more' (35 per cent).

Despite these differences our group held generally favourable
views about retirement, with 70 per cent looking forward to it
and only a small number worrying generally about problems connected
with leaving work. However, the interview did uncover areas of
uncertainty which could be explored on the course. Thirty-nine
per cent professed not to have a clear idea of retirement; 37 per
cent reported a concern with keeping sufficiently occupied after
leaving full-time work. Worries about income matters concerned
one-third of those we interviewed. There was also a small group
(11 per cent) worried about the effect of retirement upon them
personally. However, it is when we examine attitudes towards
planning and preparation that some interesting points emerge.

7.3.1. Planning and Preparation for Retirement

Most of those we interviewed claimed that they felt well
prepared for retirement (just eight per cent confessed to being
'not prepared at all'). This would appear to confirm the work of
Cokinda[1] and of Harpaz and Kremer[2] that those who participate in
PRE are already highly committed to retirement preparation.
However, it is reasonable to ask what is meant when we use the
term 'preparation'. It is certainly not long-term preparation:
only 18 per cent of those interviewed suggested periods of four
years or more as the period when planning should begin. It is not
even having a clear idea about finances in retirement (half of
those we interviewed claimed to be unsure about how much money
they would receive in retirement). Nor is there overwhelming
enthusiasm for planning as such: 44 per cent doubted whether it
is possible to plan for retirement. Rather than any of these
things, our respondents saw 'preparation' as a state of mind or
as a general philosophy: feeling right about one's finances and
about being able to cope with retirement were seen as the main
elements of planning. Our group was rather more sceptical about
the value of long term planning to improve the quality of life in
retirement.

7.3.2. Images of Retirement

There was some resistance to viewing retirement as an extended holiday (56 per cent rejecting this view); and virtually everyone we interviewed saw leaving what had been their main job or career as marking 'a new phase in their life'. However, this change of direction was interpreted in a number of ways. A minority (29 per cent) agreed that retirement could be viewed as the 'beginning of old age'. For this group, it symbolised the gathering influence of physical and social changes, at least some of which had highly negative connotations. There was some variation in the continuity which individuals perceived between their present life and life in retirement, a majority (58 per cent) visualising major changes. This is an interesting finding, given that it suggests that individuals had begun to perceive - even before the course - important alterations to the pattern of their daily lives.

7.3.3. The Post-Course Interview

In this section, we shall examine the reactions of our respondents to their courses and then discuss any changes in attitudes towards work and retirement. Criticisms of course content and structure are likely to be fairly limited given that this will have been people's first experience of retirement education. However, we did find minorities who felt that their course had come too late (27 per cent); had been too short (22 per cent); or had allowed insufficient time to discuss ideas during sessions (34 per cent). Although most people's feelings about retirement had not been affected by the course, 42 per cent had become aware of problems they had not previously considered. However, our respondents were evenly divided over whether they would do anything as a result of the course: 53 per cent mentioned specific courses of action, finance and health being the most popular items. The implication of Table 7:29 is that if courses had some success in influencing action on basic issues connected with finance and health, they had been less effective in respect of activities in retirement. What, however, of broader attitudes towards retirement? Is it possible to detect any change as a result of participation on a course. We compared responses to 27 questions exploring attitudes towards work and retirement, questions which had been repeated over both phases of interviewing. Using the McNemar statistical test, there were 10 significant changes. There were two questions relating to whether the group would seek employment after they left their current job. On both these items there was a highly significant change, with people less likely to want to return to work than was the case before the course. The group was also less likely to feel they would miss feelings of achievement gained through work (the difference between the phases was highly significant). Significantly more people felt their lifestyle in retirement would be different from their present way of life. However, examining more general attitudes to retirement the results are less straightforward. Thus, there is a significant reduction in the number who are not looking forward to retirement and amongst those who do not have a clear idea of retirement. The impact of the course seems, however, to have elicited greater response to specific questions on planning and preparation. We find highly significant

TABLE 7:29

Breakdown of 115 "yes" responses to question "Is there anything specific you will do as a result of advice received on the course?".		
Proposed Action	Number of Responses	% of all interviewed at Phase 2.
FINANCE	46	21
HEALTH/DIET/FITNESS	25	12
HOUSING	14	6
EMPLOYMENT	10	5
PERSONAL RELATIONSHIPS	7	3
LEISURE/SOCIAL ACTIVITIES	16	7
SAFETY IN THE HOME	6	3
VOLUNTARY WORK	8	4
OTHER	8	4

increases in the number reporting they were very or fairly well
prepared for retirement and an equally significant increase in
those who felt planning and preparation was possible. The
influence of one particular course (British Airways) was undoubtedly important for the former question, but change on the latter
probably reflects greater optimism generally amongst our group.

Finally, there were a number of significant changes in
scores on scales repeated over both phases of interviewing. We
had a measure with seven items covering basic knowledge about
pensions and supplementary benefits. On both the Wilcoxon matched
pairs signed-ranks test and the t-test scores showed an extremely
significant improvement over Phase 1 and 2. Table 7:30 illustrates
percentage movements over these phases. Most items show some
increase, with knowledge about age allowances perhaps the most
noticeable improvement. However, the table indicates gaps in basic
areas of knowledge remaining at the post-course interview,
noticeably on the relationship between retirement pensions and
tax and rent and rate rebates and supplementary pensions.

On the measure designed to assess resistance to retirement,
there was a significant improvement in scores. Table 7:31 confirms
the highly positive views being expressed about retirement, even
before the courses. The effect of the retirement programme is
to consolidate this positive evaluation. We included two scales
in our research examining commitment and attitudes towards work.
The former showed a significant change over the two phases, the
latter an extremely significant change. Both these results
suggest a loosening in feelings about work as a result of participation in a retirement programme.

Table 7:32 gives results from our 'facts about ageing' quiz.
The results show considerable stability over the two phases. It
is worth noting, however, the lack of knowledge about the financial situation of pensioners (item 13). It is also disturbing
that at the Phase 2 interview, one-third of those interviewed
apparently believe that 'most older people are set in their
ways and are unable to change'; one-quarter also believe that
'in general, most old people are pretty much alike' and that
'when a person retires, his health usually gets worse'.

7.3.4. Negative features of PRE

Although there is evidence for PRE having beneficial effects,
the research also uncovered some negative findings. Thus, there
is a highly significant increase in the number of people worrying
about retirement. For some of those we interviewed, it was clear
that involvement in a course may have aroused concern about the
adequacy of their financial preparation (Table 7:33). If there
had been sufficient time allotted for discussion, this may have led
to a constructive debate about possible solution to these problems.
The concern is that with only a small proportion of time allowed
for discussion, a minority of people left their course with doubts
unresolved.

It is also important to note the questions where there had
been no significant change. Thus, a minority continue to worry
over both phases about income, about keeping occupied or viewed
retirement as the beginning of old age. However, 13 people (a

TABLE 7: 30

Knowledge Scale: Comparisons of Phase 1-2 Responses						
T = TRUE F = FALSE	PHASE RESPONSE			PHASE RESPONSE		
	Correct	Incorrect	Don't Know	Correct	Incorrect	Don't Know
A state retirement pension is always free of tax. F	115 60%	47 24%	31 16%	127 66%	50 26%	14 7%
Medical prescriptions are free to men over 65 and women over 60. T	152 79%	11 6%	30 16%	166 86%	16 8%	9 5%
People may receive a supplementary pension if their income is below a certain level. T	174 90%	5 3%	14 7%	181 94%	4 2%	6 3%
People may receive rent or rate rebates only if they receive a supplementary pension. F	71 37%	76 39%	46 24%	90 47%	69 36%	32 17%
There is a scheme in existence to provide free or cheap legal advice for people who need it. T	161 83%	6 3%	26 14%	175 91%	1 1%	15 8%
After 65, people get an age allowance entitling them to a greater amount of tax free income. T	86 45%	39 20%	68 35%	132 68%	31 16%	28 15%
It is possible for people to obtain an attendance allowance when they need constant care at home. T	140 73%	6 3%	47 24%	168 87%	6 3%	17 9%

* This Table excludes respondents from EMI. No information was available on two other respondents at Phase 2.
Wilcoxon Z = 3.01   1% significant
         t = 6.67   d.f. = 190   0.1% significant

TABLE 7 : 31

Resistance to Retirement Scale: Comparison of Phases 1-2 Responses

	PHASE 1 RESPONSE			PHASE 2 RESPONSE		
	Strongly Agree/ Agree	Not Sure	Strongly Disagree/ Disagree	Strongly Agree/ Agree	Not Sure	Strongly Disagree/ Disagree
People should not be made to retire solely because of their age.	136 71%	16 8%	41 21%	131 68%	17 9%	43 22%
I am looking forward to the time off that retirement will bring.	144 75%	37 19%	12 6%	158 82%	19 10%	14 7%
If it were up to me alone, I would keep on working as long as possible.	70 36%	17 9%	106 55%	56 29%	22 11%	113 59%
I think things will go well for me in retirement.	149 77%	42 22%	2 1%	159 82%	30 16%	2 1%
Retirement is mostly good for a person.	108 56%	59 31%	26 14%	117 61%	57 30%	17 9%

* This table excludes respondents from EMI. No information was available on two other respondents at Phase 2.

Wilcoxon Z = 2.19   d.f. = 190   5% significant
          t = 2.53   5% significant

TABLE 7:32

Facts About Ageing Scale: Comparison of Phases 1-2 Responses

T = TRUE
F = FALSE

Item	T/F	PHASE 1 RESPONSE			PHASE 2 RESPONSE		
		Correct	Incorrect	No response	Correct	Incorrect	No response
For people in their 60's and 70's regular exercise can restore physical activity and reduce heart rate and blood pressure.	T	163 85%	28 15%	2 1%	162 84%	28 15%	3 2%
At least 1 in 10 of peopled past 65 live in long stay institutions (ie homes for the aged, geriatric hospitals).	F	103 53%	84 44%	6 3%	95 49%	94 49%	4 2%
Nearly three quarters of people aged 65 or more in England and Wales live in a household without a car.	T	76 46%	84 51%	4 2% *	85 52%	76 46%	3 2% *
Most older workers cannot work as effectively as younger workers.	F	91 47%	98 51%	4 2%	98 51%	91 47%	4 2%
The majority of older people are healthy enough to carry out their normal activities.	T	162 84%	28 15%	3 2%	170 88%	20 10%	3 2%
Most older people are set in their ways and are unable to change.	F	134 69%	55 29%	4 2%	126 65%	63 33%	4 2%
Old people usually take longer to learn something new.	T	157 81%	34 18%	2 1%	158 82%	32 17%	3 2%
It is almost impossible for most old people to learn new things.	F	153 79%	36 19%	4 2%	162 84%	27 14%	4 2%
One third of old people live alone.	T	133 69%	49 25%	11 6%	139 72%	50 26%	4 2%
In general most old people are pretty much alike.	F	133 69%	55 29%	5 3%	140 73%	50 26%	3 2%
People aged 60 and over make up 20% of Great Britain's total population.	T	151 78%	37 19%	5 3%	150 78%	40 21%	3 2%
When a person retires his health usually gets worse.	F	121 63%	67 35%	5 3%	136 71%	53 28%	4 2%
A majority of pensioners in Great Britain live in households below, at, or just above the official poverty line.	T	105 54%	80 41%	8 4%	98 51%	91 47%	4 2%

* These figures exclude Glasgow who were not asked this question.

TABLE 7:33

Breakdown of the 32 "yes" responses to question "What sorts of things have you been worrying about".		
Item	n	%*
FINANCE	27	84
HEALTH	3	9
PERSONAL RELATIONSHIPS (Family)	1	3
ABSENCE OF ROUTINE/LACK OF THINGS TO DO	5	16
EMPLOYMENT	2	6
MISS PEOPLE AT WORK	3	9
OTHER	3	9
TOTAL	44	

* Note: Percentages have been calculated as a proportion of the 32 "yes" responses.

drop of only four) continue to worry about the effect of retirement on them personally.

It may be that courses are satisfactory for those with very
few doubts about the areas described above. These are the people
who already feel well-prepared for retirement and who have no
worries about its social or phychological impact. However, for
those who feel insecure about their position in retirement, existing courses may do very little to allay their fears or even
provide some possible solutions to their concerns.

7.3.5. The Influence of Course Structure

So far we have identified a number of changes which participation on a pre-retirement course may have influenced. There
is the further question, however, of whether different types of
courses are more successful than others in promoting change. To
achieve a complete answer to this point we would need to allocate
people on a random basis to a range of courses. However, within
the limitations of our research design, it is possible to make
some contribution to the debate on this issue.

The major difference between our courses revolved around
their total length: the shortest lasted for 13 hours (run by
Mars and by Bristol Retirement Council); the longest for 50 hours
(run by the Scottish Retirement Council). The amount of time
allowed for discussion also varied, with most of the two or three
day courses relying on a formal lecture, with a short period for
questions allowed at the end of each lecture.

The first step in our analysis was to compare the two courses
run by the Retirement Councils, these giving us two extremes as
regards course length. We compared the programmes on 20 questions
included at the Phase 2 interview. There were two significant
differences between the groups: Bristol were _less_ likely to be
looking forward to retirement and were more likely to be worrying
about income tax problems in retirement (Tables 7:34 - 7:35). We
tried to assess whether the differences between the groups
reflected changes which had occurred between the first and second
interview or whether they were a product of differences existing
at the pre-course interview. We used a chi-squared test on the
numbers from each group who, between Phase 1 and Phase 2, had
either given the same answer or switched from positive to
negative or vice versa. Our result was _non-significant_, indicating
no statistical differences between the groups in respect of
changes between the two interviews. The inference from the result
is that the courses themselves did not contribute to the differences between the groups at the Phase 2 interview.

In fact, our analysis suggested considerable similarities
between Bristol and Glasgow at Phase 2. For example, both were
satisfied with the length of their course and the period allowed
for discussion (remarkably, the groups returned indentical
responses on this last question). Identical responses were also
given to the question: 'has the course changed your view of retirement'? (Tables 7:36 - 7:37). This result confirms our earlier
observation that people bring fairly definite views to their
programmes, views which a long course is no more likely to change
than a short course. Despite the considerable time allotted to

TABLE 7:34

"Are you looking forward to retirement"		
Response	GLASGOW (7 days)	BRISTOL (2 days)
Looking Forward	24 89%	17 59%
Not Looking Forward/Mixed Feelings	3 11%	12 41%
TOTAL	27 100%	29 100%

$X^2 = 5.1$ 　　　　　 d.f.= 1 　　　　　 5% significant

TABLE 7:35

"Are you Worried about Income Tax?"		
Response	GLASGOW (7 days)	BRISTOL (2 days)
Worried	– –	8 28%
Not Worried	26 100%	21 72%
TOTAL	26 100%	29 100%

$X^2 = 6.3$ 　　　　　 d.f. = 1 　　　　　 5% significant

TABLE 7:36

"What about the time allowed to discuss and exchange ideas during sessions?"		
Response	GLASGOW (7 days)	BRISTOL (2 days)
Enough/Too much time.	20 69%	20 69%
Not Sufficient Time	9 31%	9 31%
TOTAL	29 100%	29 100%

x^2 = 0.0   d.f. = 1   Non-significant

TABLE 7:37

"Has the course changed your view of retirement?"		
Response	GLASGOW (7 days)	BRISTOL (2 days)
Yes	8 28%	8 28%
No	21 72%	21 72%
TOTAL	29 100%	29 100%

x^2 = 0.0   d.f. = 1   Non-significant

recreation and leisure activities on the Scottish course, participants were no more likely to have thought of new things to do or feel that keeping occupied would be less of a problem.

Our next step was to divide the eight courses into two groups: (a) long courses (those lasting six days or more); (b) short courses (those lasting three days or less). We then compared the groups on 20 questions used at both interviews and found five statistically significant differences. There now appeared a significant difference on the question of leisure activities, with more of those who had attended a long course either having taken up a new leisure activity or thinking about new things to do in retirement. (Tables 7:38 - 7:39).

There was a highly significant difference on whether the two groups were worrying about income tax, those from the shorter courses having a greater number of problems in this area. The long course groups were more likely (extremely significant) to see retirement as <u>different</u> to their present way of life (although this was a <u>continuation</u> of pre-course differences). Finally, and somewhat predictably, those who had attended a short course were more likely to be critical of the length of their programme. Amongst those who had attended a long programme, seven per cent felt that it has been too short, compared with 30 per cent of those who had attended a short course (extremely significant). As before, however, the similarities between the groups were rather intriguing. There were no differences on whether the courses increased awareness of new retirement problems; allowed sufficient time for discussion; or changed people's view of retirement. Both groups had similar views on planning and preparation. Although there were differences between the groups on whether they would do anything specific as a result of the course, this did not reach the 5% level of significance.

Finally, answers were virtually identical in response to questions on whether people were looking forward to retirement; had a clear idea of their future life; or would have difficulty keeping occupied.

One additional way we tried to compare our programmes was by assigning scores to 24 questions repeated over Phase 1 and 2.

For each response given to a particular group we could arrive at a score which indicated positive, negative or no movement over the two phases. By using a chi-squared test to compare the scores of the different groups we could then make a provisional statement about whether some courses were more effective than others. Two questions showed significant differences (Table 7:40-7:41): 'Are you looking forward to the time when you will retire?'; 'How well prepared do you think you are for retirement?'

The implication of this result was that when all the groups were compared, one or more had shown a greater improvement in its views about retirement and retirement education.

TABLE 7:38

"Have you taken up any new leisure activities"		
Response	Long Courses (6 days +)	Short Courses (3 days or less)
Yes	9 13%	5 4%
No	59 87%	118 96%
TOTAL	68 100%	123 100%

$x^2 = 4.2$ d.f. = 1 5% Significant

TABLE 7:39

"Have the sort of things you have thought about doing in retirement changed since you attended the pre-retirement course?"		
Response	Long Courses (6 days +)	Short Courses (3 days or less)
Yes	14 20%	13 9%
No	55 80%	134 91%
TOTAL	69 100%	147 100%

$x^2 = 4.6$ d.f. = 1 5% significant

TABLE 7:40

Movement	NCB EXPERI- MENTAL	MARS	BRISTOL	JAGUAR	B.A.	GLASGOW	SHELL
Decreased "Looking Forward"	1 4%	– –	5 17%	– –	– –	3 11%	1 4%
No Movement	23 96%	24 80%	21 72%	13 93%	33 83%	23 85%	23 85%
Increased "Looking Forward"	– –	6 20%	3 10%	1 7%	7 18%	1 4%	3 11%
TOTAL	24	30	29	14	40	27	27

Movement of responses between phases 1 & 2 to question: "Are you looking forward to the time when you will retire?".

$x^2 = 23.3$ d.f. = 12 5% significant

TABLE 7:41

Movement	NCB EXPERI- MENTAL	MARS	BRISTOL	JAGUAR	B.A.	EMI EXPERI- MENTAL	GLASGOW	SHELL
Decreased "Preparedness"	1 4%	5 17%	3 10%	3 21%	2 5%	4 14%	5 21%	3 11%
No Movement	18 75%	19 63%	20 69%	6 43%	17 43%	11 39%	15 63%	13 48%
Increased "Prepared- ness"	5 21%	6 20%	6 21%	5 36%	21 53%	13 46%	4 17%	11 41%
TOTAL	24	30	29	14	40	27	24	27

Movement of responses over Phase 1-2 to question "How well prepared do you think you are for Retirement?"

$x^2 = 25.2$ d.f. = 14 5% significant

This finding still left us with the problem of assessing whether the improvement was in fact due to the course or whether the courses where the improvement had been greatest simply had more people registering negative views at Phase 1 (either because of (a) genuine differences at this stage, or (b) because of an abnormally negative response at Phase 1, a response which was 'normalised' at the second round of interviewing).   To resolve this problem we analysed the responses of all those who had said 'no' at Phase 1, to assess whether equal proportions had gone from 'no' to 'yes' over the two phases.   If there were statistical differences, it would suggest that one or more of the courses had been more successful on the two questions we identified; if there were no differences, it would be illegitimate to draw such a conclusion.   In fact our analysis found no statistical differences for either of the questions, and we concluded that our evidence did not give sufficient grounds for believing that a more positive response had been gained (on these questions at least) by a particular course.

7.4. Concluding Comment

These negative conclusions need to be balanced by reference to our earlier findings, particularly those reporting on the changes in attitudes amongst all the individuals we interviewed. These differences partly reflect problems in the statistical analysis of groups with small numbers, and it may be that in the comparative analysis of programmes significant changes were under-reported.   However, we do have evidence to suggest that pre-retirement education was important for many of the people we interviewed: (a) in loosening attitudes towards work; (b) in improving factual knowledge about retirement issues.   Given limitations of structure and time, however, courses could only confront fairly basic issues and problems.   Where concerns about retirement become more acute (and multi-dimensional) they appear less successful as a medium for influencing change.   In later sections of this report, we shall consider how alterations in structure and content could accommodate some of the more deep-rooted problems faced by a minority of retirees.

166

CHAPTER 7

FOOTNOTES AND REFERENCES

1. Cokinda, R.M. <u>An identification of differences between participating and non-participating automobile workers in a pre-retirement programme</u>, Ph.D. Thesis, Wayne State University, 1974

2. Harpaz, I and Kremer, Y. 'Determinants of Continued and Discontinued participation in Pre-retirement Training: An Israeli Case Study', <u>Journal of Occupational Psychology</u>, Vol. 54, pp. 213-220, 1981.

CHAPTER 8

THE IMPACT OF PRE-RETIREMENT EDUCATION

8.   Introduction

In this chapter we introduce material from our Phase 3
interviews, when the bulk of our respondents had been retired
for between six and nine months. As we noted in Chapter 3, we
were interested in whether PRE had assisted the passage from
work to retirement. Had it helped in decision-making about
finance or leisure? Did it provide a feeling of being better
prepared for retirement? We reasoned that if the long term
gains of participation in retirement education were difficult
to assess, short-term gains in easing the transition to
retirement should be possible to measure. Indeed, we would
argue that for the type of pre-retirement models studied in this
research (and they are broadly representative of courses
nationally), a minimum condition for their performance should be
that they influence behaviour in the transfer from full-time
work.

The structure of this chapter falls into three distinct
parts. First, we give a brief review of the theoretical perspectives used in understanding the transition to retirement.
This is provided to help the reader understand the variety of
interpretations that has been placed upon the experience of
leaving work; it also indicates important theoretical assumptions
which we make in the analysis of our own data. Secondly, we
compare the fortunes of our groups since their second interview,
examining the impact which the pre-retirement course has made
upon their lives. Thirdly, to strengthen our arguments about the
effectiveness of courses, we introduce our two programmes which
included control groups; the contrast between the experimental
and control subjects giving us greater confidence to draw causal
association between PRE and experiences in retirement.

8.1.   Theoretical Perspectives on Retirement

Theoretical debates in the field of gerontology have been
shaped by the work of American social gerontologists. The first
retirement programmes reflected the dominant assumptions of role
and activity theory, perspectives which associated withdrawal
from work with problems of low morale and reduced self-esteem.
A particular concern of researchers in the 1950s was looking at
how the elderly had fared in the shift from a rural to an industrial society. The general position adopted was that the elderly
had fared worse than many other groups, with their removal from
a position of "centrality" within the family being the most notable
feature. In general, the process of industrialisation was seen as
causing insecurities for older people:

> "(The elderly person).......can no longer count as a matter
> of right and moral and legal obligation on economic support
> by his children. He is less likely, if widowed, to be
> offered a home by a son or a daughter. If ill, particularly
> with a chronic ailment, his children are more and more dis-
> posed to shift his case to a hospital rather than to provide
> a bed in their home. If lonely, he must look elsewhere
> than to his descendents to provide companionship and
> sociability".[1]

The suggestion of a weakening in the social position of
the elderly was to become a common theme in the succeeding years
and, combined with the instituionalisation of retirement, the
question of developing adequate social roles for the retired
was to become a major concern. Burgess argued that the retired
man and his wife were "imprisoned in a roleless role",[2] having
no vital function to perform such as they had in rural society.
According to Burgess:

"The older person feels de-throned and devalued in the
realm of family relations where he once reigned supreme.
He can no longer count on the role of patriarch ordering
the destiny of his children and grandchildren. He cannot
even be sure of being venerated and respected. In short
he has lost his old role of dominance and has not yet
found a new one".[3]

The failure to find a new role was partly attributed to
what most researchers saw as the centrality of the work role
and the difficulty - for men - of finding a replacement.
Michelon, for example, spoke of "the rare individual who can
look ahead to the golden years, make the needed changes in
values, and substitute new vital activities for the meaning of
work."[4] This view was combined with a strong sense of pessimism
about people's ability to actually use leisure. This was
explicit, for example, in Loether's suggestion that: "One of
the serious problems facing our society is the problem of
teaching the average working man how to use his leisure".[5] And
it underlay Blau's view that:

"Ordinary men and women have relied on cultural scripts
throughout their earlier lives, and when these no longer
exist they often lack resources and the experience to
improvise new ones. Instead, many older people just
cling to life as they wait to be relieved of a lonely
and useless existence".[6]

Both role and activity theory were to have an important
and enduring influence on retirement education. Although the
more extreme positions taken by role theorists have been
modified or abandoned, the concern with maintaining activity in
retirement is still an important focus (the Scottish programme
provides a good illustration). By contrast, the disengagement
hypothesis (a theoretical approach developed in the early 1960s
by researchers at the University of Chicago) has had relatively
little influence on retirement programmes. The central postulate
of the hypothesis has been summarised by Cumming and Henry as
follows:

"Ageing is an inevitable mutual withdrawal or disengagement resulting in decreased interaction between
the ageing individual and others in the social system
he belongs to. The process may be initiated by the
individual or by others in the situation. The aged
person may withdraw more markedly from some classes of
people whilst remaining relatively close to others.
His withdrawal may be accompanied from the outset by
an increased pre-occupation with himself; certain
insitutions in society may make the withdrawal easy for

169

him. When the ageing process is complete the equilibrium which existed in middle life between the individual and his society has given way to a new equilibrium
characterised by a greater distance and an altered type
of relationship".[7]

A key assumption made in the theory is that "ego energy"
declines with age, and that as the ageing process develops,
individuals become increasingly self-occupied, and less and less
responsive to normative controls. Further, the theory contains
both social and psychological components. On the one hand, it
deals with the relationship between the individual and society;
on the other, it describes changes occurring within the individual. According to the theory, either the individual or society
may initiate the process of disengagement. When done by the
individual it is the result of ego changes; when done by society
it is the result of organisational imperatives.

As with the early role theorists the central task for men
is considered to be their work. Retirement - or the giving up
of work - means that a man's central like-task is finished, and
it is from this point that disengagement begins. The process
is made easier for the individual by the setting of fixed
retirement ages and pension schemes - developments which under-
cut individual dilemmas about when to disengage from demanding
social roles; for women, widowhood is considered to be the
formal marker of disengagement.

In addition, it is also argued that disengagement or withdrawal from social relationships will lead to the individual
maintaining a higher morale in old age - higher, that is, than
if he or she attempted to keep involved in a range of social
affairs and activities. Thus, disengagement is seen as both
natural and desirable, with a stronger sense of psychological
well-being as a result. Finally, this feature of ageing is suggested as a universal phenomenon, associated with ageing in all
cultures.

The adoption of this model on pre-retirement programmes
would have had drastic implications for existing practice.
Attempts to provide substitute leisure and work activities
would have been abandoned. Instead, the focus would have been
on how people can re-construct their lives independently of
social and community structures. This approach has been the
subject of numerous critiques (both in Britain and America) and
has never been influential in pre-retirement thinking. However,
it did provoke an important debate on the conditions likely to
precipitate withdrawal from social life (e.g. social inequalities, ageism), a discussion which could be usefully developed on
retirement programmes.

The third theoretical approach has been that of continuity
theory. This perspective arose from a range of criticisms directed at both activity and disengagement theory. The former, for
example, was seen as providing an inadequate view of how people
adjust to retirement. Rosow, for example, looked at the assumption made by theorists that social activity is positively correlated
with high morale, and he argued that we now know of many deviant
cases to this proposition - cases which call the meaning and

generality of this approach into question. He suggested a
number of grounds for this:

> "First, extensive sociological data show major class
> differences in social participation, even among the
> aged.... White-collar and middle class groups show
> much higher rates of organisational membership and
> similar formal activities than working class groups.
> Consequently, any adjustment index based on activity
> scores contains a built-in class bias which penalises
> the working class and favours the middle class. With
> this basis in middle class norms, manual groups will
> have lower and white-collar groups higher adjustment
> ratings. The very least that one can expect of an
> adjustment measure is that it gives each group an equal
> chance to score well according to its own class norms.
> But, in the face of class differences in participation,
> the middle class conception of the good, active life
> penalises manual groups arbitrarily".[8]

Secondly, empirical findings had begun to emerge which
failed to support the notion than an increase in role activites
automatically led to positive changes in life satisfaction.
Thirdly, there was increasing interest in how the response to
retirement was shaped by the kind of adjustments which individuals made during middle life and earlier. Finally, through the
influence of interactionist and phenomenological perspectives,
adjustment to retirement was related to the perceptions and
life history of the retiree, rather than pre-determined categories of need or a given model of the ageing process. Malcolm
Johnson, for example, urged that we should: "Listen to reconst-
ructed biographies in order to identify (the individual's) life
history and the way it has sculpted present problems and
concerns." Johnson went on: "In this way the individual's
own priorities for the latter end of his life will emerge - his
own losses and triumphs and fears and satisfactions and unful-
filled aspirations."[9] This approach had been echoed earlier by
Maddox in a critique of disengagement theory, where he notes
the latter's "tendency to treat as relatively insignificant
those variations in the constraints of social environment and in
the cumulative patterns of experience which constitute the
biographies of individuals". Maddox goes on to suggest that:

> "The possibility has not been adequately explored that
> an individual life-style - reflecting, for example, an
> orderly career and its correlates - developed during his
> mature years might be an important variable intervening
> between his response to retirement and the hypothesised
> .....process of withdrawal".[10]

One of the most explicit statements regarding continuity
theory has come from Robert Atchley. Describing results from
the Scripps Foundation Studies in Retirement, he writes:

> "Data from retired railroaders indicate that there are
> continuities in the situations people face that minimise
> the impact of retirement. Family, friends, church and
> other roles continue despite retirement. Cottrell's
> data suggest that ....loss of identity is minimised by

the tendency to select friends on the job from among those of one's own age. The end result of this process is to create retirement cohorts of people who have known each other on the job and who retire together. In the Scripps Foundation Studies of Retirement this phenomenon has been observed among those retired from occupations as diverse as teacher, railroader, and telephone operator. It results in a group of retired friends who have known each other for years and whose concepts of each other involve a great deal more than the mere playing of an occupational role. Nevertheless, this group is also capable of sustaining the prestige gained on the job because they know all about how this prestige was generated".[11]

8.1.1. Continuity Theory and Research on Retirement Education

For our purpose, the arguments from continuity theory suggest that when comparing retirement programmes we should guard against using activity ratings as a measure of their effectiveness; nor should we assume - as in the more extreme versions of role theory - that retirement necessarily leads to a crisis in adjustment. We should also consider the extent to which differences between individuals and groups reflect attitudes formed at mid-life or even earlier, rather than the effects of retirement per se. With these points in mind, we shall now review the results of the Phase 3 interview.

8.2. The Transition to Retirement

In the majority of cases we returned to our retirees when they had been retired for between 6 and 9 months. This was the longest period we could allow for, given the time-span of the research. However, we hoped that it would give sufficient time to provide an assessment of PRE during the transition. We returned to 153 of the 217 individuals we had originally interviewed at Phase 1. It was decided not to proceed with further interviews at Mars and Jaguar, thus reducing our total sample by 44. Very few of our Mars group would have reached retirement age before the end of our research project, and we thought it better to concentrate resources on those who had left work. At Jaguar we had already lost people through the effect of redundancies and it was decided not to risk an even smaller sample at Phase 3. From the remaining six groups, 20 people were lost through refusals and illness.

There were highly significant differences between our groups on the length of time they had been retired, although a majority of individuals in each of the six groups fell into the range of four to nine months (Table 8:1). Seven out of the 153 were still working full-time with their company (four of these from EMI); this group is, of course, excluded from the analysis of questions relating to retirement attitudes and behaviour.

There were a number of basic areas on which - using the chi-squared test - our groups showed no significant differences. There were no differences in worries about income in retirement, health, income tax, housing or the psychological impact of leaving

TABLE 8:1

Length of time	NCB EXPERI-MENTAL	BRISTOL	B.A.	EMI EXPERI-MENTAL	GLASGOW	SHELL	TOTAL
\"For How Long Have you been Retired?\"							
3 months or less	1 4%	– –	– –	3 15%	1 5%	1 5%	6 4%
4 – 6 months	9 39%	8 30%	3 9%	12 60%	5 23%	2 11%	39 27%
7 – 9 months	11 48%	15 56%	24 69%	5 25%	9 41%	13 68%	77 53%
10 months or over	2 9%	4 15%	8 23%	– –	7 32%	3 16%	24 16%
TOTAL	23	27	35*	20*	22*	19*	146

$x^2 = 28.8$ d.f. = 15   0.1% significant

(*Several individuals had not yet retired from full-time employment).

TABLE 8:2

Income Group	NCB EXPERI-MENTAL	BRISTOL	B.A.	EMI EXPERI-MENTAL	GLASGOW	SHELL	TOTAL
Retirement Income: Under/Over £4,000							
Under £4,400	20 87%	23 85%	22 65%	16 67%	15 79%	6 32%	102 70%
£4,400 and over	3 13%	4 15%	12 35%	8 33%	4 21%	13 68%	44 30%
TOTAL	23	27	34*	24	19*	19*	146

$x^2 = 20.7$ d.f. = 5   0.1% significant

(*Several individuals were unable to estimate retirement income).

work. A majority of people in each group gave positive replies
to a number of questions about health: "Do you have any particular physical or health problems?"; "Do you think leaving
work has (Improved/worsened/made no difference)to your health?".
"Do you think your health is good/fair or poor?" There were no
significant differences as to how people described their present
financial position, most groups reporting that they had "enough
to get by on". When asked to estimate their net income, however,
there were extremely significant differences between the groups.
Using two categories of under £4,400 and £4,400 plus produced
highly significant differences, the two extremes represented by
NCB (87 per cent earning below £4,400) and Shell (68 per cent
earning above £4,400 - see Table 8:2). Looking at the median
incomes of our groups (Table 8:3), the EMI experimentals were in
the lowest range; Shell International were the highest.

There were no significant differences when asked about
length of time taken to adjust to retirement. Around 50 per cent
in each group reported that they adjusted either immediately or
that they had taken a "few weeks". Taking only those who were
wholly retired (i.e. who were neither in full or part-time work)
we repeated a series of questions asked at earlier phases, designed to explore attitudes towards work. There was little
evidence to suggest that people were worried about not having a
job, or that they were missing the sense of achievement that
accompanied work. In contrast, and continuing a tendency we
identified at Phase 1, a majority in virtually all the groups
reported that they missed being with other people at work. Of
course, it must be said that this is still the early part of
retirement, and it may be that after two or three years a more
optimistic view may be expressed. On the other hand, we can
say that concern about the loss of work relationships is an
important aspect of the transition to retirement, one which was
not removed through attendance at these pre-retirement courses.

The question about whether individuals had difficulty keeping occupied in retirement revealed highly significant differences
(Table 8:4). The two extremes were Glasgow and Shell (48 per
cent of the former had difficulty keeping occupied, compared with
five per cent of the latter). We then tried to assess whether this
had developed between the first and third interviews or whether it
was a continuation of differences existing at the first interview.
Our approach to this problem was to use a chi-squared test on the
numbers from each group who - over phases 1 and 3 - had switched
answers on this topic from negative to positive or positive to
negative. Our result was non-significant, indicating no statistical differences between the groups as regards pre- and post-
retirement change on this item. The inference is that the groups
had maintained a position established at Phase 1. In fact, taking
our six groups at the first interview, Glasgow expressed the second
highest percentage of reservations on this item. The first group -
British Airways - improved quite noticeably over the two phases,
though not enough to produce a statistically significant result
when compared with the other groups.

We retained from the earlier interviews a number of questions
which explored the images associated with retirement. The groups
differed significantly on whether they viewed retirement as an
extended holiday (Table 8:5). The two extremes were represented

TABLE 8:3

Post-Retirement Income: Median Values							
NCB EXPERI- MENTAL	NCB CONTROL	EMI EXPERI- MENTAL	EMI CONTROL	BRISTOL	B.A.	GLASGOW	SHELL
£4,025	£4,025	£2,500	£3,275	£3,275	£3,275	£3,275	£5,725

TABLE 8:4

"Have there been times since you retired when you have found it difficult to keep occupied?"							
Response	NCB EXPERI- MENTAL	BRISTOL	B.A.	EMI EXPERI- MENTAL	GLASGOW	SHELL	TOTAL
Yes	3	5	5	3	10	1	27
	13%	19%	14%	15	48	5%	18%
No/Don't know	20	22	31	17	11	18	119
	87%	82%	86%	85%	52%	95%	81%
TOTAL	23	27	36	20	21	19	146

x^2 = 15.1   d.f. = 5   1% significant

TABLE 8:5

"When you think about retirement do you think of it as an extended holiday?"							
Response	NCB EXPERI-MENTAL	BRISTOL	B.A.	EMI EXPERI-MENTAL	GLASGOW	SHELL	TOTAL
Yes	14 61%	10 37%	19 54%	15 65%	14 67%	5 26%	77 52%
No/Don't Know	9 39%	17 63%	16 26%	8 35%	7 33%	14 74%	71 48%
TOTAL	23	27	35	23	21	19	148

x^2 = 11.7   d.f. = 5   5% significant

TABLE 8:6

"How would you say retirement has worked out for you? ...... Better/Worse/About the same as expected?"							
Response	NCB EXPERI-MENTAL	BRISTOL	B.A.	EMI EXPERI-MENTAL	GLASGOW	SHELL	TOTAL
Better	11 48%	15 58%	15 42%	10 59%	8 38%	2 11%	61 43%
Same/Worse*	12 52%	11 42%	21 58%	7 41%	13 62%	16 89%	80 57%
TOTAL	23	26	36	17	21	18	141

x^2 ≑ 11.9   d.f. = 5   5% significant

*A total of 7 individuals said retirement had been worse than expected.

TABLE 8:7

	Timing of Course						
Response	NCB EXPERI-MENTAL	BRISTOL	B.A.	EMI EXPERI-MENTAL	GLASGOW	SHELL	TOTAL
Too early	– –	1 4%	3 8%	– –	3 14%	7 35%	14 9%
Right time	15 65%	16 64%	24 67%	14 64%	11 50%	9 45%	89 60%
Too late	8 35%	8 32%	9 25%	8 36%	8 36%	4 20%	45 30%
TOTAL	23	25	36	22	22	20	148

x^2 = 22.6   d.f. = 10   5% significant

by Shell and Glasgow (only one-quarter of the former accepting this image, compared with over two-thirds of the latter). This finding confirms differences established in the pre-retirement phase and it is interesting to find them being retained well into the first year of retirement. We asked people whether they viewed retirement as the "beginning of old age" and, although the overall result was not statistically significant, the variation between Bristol (seven per cent agree) and the NCB (39 per cent agree) should be noted. However, there was little support for the idea of viewing retirement as a "rejection by society" and there were no significant differences between the groups on this item. We found hardly anybody who felt that retirement had turned out "worse than they expected". However, significant differences did emerge as to whether it was "better" or about the "same as expected" (Table 8:6). Only 11 per cent of Shell compared with 59 per cent of EMI were prepared to say it was better. This finding may reflect different levels of expectation between the groups, with Shell having to experience a much greater improvement in their circumstances before showing a positive response.

8.3. The Impact of the Courses

In the majority of cases over a year had elapsed between the individual's pre-retirement course and his or her final interview. This delay was crucial to our aim of assessing whether people had done anything as a result of their course. We reasoned that if no action had been taken after this length of time, then it was unlikely to occur to any significant extent in the following years. Before discussing our findings on this issue we should note the significant differences between the groups on the question of the timing of their respective programmes. Shell expressed more concern on this issue than our other groups (extremely significant), with 35 per cent feeling that the course had come too early and 20 per cent that it was too late (Table 8:7).

When we had established whether people remembered receiving sessions on finance, etc., they were asked whether they had done anything specific as a result of this advice. If they had, they were asked to describe the action they had taken (Table 8:8). Only nine per cent of the miners gave a positive answer, compared with 54 per cent of EMI. Neither course length nor distance from retirement would seem to explain the difference between EMI and NCB. Virtually all the miners were taking early retirement and this may have affected their response (although there is no obvious reason why early retirement would have reduced the number of positive responses). One possible explanation emerges when we look at the type of action taken as a result of the course (Table 8:9). Both groups received a session on investments, yet whilst none of the miners responded to this session, 11 in EMI indicated a positive response. This difference may reflect greater success on the part of the EMI programme. However, a more likely explanation - given the similarity in methods and approaches used on the two courses - might be: first, income differences between the groups (33 per cent of EMI had an income in retirement of £4,400 plus, compared with 13 per cent of NCB); secondly, pre-course attitudes towards a topic such as investments, modifications to which may be difficult to achieve within the context of a relatively

TABLE   8:8

"Have you done anything as a result of advice received on finance?"							
	NCB EXPERI-MENTAL	BRISTOL	B.A.	EMI EXPERI-MENTAL	GLASGOW	SHELL	TOTAL
YES	2 9%	5 19%	15 42%	13 54%	10 43%	7 35%	52 34%
NO	21 91%	22 82%	21 58%	11 46%	13 57%	13 65%	101 66%
TOTAL	23	27	36	24	23	20	153

x^2 = 15.7   d.f. = 5   1% significant

TABLE 8:9

Specific actions taken as a result of advice received on finance						
Action	NCB EXPERI-MENTAL	BRISTOL	B.A.	EMI EXPERI-MENTAL	GLASGOW	SHELL
Consulted DHSS	2	1	–	–	2	–
Commuted Pension	–	–	1	–	–	3
Invested Capital	–	2	12	11	4	5
Action on Taxation	–	–	1	1	1	1
Sought more advice	–	–	–	–	3	–
Saved Money	–	1	1	–	–	–
Bought house-hold goods	–	1	–	–	–	–
General	–	–	1	–	–	–
Bought House	–	–	1	–	–	–
Made Will	–	–	–	1	–	–
TOTAL	2	5	17	13	10	9

short programme.

Extremely significant differences were found on whether the groups had taken action over health: only nine per cent of British Airways had done so compared with 57 per cent of the miners. It is possible to point to differences in the way this session was handled as a factor influencing the different response of BA and NCB. The health session on the BA programme consisted of just one lecture, presenting a very general survey of health issues. The miners, on the other hand, had both a general description and a practical demonstration of a range of keepfit exercises. As we noted in our case study on the miners, these exercises appear to have made a considerable impact. (Table 8:10).

When we examine the type of response made to health talks, it is clear that action tends to revolve around either exercise or diet. There is very little response to the general advice on smoking, drinking, etc., which was given on most of our programmes (Table 8:11).

Very few individuals in our groups appear to have been influenced by advice on leisure activities (differences between groups were non-significant), a finding which confirms the trend discussed at Phase 2. There were significant differences on whether the groups had done anything as a result of advice on employment (Table 8:12). The two extremes were represented by Shell (35 per cent gave a positive answer) and EMI (four per cent).

8.3.1. Taking Action: The Courses Compared

As a very crude indicator of a "success" of a programme we examined the amount of activity our courses had generated. Considering those who had taken no action, British Airways appears least successful (47 per cent) compared with Glasgow (17 per cent) (Table 8:13). On the other hand, as Table 8:14 suggests, we find for the majority of groups, participants making one response or none at all. Approximately one-quarter in each group had taken more than one action as a result of their course. As we suggest earlier, in our analysis of responses to the health course, this indicates the very selective way in which people respond to retirement programmes. Our evidence indicates that there is much sifting of information before people finally arrive at an area of advice which is considered "useful" and "relevant".

8.4. Planning and Preparation: Course versus control groups

Although we have found a number of significant differences between our groups this still leaves open the question of whether course participants had done more preparation in comparison to those who had not received a course. In the case of two of the groups we have been discussing (EMI and NCB), we formed experimental and control groups (see below for sampling details). We compared the responses of the six course groups and two controls to a number of questions related to planning and preparation. When we asked: "How well prepared do you think you were for retirement?". no significant differences were found between the groups. A

TABLE 8:10

"Have you done anything as a result of advice received on health?"							
Response	NCB EXPERI-MENTAL	BRISTOL	B.A.	EMI EXPERI-MENTAL	GLASGOW	SHELL	TOTAL
Yes	13 57%	15 56%	4 11%	6 25%	9 39%	4 20%	51 34%
No	10 44%	12 44%	31 89%	18 75%	14 61%	16 80%	101 66%
TOTAL	23	27	35 *	24	23	20	152

x^2 = 21.7   d.f. = 5   0.1% significant

* One person did not recall receiving advice on health.

TABLE 8:11

Specific actions taken as a result of advice received on health.						
Action	NCB EXPERI-MENTAL (n=23)	BRISTOL (n=27)	B.A. (n=36)	EMI EXPERI-MENTAL (n=24)	GLASGOW (n=23)	SHELL (n=20)
Exercise	13 57%	7 26%	4 11%	3 12%	8 35%	2 10%
Diet	1 4%	11 41%	1 3%	4 17%	2 9%	4 20%
Smoke less	1 4%	–	–	–	–	–
Keep Warm	–	1 4%	–	–	–	–
Accident Prevention	–	1 4%	–	–	–	–
General	–	–	1 3%	–	–	–
Drink less	–	–	–	1 4%	–	–

Note: Percentages are expressed as a proportion of respondents in each group.

TABLE 8:12

"Have you done anything as a result of advice received on employ-							
Response	NCB EXPERI-MENTAL	BRISTOL	B.A.	EMI EXPERI-MENTAL	GLASGOW	SHELL	TOTAL
Yes	– –	3 12%	6 18%	1 4%	3 14%	7 35%	20 14%
No	22 100%	22 88%	28 82%	22 96%	19 86%	13 65%	126 86%
TOTAL	22	25	34	23	22	20	146

x^2 = 13.4   d.f. = 5   5% significant

TABLE 8:13

Comparison of Activity Levels: No Action versus Action							
ACTIVITY LEVEL	BRISTOL	B.A.	EMI EXPERI-MENTAL	NCB EXPERI-MENTAL	SHELL	GLASGOW	TOTAL
Course length	2 days	2 days	2 days	3 days	6 days	7 days	
No Action	12 44%	17 47%	10 42%	9 39%	7 35%	4 17%	59 39%
Action	15 56%	19 53%	14 58%	14 61%	13 65%	19 83%	94 61%
TOTAL	27	36	24	23	20	23	153

x^2 = 6.1   d.f. = 5   Non-Significant

TABLE 8:14

Comparison of Activity Levels: No Action versus One Action versus Two or More Actions							
ACTIVITY LEVEL	BRISTOL	B.A.	EMI EXPERI-MENTAL	NCB EXPERI-MENTAL	SHELL	GLASGOW	TOTAL
Course length	2 days	2 days	2 days	3 days	6 days	7 days	
No Action	12 44%	17 47%	10 42%	9 39%	7 35%	4 17%	59 39%
One Action	8 30%	9 25%	7 29%	13 57%	8 40%	14 61%	59% 39%
Two or more Activities	7 26%	10 28%	7 29%	1 4%	5 25%	5 22%	35 23%
TOTAL	27	36	24	23	20	23	153

x^2 = 15.9   d.f. = 10   Non-significant

TABLE 8:15

"How well prepared do you think you were for retirement?"							
Response	NCB EXPERI-MENTAL	NCB CONTROL	EMI EXPERI-MENTAL	EMI CONTROL	BRISTOL	B.A.	GLASGOW	SHELL
Very/Fairly Well Prepared	22 96%	19 79%	18 75%	23 74%	21 78%	29 83%	19 86%	16 80%
Not Very Well/ Not Prepared At All	1 4%	5 21%	6 25%	8 26%	6 22%	6 17%	3 14%	4 20%
TOTAL	23	24	24	31	27	35	22	20

x^2 = 5.4   d.f. = 7   Non-Significant

TABLE 8: 16

"Do you feel you can plan and prepare for retirement?"							
Response	NCB EXPERI-MENTAL	NCB CONTROL	EMI EXPERI-MENTAL	EMI CONTROL	BRISTOL	B.A.	GLASGOW	SHELL
Yes	16 70%	13 54%	18 75%	20 63%	18 67%	26 72%	11 48%	14 70%
No/Don't Know	7 30%	11 46%	6 25%	12 37%	9 33%	10 28%	12 52%	6 30%
TOTAL	23	24	24	32	27	36	23	20

x^2 = 6.7   d.f. = 7   Non-Significant

TABLE 8:17

"How long before retirement do you think people should start planning and preparation?"							
Response	NCB EXPERI-MENTAL	NCB CONTROL	EMI EXPERI-MENTAL	EMI CONTROL	BRISTOL	B.A.	GLASGOW	SHELL
18 Months Or Less	10 63%	6 46%	6 33%	5 25%	6 33%	7 27%	6 55%	3 21%
Over 18 Months	6 37%	7 54%	12 67%	15 75%	12 67%	19 73%	5 45%	11 79%
TOTAL	16	13	18	20	18	26	11	14

x^2 = 10.5   d.f. = 7   Non-Significant

TABLE 8:18

"Can you think of any particular thing you did to plan for retirement which you have found beneficial?"								
Response	NCB EXPERI-MENTAL	NCB CONTROL	EMI EXPERI-MENTAL	EMI CONTROL	BRISTOL	B.A.	GLASGOW	SHELL
Yes	10 67%	7 54%	13 72%	13 81%	12 67%	14 54%	6 67%	10 77%
No	5 33%	6 46%	5 28%	3 19%	6 33%	12 46%	3 33%	3 23%
TOTAL	15	13	18	16	18	26	9	13

$x^2 = 5.3$ d.f. = 7   Non-Significant

TABLE 8:19

Comparison of Phase 1-3 feelings of "preparedness for retirement"						
	NCB EXPERI-MENTAL	BRISTOL	B.A.	EMI EXPERI-MENTAL	GLASGOW	SHELL
Less prepared at Phase 3 than at Phase 1	2 9%	3 11%	7 19%	5 21%	2 9%	3 15%
No change in feelings of preparedness	19 83%	16 59%	11 31%	11 46%	8 36%	7 35%
More prepared at Phase 3 than at Phase 1	2 9%	8 30%	18 50%	8 33%	12 55%	10 50%
TOTAL	23	27	36	24	22	20

$x^2 = 22.1$ d.f. = 10   5% Significant

similar result also emerged when we looked at responses to the
questions: "Do you feel you can plan and prepare for retirement?",
and "How long before retirement should people start their planning
and preparation?". We also compared replies to the question: "Can
you think of any particular things you did to plan for retirement
which you have found beneficial?" This is a useful question
because it focuses upon concrete items of planning instead of very
general commitments to the idea of preparation. Once again, we
found no significant differences between our groups (Tables 8:15-8:
18). This provides a hint that our control group is at least as
committed to preparation for retirement as are the experimentals.
This conclusion is confirmed below, in our more detailed examination of the experimental and control groups. Indeed, in the case
of the EMI control group, 54 per cent claimed to have done preparation in the area of finance and leisure, a figure which compares
favourably with the activity of the experimental groups.

8.5. Course Differences

We compared the performance of the six courses by examining
how responses had changed over the pre- and post-retirement
interviews. For each response given by a particular group we
could arrive at a score which indicated positive, negative, or
no movement over the period. By using a chi-squared test we
could then make a provisional statement about whether some courses
were more effective than others. On only one question - "How
well prepared do you think you (are/were) for retirement?" were
there significant differences between the groups. The implication
of this result was that when all the groups were compared, one or
more had shown a change in its confidence about retirement preparation. (Table 8:19).

This finding still left us with the problem of assessing
whether the improvement was due to the course, or whether the
courses where the improvement had been greatest simply had more
people registering negative views at Phase 1 (either because of
(a) genuine differences at this stage or, (b) because of an
abnormally negative response at Phase 1, a response which was
"normalised" at the second round of interviewing). To resolve
this problem, we analysed the responses of all those who had
said "no" at Phase 1, to assess whether equal proportions had
gone from "no" to "yes" over the two phases. If there were
statistical differences, it would suggest that one or more of
the courses had been more successful in the area identified; if
there were no differences, it would be illegitimate to draw such
a conclusion. Our anlysis found no statistical differences
between the groups of this item, and we concluded that our evidence
did not give sufficient grounds for believing that a more positive
response had been gained (on this question at least) by a particular course.

8.5.1. Comment

Although we found some differences between our six courses,
many of these could be traced to differences established at the
first interview rather than to strengths or weaknesses of a particular programme. There were significant differences in respect
of action taken as a result of advice, although the reasons varied
according to subject area. The introduction of our control groups

suggested that the courses had not significantly increased commitment to retirement preparation nor extended the amount of planning activities. We shall now explore this point in greater depth: first, by pooling the data from our six courses; secondly, by comparing the responses of our experimental and control groups.

8.6. From Work to Retirement: the Role of Pre-Retirement Education

In this section we shall pool together the 153 individuals attending our six pre-retirement courses who were interviewed in Phase 3. This will enable us to gather additional information on the role of PRE in the experience of retirement. We shall also look at the extent of any planning arising out of particip- ation on a course.

The Transition to Retirement

Withdrawal from the work-force is a complex phenomenon. For some individuals it may arouse feelings of anger and loss, with a sense of being rejected by society. Others may view it as a satisfactory end to a long working life: retirement as a "reward" for 40 or 50 years of labour. In our group of 153 subjects, 71 per cent had been retired for between six and nine months by the time of the final interview. Eighty-four per cent reported having a retirement party, an event organised either by their workmates (59 per cent), or the firm itself (37 per cent). Three-quarters had been back to the firm since leaving work, mostly to see friends and former work colleagues.

Of the 138 leaving early or going because of a fixed retire- ment age, 35 reported that they would have preferred to have stayed on longer with their company. There is some evidence to suggest that the entry into retirement had been negotiated with relative ease by most of those we interviewed. Forty-seven per cent agreed that it had taken them "no time at all" to adjust to retirement; 29 per cent thought that it had taken a few weeks or a few months. Seventy-three per cent reported "feeling happy" when they first retired.

However, the minority experiences also deserve comment. Thus, 16 per cent were "still not adjusted" to retirement and 19 per cent had mixed feelings or were unhappy during the first days of leaving work. Clearly, a minority of those we inter- viewed had - regardless of their course - sufficient doubts about retirement to create difficulties in the period of transition. Part of their difficulties may have been related to the way in which they viewed retirement. For example 17 per cent still regarded retirement as "the beginning of old age"; eight per cent viewed it as a "rejection by society". It must be stressed that the numbers involved are relatively small, but it is import- ant to observe how such images can be retained throughout the transition and despite participation on a retirement course.

8.6.1. Planning and Preparation in the Transition

On a more positive note we find three-quarters saying that they were having no problems "keeping occupied". Eighty-two per cent said that they had been "very" or "fairly well prepared" for retirement and over two-thirds felt that it was possible to plan and prepare for retirement. However, it is also clear from our data that much of this preparation had taken place independently of the course. It is worth noting the substantial minority (39 per cent) who were critical of the timing of their programme (mainly that it had come too late). These reservations appear to have hardened since the second interview. Apart from in the areas of health and finance the response to the courses had been somewhat limited. Thirty-four per cent had done something as a result of the financial advice; 34 per cent as a result of the health information. In the area of leisure, just eight per cent had made a positive response; advice on employment attracted 14 per cent. We phrased our questions carefully to screen out those who would have taken action regardless of the course. However, our figures may still over-estimate the response to PRE. To set against this, there were many people who told us that their programme had given substance and meaning to ideas they had begun to consider, and the value of this should not be discounted.

We examined in some detail the background of those who had taken some action as a result of PRE. Our sample divided between 39 per cent who had taken no action and 61 per cent who had undertaken one or more activities. These two groups were then compared at the Phase 1 interview, in relation to the following areas: class, gender, expectations of retirement, worries about keeping occupied, worries about income and level of retirement preparation. On none of these items did the chi-squared statistic reach the five per cent level of significance.

We then compared the two extremes: those who had taken no action (39 per cent) and those who had undertaken two or more activities (23 per cent). There were three statistically significant differences. Those doing two or more activities were more likely to be looking for work (highly significant); less likely to be looking forward to retirement (significant); more likely to feel that it was possible to plan and prepare for retirement (significant – see Tables 8:20-8:22).

8.6.2. Attitude Change in the Transition

We examined the extent of attitude change over the pre- and post-retirement phases. Out of 32 items, there were 11 significant changes (Table 8:23). Some of the items on Table 8:24 suggest consolidation of changes detected between the Phase 1 and Phase 2 interviews, with fewer people looking for work; greater confidence about preparation for retirement; fewer people worrying about losing the sense of achievement that is sometimes associated with work. In these instances, the impetus provided by the course appears to have been given a further boost by retirement itself. However, there are also changes which reflect benefits arising out of the initial experience of leaving work, e.g. fewer people were worrying about money; fewer had problems about keeping occupied than they thought would be the case.

From our review of the experience of 153 subjects, there is some evidence to suggest that a movement towards greater optimism had occurred over the main phases of interviewing. However, the question we must now ask is whether those without the benefit of a retirement programme experienced more problems in negotiating the

186

TABLE 8:20

"Do you think you will look for work after you retire?"				
Response	No Activity		2+ Activities	
	n	%	n	%
Yes	22	37	23	66
No	37	63	12	34
TOTAL	59	100	35	100

$x^2 = 7.1$ d.f. = 1   1% Significant

TABLE 8: 21

"On the whole, are you looking forward to retirement?"				
Response	No Activity		2+ Activities	
	n	%	n	%
Yes	46	78	19	54
No/Mixed	13	22	16	46
TOTAL	59	100	35	100

$x^2 = 5.8$ d.f. = 1   5% Significant

TABLE 8: 22

"Do you feel you can plan and prepare for retirement?"				
Response	No Activity		2+ Activities	
	n	%	n	%
Yes	27	46	24	69
No	32	54	11	31
TOTAL	59	100	35	100

$x^2 = 4.6$ d.f. = 1   5% Significant

TABLE 8: 23

Phases 1-3 Significant Items on McNemar Tests of Significance of Changes		
SIGNIFICANT (5%)	HIGHLY SIGNIFICANT (1%)	EXTREMELY SIGNIFICANT (0.1%)
"Do you miss any feelings of usefulness or achievement which work may have provided?"	"Have you taken up any new leisure time activities?"	"Do you plan to look for any kind of paid work?"
"When you think about retirement, do you think of it as a life similar to when you were working?"	"Since you retired, have you found times when it has been difficult to keep occupied?"	
"Do you ever worry about Income Tax?"	"When you think about retirement, do you think of it as an extended holiday?"	
"How would you describe your present financial position - Difficult to make ends meet; Enough to get by on; well off; or very well off?"	"How well prepared would you say you were for retirement?"	
	"Do you feel you can plan and prepare for retirement?"	
	"Do you ever worry about your income in retirement?"	

transition from work. For evidence on this point, we now turn to our comparison between experimental and control subjects.

8.7. Experimental and Control Groups

So far our discussion of changes at Phases 1-2 and 1-3 has relied upon a comparison between a number of non-equivalent groups, all of whom received pre-retirement education. This raises the question, however, of how a group of retirees without a course would have responded to the kind of questions we asked in our interviews. To gain information on this point we tried wherever possible to form control groups of subjects. We managed to achieve this for two groups: the miners and the workers at EMI. With the former, our control group was created by using retiring miners from the North Nottinghamshire Area of the National Coal Board. In the case of EMI, individuals were allocated to their group on a random basis; we shall now discuss the results of this part of our research.

8.7.1. The Miners

The control group was taken from the North Nottinghamshire area of the NCB, with the sample being drawn from a group of collieries where PRE had not been made available. The emphasis, as in South Nottinghamshire, was on those taking voluntary early retirement. Letters were sent to all those retiring between April and September 1982 asking if they would be interested in participating in a survey on retirement. Included with the letter was a stamped addressed card asking people to state whether or not they were interested in helping with the study or whether they would be continuing with the NCB. Phase 1 interviews were completed with 25 of the 55 eligible for inclusion in the survey.

8.7.2. Results

Chi-squared statistics were calculated for 36 questions given to both groups at the Phase 1 interview. These covered a range of items covering attitudes towards work and retirement and financial position before and after retirement. The results revealed only one statistically significant difference between the two groups.[12] The control gave a more pessimistic evaluation of their likely financial situation in retirement (see Table 8:24). Before comparing the two groups at the Phase 3 interview we ran the McNemar test to assess the extent of any changes in the pre- and post-retirement period. The experimental group said they were less likely to be worrying about health and income (significant at 10 per cent). The control group were significantly more likely to say in their final interview that they were poorly prepared for retirement.

We then compared the two groups at the Phase 3 interview. Out of 21 items, there was just one significant difference: the control group had more health problems (significant at five per cent). Tables 8:25 - 8:28 illustrate the similarities between the groups on a range of questions.

189

TABLE 8:24

NCB PHASE 1: PRE-RETIREMENT FINANCIAL POSITION				
Response	EXPERIMENTAL GROUP		CONTROL GROUP	
	n	%	n	%
Difficult/Enough	12	50	20	83
Well off/Very well off	12	50	4	17
TOTAL	24	100	24	100

$x^2 = 4.6$ d.f. = 1   5% Significant

TABLE 8:25

NCB PHASE 3: "Do you have any particular physical or health problems?"				
Response	EXPERIMENTAL GROUP		CONTROL GROUP	
	n	%	n	%
Yes	5	22	13	57
No	18	78	10	43
TOTAL	23	100	23	100

$x^2 = 5.8$ d.f. = 1   5% Significant

TABLE 8:26

NCB PHASE 3: "Do you worry about not having a job to do?"				
Response	EXPERIMENTAL GROUP		CONTROL GROUP	
	n	%	n	%
Yes	18	90	19	90
No	2	10	2	10
TOTAL	20	100	21	100

$x^2 = 0.0$ d.f. = 1   Non-Significant

190

TABLE 8: 27

NCB PHASE 3: "When you think about retirement, do you think of it as... the beginning of old age?"				
Response	EXPERIMENTAL GROUP		CONTROL GROUP	
	n	%	n	%
Yes	9	39	7	30
No	14	61	16	70
TOTAL	23	100	23	100

$x^2 = 0.4$ d.f. = 1   Non-significant

TABLE 8:28

NCB PHASE 3: "I enjoy the time off that retirement allows".				
Response	EXPERIMENTAL GROUP		CONTROL GROUP	
	n	%	n	%
Strongly Agree/Agree	23	100	22	100
Not Sure/Undecided	-	-	-	-
Disagree/Strongly Disagree	-	-	-	-
TOTAL	23	100	22	100

$x^2 = 0.0$ d.f. = 1   Non-Significant

8.7.3. EMI and Legal and General

With the EMI group, we used an experimental approach, with individuals being allocated on a random basis to their particular group. In this instance our control group received a number of leaflets and books on retirement (e.g. Money and your Retirement by Edward Eves: The Time of your Life by Aleda Erskine; Your Rights by Age Concern). The comparison was now between one group who had received a pre-retirement course (organised by Legal and General Assurance Limited.) and another who had been given literature available in book shops or via the Pre-Retirement Association. At the West London site chosen for the research, 86 people were due to retire in the 12 months from June 1981. Sixty-four (73 per cent) agreed to participate after being contacted by letter. At least half the refusals were from people already on long-term sick leave. The group was stratified according to age, sex and social class. Allocation to the experimental or control group was made by toss of a coin.

8.7.4. Results

Chi-squared statistics were calculated for 36 questions given to both groups at the Phase 1 interview. There were two significant differences between the groups. The control group were more likely to worry about the prospect of not having a job in retirement; they were also more likely to give a period of 18 months or more as the time when people should begin planning and preparation for retirement.

Before comparing the two groups at the Phase 3 interview, we assessed the extent of any changes in the pre- and post-retirement period. Out of the 21 items, each group showed two changes.[13]

At the post-retirement interview, experimentals and controls showed just one significant difference: the experimental group were more likely to see retirement as an extended holiday (significant at five per cent). Apart from this item, as Tables 8:29 - 8:31 illustrate, the two groups showed striking similarities.

8.7.5. Comment

Our findings have uncovered very few differences in the experience of control and experimental subjects in the transition to retirement (a result supported by the equivalent American research). This result does not, however, invalidate the necessity of some form of retirement preparation. First, it serves as an indication that existing retirement programmes exercise a limited influence on behaviour and attitudes: alternative models - for example, those beginning at mid-life - may achieve a more positive response. Secondly, there is empirical evidence to suggest that anxieties can increase as retirement approaches, so educational programmes may thus play an important role in reducing worries about leaving work. Thirdly, our research found - amongst both experimental and control groups - important deficiencies in knowledge about pensions, taxation and general facts about ageing. Given the increasing complexity of pension arrangements and the emergence of early retirement, the need for retirement preparation is likely to increase. Fourthly, it is worth remembering that the small size of

TABLE 8:29

EMI PHASE 3: "Have you found times since your retirement when it has been difficult to keep occupied?"				
Response	EXPERIMENTAL GROUP		CONTROL GROUP	
	n	%	n	%
Yes	3	15	4	17
No	17	85	19	83
TOTAL	20	100	23	100

x^2 = 0.0   d.f. = 1   Non-Significant

TABLE 8:30

EMI PHASE 3: "How well prepared do you think you were for retirement?"				
Response	EXPERIMENTAL GROUP		CONTROL GROUP	
	n	%	n	%
Very/Fairly Well	18	75	23	74
Not Very Well/Not At All	6	25	8	26
TOTAL	24	100	31	100

x^2 = 0.0   d.f. = 1   Non-Significant

TABLE 8:31

EMI PHASE 3: "Do you think you can plan and prepare for retirement?"				
Response	EXPERIMENTAL GROUP		CONTROL GROUP	
	n	%	n	%
Yes	18	75	20	63
No	6	25	12	37
TOTAL	24	100	32	100

x^2 = 0.5   d.f. = 1   Non-Significant

our sample <u>may</u> understate the effect of retirement programmes. Finally, our analysis may not be able to capture more subjective benefits which arise from a course.

8.8. The Transition to Retirement: Crisis or Continuity

At the start of this chapter we discussed a number of theoretical models which could be used to interpret the transfer from work to retirement. One of these - role theory - suggests that withdrawal from work may lead to various social and health problems, an increase in mortality and morbidity being one possible outcome. On the other hand, continuity theory would caution against exaggerating the effects of retirement, and would point out the influence of other experiences in the life-cycle. Our data allow us to make some comment on the immediate impact created by the loss of a full-time occupation.

We examined responses to a number of questions on health which were asked at the Phase 1 and Phase 3 interviews:

"On the whole, would you say your health was good/fair/ poor?"

"How long ago did you last consult your doctor?"

"Have you taken medicines or tablets for any of the following:-

(a)   To help you sleep at night?
(b)   As a tonic to buck you up?
(c)   Anything for your nerves? (including tranquillisers)?
(d)   Anything to get relief from pain?
(e)   Any tablets or medicines for anything else?"

"Could you tell me whether you have had <u>frequent</u> difficulty with any of the following:-

Problems with sleeping?
Loss of appetite?
Always feeling tired?
Indigestion?
Shortness of breath?
Spells of depression?
Rheumatism?"

For all of our groups (course and controls) we find stability over the pre- and post-retirement phases. In the majority of cases, where movement did occur, this was in a positive direction.

We then examined levels of worry expressed by each group before and after retirement. Scores were computed from the follow-question:

"Do any of the following matters worry you:

Retirement income?
Your health after you retire?
Income tax in retirement?
Your housing in retirement?
Your relationship with family or friends?
The effect of retirement on you personally?".

194

TABLE 8:32

LEVELS OF WORRIES PHASE 1 – 3								
	NCB EXPERI-MENTAL	NCB CONTROL	EMI EXPERI-MENTAL	EMI CONTROL	BRISTOL	B.A.	GLASGOW	SHELL
Increase in Worries	1 (4%)	6 (26%)	7 (29%)	8 (27%)	3 (11%)	7 (20%)	5 (25%)	3 (16%)
No Change	12 (52%)	11 (48%)	11 (46%)	14 (46%)	11 (41%)	17 (49%)	9 (45%)	9 (47%)
Decrease in Worries	10 (43%)	6 (26%)	6 (25%)	8 (27%)	13 (48%)	11 (31%)	6 (30%)	7 (37%)
TOTAL	23	23	24	30	27	35	20	19

x^2 = 10.8   d.f. = 14   Non-significant.

When the six course groups and two controls were compared over Phase 1 to Phase 3 differences in changes over levels of worry were not statistically significant (Table 8:32). However, when we pooled the group together, we found that individuals were less likely to worry about retirement at Phase 3 in comparison to their feelings before leaving work (highly significant).

Finally, we compared our groups for activity levels before and after leaving work. An increase in activities around the home was characteristic of virtually all those interviewed. Activities outside the home were sustained at their pre-retirement level. In terms of items which had been reduced, only small amounts were reported by each of our groups. The EMI experimentals and controls returned a virtually identical pattern of response; the NCB controls, however, showed higher levels of loss than the experimentals. One interesting feature was that 14 out of the 36 in the British Airways group had reduced their amount of driving since retirement. This probably reflects the absence of commuting; however, given the worries about income expressed at the first interivew, the cost of driving may have been an importance factor for this group.

Our findings support an earlier British study by Crawford, the majority of whose subjects 'still felt themselves to be active members of the community .... (and were) not disengaging psycholog-ically from the social system'.[14]

It must be said, however, that there is little evidence from our results to support the thesis that participation on a convent-ional lecture-based course has greatly contributed to adjustment in retirement. Neither the reports from our course participants, nor the comparison between experimental and control subjects, would appear to support this position. If courses are to play a more dynamic role, then some major changes will need to be considered. In Chapter 10 we discuss the range of reforms we would like to see introduced.

CHAPTER 8

FOOTNOTES AND REFERENCES

1. Burgess, E.W. (Ed.). Aging in Western Societies, University of Chicago Press, 1966, p.17.

2. Ibid, p.20.

3. Ibid, p.272.

4. ·Michelon, L.C. 'The New Leisure Class', American Journal of Sociology, Vol. 59, 1959, p.371.

5. Loether, H.J. Problems of Aging, Dickenson, First Edition, 1975, p.91.

6. Blau, Z. Old Age in a Changing Society, New Viewpoints, 1973, p.177.

7. Cumming, E and Henry, W. Growing Old, Basic Books, 1963, pp. 14-15.

8. Rosow, J. 'Adjustment of the Normal Aged', in William R. et al (eds). Processes of Aging, Vol. 2. Atherton Press, 1963.

9. Johnson, M. 'That Was Your Life: A Biographical Approach to Later Life', in Carver, V. and Liddiard, P. An Ageing Population. Hodder and Stoughton in association with the Open University Press, 1978, p.111.

10. Maddox, G. 'Retirement as a Social Event' in McKinney, J.C. and de Vyver, F.T. (eds.), Aging and Social Policy, Appleton-Century-Crofts, 1966.

11. Atchley, R.C. 'Retirement and Leisure Participation: Continuity or Crisis', Gerontologist, Vol. 11, 1971, p.15.

12. It should be pointed out that, on the basis of chance alone, we would have expected two significant differences.

13. ditto.

14. Crawford, M.P. 'Retirement as a Psycho-Social Crisis', Journal of Psychosomatic Research, Vol. 16, No.5. p.280, 1972.

SECTION 4

In this final section we try to summarise the central findings
of our research. We also develop a series of arguments and
suggestions for improving the practice of pre-retirement
education.

CHAPTER 9

THE EXPERIENCE OF PRE-RETIREMENT EDUCATION:
A summary of the research findings.

9. Experiences

"It made me feel less confident - I thought I had it
'all buttoned up' but the course made me think again
and more carefully about certain aspects of retirement.
Nevertheless, I am quite happy with the decision to
retire, but I shall now make more effort to get things
done."
(Administrative Assistant, Female, Age 55).

"I was the only single lady on the course and I feel
it would have been a good idea if it could have been
so arranged that there were some other single ladies
on it at the same time. The problems we face and some
aspects of our retirement are totally different to those
of the married people".
(Secretary, Female, Age 54).

"Pensioner....was from another world. I said to the
chairman at one dinner time "don't you think we should
have somebody more like myself - a working man". We
should have somebody from the other end of the scale.
He (the speaker) wasn't much good to me....(he) went on
about his index-linked pension. As much as he wanted
to - that man couldn't help. We are living in different
worlds".
(Plant Maintenance Worker, Male, Age 65).

"I thought the course was very well put together, one thing
I should say, it was a course designed to give encouragement to people about retirement. It seems to depend,
however, on all the parts fitting into a satisfactory
pattern - on having a company pension, getting state
benefits. It didn't give any comfort to younger retirees
who were some years before retirement and who were not
going to get many of the benefits. The course was
designed around people taking an average retirement".
(Purchase Accounts Supervisor, Male, Age 58).

"Course was basically for people who had attained state
retirement age....less so for people experiencing premature
retirement and redundancy. When one is going on premature
retirement the worry is how is one going to manage. I
can't say I really grasped what I could get (i.e. in the
way of financial and social security benefits").
(Cashier, Female, Aged 59).

"It's made me treat it with more respect. I think one of
the things it's taught me is to talk with my wife more
about what we are going to do - joint ventures, for
example. It's certainly going to make an impact on eating
habits. I'm not going to let my wife do everything. My
dinner won't be just there all the time".
(Sheet Metal Worker, Male, Age 55).

"It settled me more .....going with others.....I wasn't alone. They are all in the same position. I feel now that perhaps retirement isn't so bad".
(Senior Waitress, Age 59).

"I would like to have had more time on the financial talks and more time to discuss things. The social security dragged things out too much. It should have been a more compact lecture and we would have remembered it better. I also felt that it was rather 'male orient- ated' and that as a woman I was being left out a bit. However, apart from this I thought it was well done and useful'.
(Assembly line worker, Woman, Age 60).

"It was excellent in every way".
(Engineer, Man, Age 64).

"They didn't provide much help for lower paid people. It was for people who are fairly well off".
(Assembly line worker, Man, Age 59).

"In the money region they were giving us the idea that you were going to get thousands, but you have to pay the bills. You can't invest it because you need all you get. The man was talking about £30,000. We needed more advice about what to do with a small amount'.
(Assembly line worker, Woman, Age 59).

"They started telling us about courses at University - in French and German - people around here would find you ridiculous (if you went to them). To be honest our attitude towards the course was 'well that's one day less at work ..... only four days to go'. It's working class people who go on these courses and there is a feeling 'well at least it's a day off work'. The course hasn't been a lot of good to me. Most of us went along and listened to the lectures and said 'well that was quite an interesting lecture but it won't affect my retirement very much'. They lectured at you, they should ask you first what your problems are".
(Progress Chaser, Male, Age 64).

"I was pleasantly surprised at how comprehensive it was ... I couldn't improve on it. Seeing people in a similar situation to yourself was very helpful. The course made you feel that there were people concerned about you - that made you feel good".
(Lathe Operator, Male, Age 64).

9.1. Information 'overload'.

In the previous two chapters we concentrated upon the instrumental value of PRE: Does it increase knowledge about retirement and ageing? Does it stimulate more positive views? However, as some of the above quotations might indicate it is unfair to concentrate solely on the direct value of PRE. Retirement programmes may have other benefits less easily articulated within the framework of a structured interview. For example, they may give a shape and focus to retirement and, along with the retirement celebration itself, become a significant element in the 'rite de passage' from a full-time occupation.

The capacity of a course to provide this framework will, however, depend upon the space which individuals are allowed to insert their own ideas and biographies within the time allowed by the course. This was a source of tension in virtually all of the courses we studied, regardless of their length. Even a six or seven day programme can be so crowded with sessions and ideas, that participants can feel 'breathless' and overtaken by the weight of information by the end of the programme. Simply to expand courses by a given number of days does not, therefore, resolve the problem of 'information overload'. It can only help when done in conjunction with greater discrimination about the relevance of given areas of knowledge and in the context of clearly defined objectives both for individual sessions and the course as a whole.

9.2. Pre-Retirement Education and Personal Biographies

One of the problems faced by our courses was that, in the majority of cases, they arrived towards the end of the individual's own dialogue with partners, workmates and friends about the nature of retirement and the value of preparation. Thus, the timing of the programme was a problem for many whom we interviewed. It was particularly acute for our women retirees, some of whom foresaw social and financial problems arising through leaving work (the feeling of missing people at work was given considerable emphasis by the women). Most of those we interviewed, however, had accepted the reality of compulsory retirement. Certainly, we found many who would have preferred to have remained at work for perhaps another year. But the limited opportunities for this had been largely accepted and there was no evidence for any sense of bitterness or rejection underyling the views of our sample. On the other hand, the lateness of the programme meant that it could only have a marginal influence on beliefs about the value of planning and preparation. In essence, planning was seen both before and after the course as a form of mental adjustment rather than a conscious attempt to control an external environment (the exceptions to this were drawn from the white collar groups in our sample).

In some respects, the attitudes of the sample mirrored many of the assumptions of pre-retirement educators. Yet it departed from these in terms of a broader view about the extent to which a change could be made in a given financial position or a balance of family and leisure activities. On the subject of leisure especially our programmes met with little success, suggesting the need for a fundamental re-think of work in this area. As regards financial advice, the selective way in which individuals responded to information raises some important issues. Advice on investments did receive some support, but only in situations where - predictably - a surplus was available. Unfortunately, course organisers were occasionally insensitive to the financial realities facing some of their audience, and were unable to present more relevant information. Information about state benefits and local authority concessions for pensioners was seen as useful and relevant by our respondents, but there were many complaints about the quality of presentations, particularly about speakers from the Department of Health and Social Security. Information on health was received with considerable interest, but its impact on behaviour was restricted to lectures which set clear and practical objectives.

9.3. The Impact of Retirement Education

As the above comments may indicate, what happened on most of the courses we studied was not a change in behaviour, but a consolidation of existing views. People would sometimes say to the interviewer: 'I feel more settled now' or 'The course has told me which of my plans was right and which was wrong'. However, we should also note a minority of people who worry more as a result of their involvement in a programme. In these instances, something happened in the few days of the course to suggest that all was not right in their approach to retirement or that something was missing in the financial package which they had put together. It may be that these people are amongst the group who told us that they wanted more time for private counselling during their course, either about financial problems or concerning a personal issue (in one case anxiety about a wife who suffered from her 'nerves' and was on tranquillisers).

In the above examples it seemed to us that the research had illuminated an important feature of PRE: namely, that even in only two or three days a programme could release quite urgent worries. However, we found that these could rarely be resolved within the framework of a conventional course. Indeed, we can say that where people did have deep-seated problems (or became aware of such problems as the course unfolded) then existing programmes could offer very limited guidance or constructive help. The problems may have been associated with fears about losing the companionship of colleagues at work. Alternatively, they may centre around personal difficulties. For example, one of our respondents at her first interview, expressed distress at losing the security of her job and returning home to a marriage which was the cause of much unhappiness. In this instance, when we returned to our respondent at the third interview, we found her in much distress, locked into a highly oppressive domestic environment. Of course, it is not fair to say that her particular programme had failed; retirement education obviously cannot resolve what may be life-long strains within a marriage. But it should at least provide a supportive environment, where personal, marital and financial concerns are recognised. The suspicion we have from our research is that too many courses convey an idealised picture of retirement to the participants, rarely admitting to be disturbances created by unhappy marriages, poverty and ageist beliefs and practices within society.

Actually, the picture is more complex than we have described it, since PRE is currently operating with two diametrically opposed models of retirement. One of these is receding in importance, but was dominant in the early history of the movement. This perspective suggests that withdrawal from work leads to a psycho-social crisis, one which can only be resolved through returning to work or finding substitutes for a full-time occupation. The other model, dominant in the PRE literature (particularly 'Choice' magazine), and of increasing influence on courses themselves, places less emphasis on the negative psychological impact of retirement. Instead, leaving work is seen as creating opportunities for the exploitation of leisure and hobbies; for creating a perfect home environment; and for re-engaging in the social and cultural sphere. The positive aspect of this model is the greater recognition that work can be experienced as a burden - particularly in late middle age. The negative aspect is its insensitivity to those without a significant occupational pension or with limited savings. Thus the new approach to PRE is adequate if you can participate in the consumer market aimed at the more prosperous retirees. If you are outside this market, dependent upon resources provided by the state, then retirement education has much less to offer.

9.4. The Social Composition of Courses

As the above arguments might suggest, a critical issue facing organisers is how to respond to the social and economic stratification amongst people facing retirement. In our individual evaluation reports, we referred to the problem of heterogeneity, i.e. divisions of social class, gender, marital status, income level and retirement age. In all these areas our courses had faced enormous change over the decade of the seventies, their participants showing much greater diversity than in the preceding decades. This was an issue faced most acutely by retirement councils. However, even in private companies the range of circumstances could be very wide.

This development has created three problems: First, meeting the information needs of a substantial portion of the audience is increasingly difficult if there is reliance upon a lecture-based model for transmitting information. This approach is dependent upon general statements and principals, many of which may be irrelevant to a high proportion of course members. Secondly, there is a view - particularly in British PRE - that diversity is a bonus; that mixing people of different ages and backgrounds increases the quality of discussion. Our research, however, showed some resistance to this on the part of participants and we think that organisers need to recognise the tensions created by mixed social groups. Thirdly, where there is no active chairing on courses - as seems to be the case in most of those we have observed during the life of the project - the problem of heterogenity is exacerbated. It is no use making a virtue of having everybody from the cleaner to the managing director on a course if organisers then sit back and let participants muddle through on their own. In the real world cleaners rarely talk to managing directors (if only because they tend to turn up for work at different periods in the day); at the very least, constructive talk will only happen if there is somebody actively promoting debate and discussion. In fact, cleaners and managing directors rarely come to courses (though for different reasons) and communication is usually between blue collar workers and lower middle grade white collar employees. Even within the narrow band of social class III, however, income differentials and life styles can still be very wide.

However, we are not just talking about categories of class and
income. Retirement age is a crucial variable and we found many
of our early retirees saying they would have preferred a programme to themselves, where their distinctive needs could have
been met. There was a feeling amongst some that they had no
identification with the label 'retired' and that the course -
by placing them with a group of people 10-15 years older (in
some instances) than themselves - was forcing them into acceptance of this category. It seemed to us from these comments
that there was a case for organising separate programmes for
early and normal age retirees, although we recognise the problems
this may create for organisers. Finally, it is clear that PRE
has yet to respond to the needs of the growing number of women
employees; or, indeed, to promote courses for women in the
community (The Scottish Council remains an important exception).
There remains a male bias in PRE, one which is partly sustained
by the numerical dominance of men as chairmen and organisers,
but also because of a view that leaving work is a more damaging
experience for men than it is for women. Yet we do have
sociological evidence indicating a change in women's attitudes
to retirement, with those who return to part-time or full-time
employment showing some resistance to the prospect of leaving
work. They do, of course, face a much longer time in retirement;
they will experience widowhood; and their income is likely to
decline quite sharply as they enter their 70s. For all these
reasons women need, not necessarily separate courses, but individual sessions within programmes, to discuss some of the
problems they are likely to face.

9.5 What are we trying to do in Retirement Education?

One of the difficulties we faced as researchers was trying
to relate our findings to the objectives of the courses we
examined. With two exceptions, none of the courses which we
studied in detail appeared to have provided either a clear
statement of the general aims of their programme, or the purpose
of individual sessions or lectures. The introduction to courses
rarely provided an insight into what organisers thought they
were trying to achieve. In some instances, ambiguity was
increased by contradictory advice from different speakers.
Participants were therefore often faced with at least two
problems in the lecture-room: first, they had to sort through
a substantial volume of material; secondly, they had to decide
upon what was 'good' and 'bad' advice or information which was
supported by knowledge and experience as opposed to items which
were based upon 'personal opinion'. If one remembers that many
participants will not have received formal 'education' for a
very long period of time, one begins to appreciate the formidable
problems involved in organising a successful course. Yet good
practice is possible to achieve. Among our eight courses, there
were three presentations which - in adult education terms - were
a model of clarity and exposition. In each case, the speaker
began with a clear statement of objectives, developed participation
from the audience and outlined the practical benefits of the
suggestions which were made. These were the sessions which - 12
or more months after the event - were still having an impact on
those who took part. However, these sessions were also a minority
of all those studied and observed over the three years of the
research. In the majority of cases, basic rules of how adults
learn were ignored, although this must partly reflect the way adult

education has itself ignored the question of education for older people.

9.6 Chairmanship

The problems we have identified must be related to the effective chairing of courses. We found that few chairmen saw their position in terms of intervening where speakers gave inaccurate or irrelevant information. Most adopted a largely passive role, viewing their function in terms of making introductions and organising meal and tea breaks.

We would argue that improving the effectiveness of course chairmen would raise both the quality and productivity of courses. Our evidence suggests that the latter is fairly low at present, i.e. that the number of identifiable responses made to PRE is very restricted. In making this statement we would put forward two qualifications. First, as suggested earlier, to judge programmes solely in instrumental terms is misguided. A course is more than the sum of various lectures and discussions. It may, for example, provide alternative ways of seeing the world beyond full-time work. It may even provide the beginning of a new philosophy regarding personal and social relationships. The second problem with an instrumental approach is that many people who attend courses are already highly motivated for retirement. In other words, 'productivity' may be low if only because the 'non-participants' may be those who do need substantial help and advice. But with these qualifications, we still met a very limited response to the variety of programmes which were studied. We would argue that where chairmen become more actively involved and more responsive to the individual needs of course members, a positive outcome would be an increase in those who feel able to respond to the advice given on courses.

The problem of chairmanship must also be related to the stated objectives of pre-retirement courses. It is unsatisfactory to claim that courses are about changing attitudes or promoting adjustment if they are organised a few months before retirement and consist of a number of 50 minute lectures. Such an approach is useful for disseminating quick, first-aid advice - a task which is useful and important. However, if there is a desire to intervene and influence retirement attitudes in a more direct way, then different procedures are needed. It is this issue which we shall discuss in our next chapter.

CHAPTER 10

PRINCIPLES AND PRACTICE FOR
PRE-RETIREMENT EDUCATION

10. Introduction

In this concluding chapter we shall discuss a number of recommendations for improving the practice of PRE. In developing our arguments we shall draw upon findings from the existing PRE literature (as reviewed in Chapter 3) and findings from our own survey. We shall also use sociological theory to illuminate the aims and objectives of retirement planning. In this context our approach should be seen as complementary to Allin Coleman's survey of PRE.[1] His research uses the conceptual vocabulary of adult education to examine retirement programmes. We shall use sociological theories about the process of retirement to interpret data concerning the effectiveness of courses. Before presenting our arguments, we shall list the key recommendations which arise from our work:

Recommendations for Good Practice

1. Equal relationship between teacher and students. (10.1)

2. Separate courses for early and normal age retirers.(10.2)

3. Sessions for groups to discuss problems of mutual concern. (10.2)

4. Development of case study materials. (10.2)

5. Different individuals to perform roles of course chairman and course coordinator. (10.2)

6. Introduce counselling element on all pre-retirement courses. (10.3)

7. Identify concerns of participants in advance of the course. (10.4)

8. Identify facilities in the community of key importance for retired people. (10.5)

9. Introduce participants to self-help and community organising skills. (10.5)

10. Courses should devote greater time to discussing stereotypes of ageing and retirement. (10.6)

11. Organisers must critically examine their own beliefs about the process of ageing and the experience of retirement. (10.6)

12. Audio-visual aids should be more widely used, particularly as an aid for further discussion. (10.7)

13. Course material should be distributed in advance of the course. (10.7)

14. Organisers should give greater emphasis to the efficient chairing of courses. (10.7)

15. The lecture model should be drastically modified. Emphasis should be placed upon a short (10-15 minute) talk supported by audio-visual aids and hand-outs as a stimulus for question and answer within the group. (10.7)

16. Creation of peer group support networks. (10.8)

17. Development of mid-life planning courses (10.9 and 10.10)

18. Organisers must develop a more experimental approach to the design and presentation of courses. (10.11)

10.1 <u>Creating Equal Relationships on Courses</u>

In Chapter 8 we noted the influence of role theory on the structure and content of retirement courses. An important derivative of this model is a crisis approach to retirement education, one in which the aim of the programme is to find new identities and meanings to replace those formed within the workplace. This approach has been subjected to number of critiques within sociology.[2] Emergent approaches emphasise the variety of responses individuals make to retirement, and suggest the need for isolating specific (rather than general) forms of strain and disruption. In addition, retirement is viewed as a process rather than a single traumatic event, the research problem becoming one of identifying a number of points of strain and tension running throughout later life. Finally, reaction to retirement is conceived as a variable (rather than a social event with a single meaning), one which must be set within the context of a variety of experiences which make up an individual's biography.

This theoretical debate has important practical implications for the organisation of retirement programmes. We would argue that courses organised around a "crisis approach" will have diminishing relevance for new cohorts of retirees (particularly men retiring at the statutory age). Of course, some individuals and groups will continue to benefit from an approach of this kind; however, in general terms, PRE will become less concerned with problems of substituting for a work-based identity. Instead, the focus will be upon realising the potential of an existing lifestyle, within a relatively stable network of activities and relationships. Where retirement is perceived in crisis terms, the didactic approach to PRE (see below) will be replaced by one emphasising an open discussion of retirement problems. The implications for the structure and content of programmes may be summarised as follows:

Theoretical model	Style of Presentation	Programme content
Retirement as a psycho-social crisis.	Didactic/Authoritarian	Suggestions for new activities and relationships.
Retirement as continuity	Interactionist/ Egalitarian	Advice based upon knowledge of individual needs and biographies.

The crisis model, as noted in Chapter 8, was influential in the early history of PRE, having an impact both upon teaching style and course content.   Whilst this model could have encour-- aged considerable interaction between tutor/teacher and audience, in reality, the dominant style was authoritarian and didactic. In the typical presentation, the lecturer attempted to define a "correct" set of attitudes for retirement; in addition, on some courses, there would be a "model" retired person, someone who had successfully negotiated the transition from full-time work.   In the second model, however, there is a radical change of emphasis.   First, there is a more egalitarian relationship between teacher and student.   We have described this as "inter- actionist", since the retirement course would not define issues in advance.   Instead, the course would be developed within the context of individual questions raised by the group.   Secondly, the topics selected for discussion would change from group to group, hence there would be greater diversity in course curric- ulum.

 Our arguments would support a pluralist approach to retire- ment education, with organisers re-working their programmes in the light of trends in social policy and demographic and labour market conditions. However, within this perspective, we can outline some additional proposals for good practice.

 10.2 The Need for Homogeneity in the Composition of Programmes

A major concern of organisers must be to improve the extent of group participation on courses.[3] One way of achieving this would be through reducing class and status differences within groups.   This is not to suggest separate courses (although this may be necessary for early and normal age retirees);   rather, it should be possible for groups on a particular course to discuss - in separate sessions - areas of mutual concern (e.g. single women may want a specialised session on finance; unskilled workers with no occupational pension may need detailed advice on supplementary benefits; a group of married couples may feel the need for a more detailed discussion about the impact of retire- ment on personal relationships).   Special provision may also be necessary for ethnic minority elders, for whom racial discrim- ination joins with age-related inequalities.[4]

To achieve constructive groupwork along the lines we have indicated, will require spreading courses over a longer period of time.   Our research found that short courses were criticised for insufficient discussion time, complaints about the "cramming" of information being relatively common. Organisers should attempt wherever possible, therefore, to move away from very short prog- rammes.   Greater homogeneity will also help resolve tensions regarding course content, i.e. conflict between generalised information and an audience with diverse needs and interests. Developing specialised sessions will require organisers to (a) develop case study material; (b) draw upon a much wider pool of speakers; (c) distinguish between the role of programme co-ordin- ator and that of course tutor. (The former would be concerned with basic requirements for rooms, refreshments, etc.; the latter would facilitate group discussion and would clarify points of ambiguity in presentations from speakers).

10.3 The Counselling Element in Retirement Education

Many of the people we interviewed expressed the need for personal counselling to be brought into their course. The importance of the counselling element has been discussed by a number of British and American writers, and use of this approach can greatly increase the range of problems discussed on courses.[5] There are at least two ways in which counselling could be organised. Firstly, on a one-to-one basis with speakers, course facilitators and representatives from within the employing organisations (e.g. trade unions and welfare departments). Secondly, programmes could use a group interaction model (as outlined by Manion) to allow greater space for retirees to identify anxieties in the pre-retirement period. Some of the key elements of this model are:

1. "Development of self-diagnostic skills - helping the older employees to become aware of their fears and of their strong motivational needs, and to relate these to their own retirement planning".

2. "Development of communication and interpersonal relations skills".

3. "Development of skills in life planning".

4. "Development of skills and attitudes for effective problem solving (which are considered necessary tools for adequate retirement adjustment)".[6]

The importance of this approach is that it emphasises the value of counselling in a peer group setting, allowing the individual to relate his or her own problems to a wider economic and social environment.

10.4 Identifying Key Issues and Concerns

Whether a counselling element is adopted must be a pragmatic decision, depending on the range of concerns individuals bring to their course. This point illustrates a key finding to emerge from our work: namely, that retirees will only respond to issues which they perceive as relevant to their particular problems. Identifying these areas must be done before the start of any course, and the priorities of the group must be reflected in all aspects of course planning. In this respect our research supports the conclusions from the work of O'Rourke and Friedman:

"The attitudes of workers towards retirement should be ascertained before a training program is constructed. In this way, the program content may be designed for and aimed at those areas of attitudes and knowledge most critical for the worker and most susceptible to change. The question of how critical is an area of ignorance is a matter of subjective estimate for program planners; the question of susceptibility to attitudinal change is a matter of continued basic research".[7]

Gaining knowledge of group concerns in advance does raise organisational problems. However, there are some straightforward measures available to acquire this information. For example,

questionnaires could be distributed <u>prior</u> to attendance at a
course. The information from could be used to draw both a sociological profile of course participants, and a check-list of responses to questions about key worries or concerns regarding
retirement. Alternatively, retirees could be encouraged to see
a company or trade union representative to indicate the type of
issues they would like discussed on the course. The organiser
would thus have some familiarity with the needs of participants in
advance of the actual programme. This knowledge could be used to
modify the design of the course e.g. reducing or increasing the
proportion of time spent on discussing financial issues; expanding
the counselling element; introducing new subject matter.

10.5. <u>Retirement in the Community</u>

Both Woodrow Hunter and Mannes Tidmarsh have argued for a
community orientation to retirement courses.[8] This could be done
by: (a) running courses for people retiring to the <u>same</u> neighbourhood; (b) providing "contacts between the older workers in the
programme and leaders of community programmes and services of
special value to older people".[9]

This community approach has important implications for the
structure and content of PRE. We would argue for more time to be
spent on courses examining the range of services available in the
community. This could have an action component as well as presenting basic information. The former would explore how older people
can work together to develop facilities which do not yet exist but
which could improve the quality of life in retirement. It would
also examine how retired people can organise to maintain and improve
existing services (e.g. in the area of health and leisure). A
community focus to PRE would thus need to examine questions relating
to <u>self-help</u> in the individual's own neighbourhood, with workshops
looking at the basic skills required for organising within the
community.[10]

10.6 <u>Developing a Positive Image of Retirement</u>

From a historical perspective we find considerable ambivalence
in the way British society has traditionally viewed retirement. On
the one hand, where labour is in short supply, it has discouraged
withdrawal from the labour market; on the other hand, where there
is a surplus of employees inducements are provided to encourage
individuals to leave work. This social ambivalence has created
contradictions in the way retirement is experienced. It may be
perceived as a partial reward for long service; at the same time
it may also stimulate feelings of guilt, a sense that being a
worker is a more legitimate position than that gained through
withdrawal from a full-time occupation. Such tensions confirm the
need for courses to help individuals develop positive feelings
about life in retirement. Indeed, as Dennis Lumsden has recently
reminded us, Thompson's research in the 1950s showed how attitudes
and beliefs about retirement can determine the effectiveness of
pre-retirement planning. The research concluded that:

> "....planning for retirement was relatively unimportant
> for successful adjustment compared to having an accurate
> preconception of retirement and a favourable pre-retirement
> attitude. Planning seemed to be important only when the

individual had a favourable pre-retirment attitude and
an accurate preconception. If the opposite were true,
planning did not increase his chances of making a successful adjustment".[11]

There are at least two observations which follow this kind
of research. First,   developing accurate preconceptions will
involve confronting sociological and psychological stereotypes
of growing old. In a society where there are political, economic
and cultural pressures to define old age as a form of dependency,
retirement itself may be seen as a devalued status.[12] In our
research, we found a substantial minority of individuals who
associated retirement with the beginning of old age or who be-
lieved that retired people become set in their ways and unable
to change. These beliefs were, in many instances, sustained
even after attendance at a retirement programme, indicating the
problems conventional courses face in tackling ageist beliefs
and practices. We would argue that PRE must devote a greater
proportion of time to discussing stereotypes about ageing and
retirement, and that organisers must critically examine to what
extent they themselves reinforce, rather than challenge, such
attitudes.

A second observation we can make stems from an important
finding of the Keele research: namely, that those who attend
courses may already have positive views about retirement and may
not identify with the more extreme stereotypes of old age. What,
however, of the "non-participants"? Do they exhibit a similar
profile, or are some more disturbed by the prospect of with-
drawing from work? If the latter is the case, what has prevented
their participation on the retirement course? This raises the
question of how effectively we communicate the existence of
programmes. It is surely disturbing that in Stanley Parker's
survey of older workers, 38 per cent of those interviewed had
no knowledge of the existence of courses.[13] Our own research
found instances where the publicity about a course was very
haphazard, dependent upon chance meetings or notices pinned to
factory notice boards.

However, as well as improving methods of communication,
we also need to think about the style of presentation. The
problem for PRE, as we have indicated in earlier chapters, is
that it must now try to appeal to a much broader constituency
of men and women. This situation places considerable pressure
on its public image and methods of communication. Does PRE
appeal to people in their mid-fifties? Does it appeal to working
women? Our research often produced negative answers to these
questions. Part of the problem, we suspect, is that the movement
has not been sufficiently critical about the impact of its work.
The "natural history" of many courses is for experimentation and
innovation to occur only in the initial stages of course development. Rather than view each course as an experiment in "objectives,
content and method", organisers have been happy to remain with an
estblished formula. If the "success" of the arrangement is confirmed by questionnaires administered directly after the course, so
much the better; even if the questionnaires do not come up with
the desired replies they can be safely ignored or attributed to an
"exceptional" or "difficult" group.

We would argue that it is important that organisers recognise that courses do sometimes "fail"; that communication with participants is occasionally defective. Without this recognition, establishing what constitutes a "successful" course becomes virtually impossible.

10.7. Lecture versus Discussion Groups

So far we have discussed issues concerning the organisation of PRE without committing ourselves to a statement about the value of the lecture model (the form of organisation which has dominated most retirement courses). There is now emerging powerful evidence to suggest there are considerable problems in relying on a 40-50 minute lecture as the medium for transmitting information. Tiberi et al., in a comparative analysis of four PRE models, found that the lecture-based model and one using video-tapes were the least appropriate for transmitting information on retirement. They argued that:

> "If retirement in our society is an emotionally loaded concept, then, a motive for these people to participate in a pre-retirement program is indicative of a need to express, share, and deal with the feelings and apprehensions concomitant with the retirement experience. A pre-retirement program that does not provide specific processes to work with these feelings and apprehensions will probably be perceived as frustrating and depressing".[14]

This finding is supported by the work of Christrup and Thurman. The researchers found that:

> "Factual presentations by guest speakers in a large auditorium and the distribution of published materials were found to be far less effective than informal meetings? in small groups with maximum involvement by participants who were encouraged to discuss their psychological and emotional feelings about retirement as a prelude to planning for their retirement years".[15]

Our research confirmed the difficulties accompanying a formal lecture, particularly where it was given by an individual with no experience of adult education. Thus, although there may be short-term action arising from a course, response over a longer period may be much more limited, i.e. whilst people may appear more competent after experiencing pre-retirement education, comprehension of a complex set of data and ability to set long-term goals may not have improved.

At the same time, our research would question whether simply injecting more discussion time into courses is the complete answer. Of all our courses, the Shell International programme devoted a considerable part of its six days to group discussion. Yet this was also the course with the highest number of complaints about inadequate time for exchanging views. This may reflect, as we suggested earlier, the high expectations of a white collar group. It may also indicate that an extended period of discussion-time is still unable to cope with an extensive amount of information presented during the lecture period.

However, the major problem with the lecture model is how it responds to a group with widely differing needs. We tried to gain information on this in the analysis of our results. Using a statistical test known as chi-squared for linear trend (see Appendix 1 for a definition of this statistic), we examined whether the proportion of manual to non-manual workers on a course influenced the amount of action arising from the programme. We found that programmes with the highest proportion of <u>manual</u> workers were <u>least</u> likely to respond to advice on finance (Table 10.1). Conversely, those with the highest proportion of <u>non-manual</u> workers were least likely to take action on health (Table 10:2). The first finding is particularly disturbing, suggesting that those most in need of help (judged in terms of financial resources) are the least responsive to PRE. The inference, in our view, is that the lecture model is insufficiently flexible to respond to the problems faced by manual workers. On the other hand, it must be noted that only one of the groups had more than 50 per cent of participants taking action on finance. Even for the more middle class groups, therefore, the response to the sessions on finance had not been overwhelming.

We would suggest that some of the problems we have discussed could be resolved by combining a short lecture with regular periods of discussion.[16] This approach would use a 10-15 minute talk (supported by audio-visual aids and handouts) as a stimulus for question and answer within the group. For this method to work, three conditions would have to be satisfied: (1) sessions must be supported by extensive use of visual aids, e.g. trigger films with brief retirement case studies; (2) hand-outs should be distributed prior to the course to ensure maximum participation in discussions; (3) firm and positive chairing should be encouraged, particularly in respect of stimulating discussion.

This approach should be of particular benefit to courses which rely upon untrained speakers. At the present time, these speakers are attempting to present a 40 or 50 minute lecture, to audiences of 20 or more people. Unfortunately, communicating complex issues in the field of health, finance, etc. demands a high level of teaching ability and technique. Our research indicates that many people were not able to meet these demands and, not surprisingly, left feelings of confusion and uncertainty in the minds of participants.

10.8 Peer Group Support Networks

The difficulty with the lecture model revolves around how people respond to information in the seminar or class room. The view that it is best achieved via a verbal presentation ignores the difficulties faced by individuals in differentiating between a number of recommendations or sorting through conflicting areas of advice (campaigns on health education have provided supporting evidence for this point). Instead, if communication is to be effective it must, first, be perceived as relevant to the particular situation facing the group; secondly, it must be presented by a credible source, one with whom the listener can identify. The latter raises particular problems for PRE. Many of the speakers used on courses (e.g. bank managers and doctors) may generate antipathy amongst the audience, maintaining a professional reserve which the listener finds alienating. They may also give advice which departs from their own sphere of competence, creating doubts as to the accuracy and relevance of some of their views.

TABLE 10.1

Response	NCB Experimental	Bristol	B.A.	EMI Experimental	Glasgow	Shell
"Have you done anything as a result of advice received on finance?" (Ordered by Social Class).						
Yes	2 9%	5 19%	15 42%	13 54%	10 43%	7 35%
No	21 91%	22 82%	21 58%	11 46%	13 57%	13 65%
Total	23	27	36	24	23	20

Conventional x^2 = 15.7   d.f. = 5   1% significant
x^2 Linear Trend = 7.4   d.f. = 1   1% significant

TABLE 10.2

Response	NCB Experimental	Bristol	B.A.	EMI Experimental	Glasgow	Shell
"Have you done anything as a result of advice received on health?" (Ordered by Social Class).						
Yes	13 57%	15 56%	4 11%	6 25%	9 39%	4 20%
No	10 44%	12 44%	31 89%	18 75%	14 61%	16 80%
Total	23	27	35	24	23	20

Conventional x^2 = 21.7   d.f. = 5   1% significant
x^2 Linear Trend = 6.6   d.f. = 1   1% significant

215

One alternative approach to this problem would be to create networks of peer groups – i.e. people retiring at roughly the same time – within a factory or office. The task of the welfare, training or personnel department would be to service these groups with relevant brochures, leaflets, etc.; provide facilities for meetings; respond to calls for specialist speakers. The groups could function over a period of years or they may only be active in the months preceding retirement. Obviously, this kind of arrangement is more appropriate for fairly large companies. However, we would like to see such networks formed in a variety of industrial contexts, with a research input to monitor their effectiveness.

10.9 Mid-Life Planning

Proposals to organise courses at mid-life have been the subject of some debate inside PRE. A number of researchers have, for example, called for mid-life planning courses to begin at 40 or 50 years of age. At present very few organisations are developing such programmes and many questions remain unanswered about how they should be organised. As part of the Keele research (and in co-operation with Mannes Tidmarsh, formerly of Sheffield Polytechnic) we organised two courses for men and women in their mid-fifties in a large manufacturing company in Manchester. The firm had previously experimented with a policy of phased retirement but were interested in extending their interest in the direction of PRE. In this chapter, we shall examine both the background to the course and the way it was organised; as well as examining the broader implications of taking PRE into middle age.

10.9.1 The case for earlier courses

The case for earlier programmes can be supported by a number of arguments. First, middle age may bring important changes in the areas of occupation, health and family life. The adaptations made to these changes are likely to have a formative influence on attitudes towards planning and preparation for retirement.[17] Secondly, there are a number of planning decisions - particularly those connected with finance - which can only be made around middle age; if left to a later period their influence upon retirement is likely to be marginal. Finally, altering a particular balance between leisure and family activities may be more easily achieved in the early pre-retirement phase than if left until retirement.

Given these arguments, we were interested in exploring how people would respond to a mid-life planning course. The next section of this chapter examines the development and organisation of such a programme.

10.9.2 A Mid-life planning course

In Autumn 1981 and Spring 1982 we ran a mid-life planning course for nearly 60 employees at a manufacturing company in Manchester. The underlying aim of the programme was set out in a brochure distributed in a letter of invitation to 105 people in the 55-57 age group.

At certain stages in life we are called on to adapt
to major changes in ourselves and our personal and
social relationships, e.g. at adolescence, marriage,
starting a family, retirement, and so on. Middle
age, though more extended and gradual than any of
those, requires a great deal of adjustment if we are
to go on to enjoy the second half of our lives. This
course aims to look at some of the changes that we
may be subjected to at middle age and some of the ways
we can adapt so as to leave open the possibility of
further development in the future. As well as examining
changes in middle-age, the course will provide assistance for long-term retirement preparation. Speakers
will be provided to advise on areas such as finance,
health and leisure opportunities. The emphasis throughout the programme will be on discussion and the exchange
of ideas. The atmosphere will be made as relaxed and
informal as possible, and it is hoped that the course
will be both stimulating and enjoyable.

From the 105 people in this age group, 62 (59 per cent)
responded positively both to the invitation to the course and
to a pre-course interview to discuss their views on mid-life
change. For this interview we had designed a short questionnaire to assess attitudes towards mid-life. Fifty-six people
attended the interview which was held (along with the course)
in the factory. The group was evenly divided between manual and
non-manual workers, and was composed predominantly of men. We
first asked a number of questions about whether people were
experiencing more stress in the key areas of work, family and
health. Health emerged as the area which had triggered most stress
(35 per cent agreed that they were aware of more stress; 32 per
cent felt less physically fit than they were five years ago; 29
per cent were worrying about their health). Forty-one per cent
agreed that they saw 'new directions or possibilities' opening
in mid-life; 52 per cent confirmed that they had experienced a
greater sense of freedom in this period. On the other hand
only 18 per cent could identify 'specific opportunities' which
might become available (a finding which supports a review of
leisure and adult education facilities relevant to this period).

It is clear from our interview that even without a course,
the group had already begun to make various adjustments both to
mid-life and to their future retirement. Thirty-six per cent
agreed that they had made adjustments to cope with changes in
middle age. Seventy-one per cent claimed to be looking forward
to retirement; 36 per cent, however, admitted shortcomings in
their preparation for retirement.

The response both to our initial letter and to the questionnaire, indicated that there was some interest in the idea of
mid-life planning. Given a background of high unemployment, our
group had already started to think about life beyond full-time
work. This aspect was confirmed during the discussion periods
of both the courses which we organised.

10.9.3. The organisation of a mid-life planning course

In Table 10:3 we show the structure and content of our
course. The introduction included a period for exchanging views

TABLE 10:3   MID-LIFE PLANNING COURSE

DAY 1	DAY 2	DAY 3
9.00 - Introducing the Course	9.00 - 10.00 The Company Pension.	9.00 - Opportunities at mid-life: Adult Education.
10.15 Video Film - Changes in Mid-Life.	BREAK	10.15 Voluntary Work.
BREAK	10.15 - 11.30 Financial Planning: Guide to Savings and Investments; Tax problems: Social Security.	BREAK
10.30 - 11.30 Discussion Period		10.30 - 11.30 Course Review and Discussion
BREAK	BREAK	BREAK
12.00 - 1.00 Health in Middle Age and Later Life.	12.00 - 1.00 Discussion.	COURSE ENDS.

about the purpose of the course and the organisation of the
sessions. A 60 minute video was then used as means of opening
a discussion about some of the main interests and concerns of
the group. The video examined mid-life change and retirement
and was an episode from the London Weekend Television series
"The Seven Ages of Man". The film opened with a number of
couples discussing their feelings about entering mid-life, e.g.
the menopause, career change and alterations in family relationships. The second part concentrated on the transition to
retirement presenting case studies of people who had taken early
retirement; a retirement party; and the initial impact and
experience of retirement.

The advantage of the film was that it dealt with the issues
of immediate relevance to our group. Its main disadvantage
(which was commented upon by a number of individuals) was that
the first half presented only a limited range of experiences,
the majority of case studies taking their examples from white
collar and professional groups.

One interesting feature was that in the session following
the video most of the discussion focused on retirement. Thus,
although the course was labelled 'mid-life' planning, most of
the attention switched to the pre- and post-retirement phase.

The session on health in middle age and later life was
treated differently in each of the two courses. In the first
talk we had a 30 minute lecture followed by a discussion. The
talk followed the usual format, covering items on nutrition and
physical fitness. The talk on the second course focused almost
exclusively on physical fitness and included material about
pensioners running their own keep-fit groups.

The financial presentation covered talks on the company
pension, social security and investments. A representative
from the firm discussed benefits available from the company
pension; commutation; additional voluntary contributions; and
financial aspects of early retirement. The investment talk
was a brief presentation from a financial consultant who listed
the main options available for investing money. He also
contributed to the discussion on commutation and additional
voluntary contributions. Information on social security was
presented by a worker from a Citizen's Advice Bureau. His
initial focus was on the stigma surrounding state benefits. He
went on to discuss the conditions for receiving a range of
benefits, including invalidity allowance, mobility allowance,
sickness benefits and attendance allowance. One of the features
of the discussion which followed this talk was the number of
people who thought their own elderly relatives might be eligible
for the benefits described. Finally, we had two sessions from
people involved in Adult Education. The first of these looked
at the meaning and relevance of education in later life. It
tried to show how involvement in education could help the individual to: (a) learn new skills; (b) communicate their existing
skills and knowledge to a particular group or class; (c) gain
knowledge about changes within their own neighbourhood and in
society. The second sessions worked from the stated interests
of the group, examining how these could be met by adult education
facilities within the Manchester area.

10.9.4. Discussion

Although described as a course relevant for 'mid-life' the sessions probably came too late to influence changes in this period. On the other hand, it did provide an early opportunity to discuss retirement, a feature which met the needs of many people in the group. Interest in the course seemed to be sustained throughout the various sessions. Indeed, our experience confirmed that there is considerable support for the idea of running courses well in advance of leaving work. However,this raises the question of the type of course structure we need to develop.

At the first Keele seminar on retirement preparation, Mannes Tidmarsh put forward the case for three phases of retirement preparation.[18] The first coming at 45-50 (concentrating on personal and family change); the second at 50-55 (concentrating on domestic and financial planning); the third during the final years of working life, examining areas of immediate and practical concern. Our pilot course suggests that this type of format would receive considerable support. It would also resolve problems connected with making courses relevant to early retirees, as well as clarifying the role of retirement councils in PRE. However, some major re-thinking must be done if an extended period of retirement preparation is to become a reality. For the remainder of this chapter, we shall consider the basis for this proposal.

10.10 The Case for Mid-life Planning

The development of early retirement has become so crucial over the past five years that a strong case can be made for planning to begin at 40. However, we would like to see two elements in this initial phase. First, there would be a mid-life planning element, focusing upon changes at work and within the family. This aspect would examine individual attitudes and changes wthin the individual's own social system. The second area would focus upon collective issues: namely, reforms which must be made in the individual's living and work environment, to guarantee a satisfactory period of retirement. This second element has a vital pre-condition at the level of government legislation and social policy. We would suggest that the potential of retirement education will only be realised if retirement itself is recognised as a basic human right; with society recognising its obligation to provide people with sufficient resources of health, income and education.

Viewed historically, society has displayed contradictory attidues towards retirement. Moreover, it has done remarkably little to modify a situation where class differences still influence both the individual's chances of reaching retirement and the quality of life he or she enjoys in this period.[19] The structural and ideological limits affecting retirement have influenced PRE in two ways: first, they have restricted its growth in both quantitative and qualitative terms; thus, set beside the demographic and economic reality of retirement, the movement has - despite the energy of its promoters - failed to secure a firm base within the industrial and educational establishment. Amongst those organ-

isations who have been supporters there has been little
enthusiasm for innovation in programme design and even fewer
advocates of a multi-staged approach. Secondly, PRE has had to
grapple with the numerous social and class inequalities which
disturb the individual's experience of retirement. Unfortunately,
the movement has failed - in our view - to acknowledge the major
constraints such inequalities place upon the effectiveness of its
work. Indeed, it has too often indulged itself with the view
that such phenomena do not matter; that the period of retirement
acts as a social leveller. The fact is that the gap in financial
experiences between the working and middle classes is sufficiently
wide to make nonsense of this statement. Layard et al in their
work for the Royal Commission on the Distribution of Income and
Wealth, found that the occupational pension for those from professional and managerial groups averaged £20; for those from unskilled manual occupations it averaged £5.[20] All the available
evidence suggest that in the years ahead such inequalities are
unlikely to diminish.

These arguments have been made to underline our case for a
retirement policy which gives people the right to leave work
with personal resources which have not been diminished by their
social and work environment. At the initial stage, therefore,
of our multi-stage course we would be concerned with questions
of a collective nature: what are the factors in the individual's
present environment, whether at work or in the community, which
are inimical to long life? We would be concerned with examining
how long people had been in jobs which, on the available evidence,
were deleterious to health. We would also be concerned with
aspects of their social and work roles which influenced behaviour
likely to cause ill-health. As David Tuckett has pointed out, we
know that smoking is much more common amongst the working than the
middle class, but whether this is due to a failure to appreciate
the risk of cigarette smoking or a generally low level of morale
and self-esteem among people forced to undertake and adjust to
dangerous, dirty and repetitive jobs, with restricted life changes,
is unknown.[21] What is reasonably clear, is that diatribes against
smoking (a common feature of PRE courses) are useless unless
related to reform within the individual's social and working environment. Around the age of 40, therefore, there is a need for
comprehensive review of 'danger points' in the individual's social
environment.

The second phase would consist of a course along the lines
described in the first section of this chapter. We would once
again, be interested in questions of mid-life change, with a major
focus on the issue of long-term financial planning.

In the final phase, the period immediately before retirement,
practical issues would become the major theme, together with the
development of ideas concerning community-based resources. It is
at this point that we can identify an important organisational
principle under-pinning our arguments. The two previous stages
we see as the concern of the employer, with the courses themselves
taking place in the individual's factory or office. However, at
this third stage, where we are proposing a major community element,
there is obviously a case for co-operation between the employer and
the Retirement Council or equivalent body. This structure would,
we believe, remove a number of problems faced by those organising

courses. Where organisers are presenting a conventional programme, the sheer weight of information to be conveyed can pose major difficulties. Retirement Councils face numerous questions about pensions and taxation which their often untrained staff find difficult to answer. On the other hand, companies have difficulty in developing a community focus, providing general talks on leisure and health, when it may be more appropriate to develop practical discussions about leisure and health facilities within particular communities.

We would suggest, therefore, a division of labour in the organisation of retirement education:

(1) The first two stages of the PRE model sketched above would be the responsibility of the Government and the employer. They would provide a financial, health and counselling element in the early pre-retirement phase.

(2) The third stage would be the responsibility of the company with the relevant community organisation (retirement councils or other voluntary bodies). This policy should remove some of the burdens being placed upon the voluntary sector. At present, it is attempting to deal with too many aspects of an increasingly complex period in the life cycle. We believe that it should concentrate on the area where it can be most effective: namely, introducing people to the network of resources available within the community. Alternatively, where deficiencies are identified, the course should introduce people to the basic skills of community action. In this way, the programme could make a major contribution to achieving continuity between the pre- and post-retirement periods.

10.11 Conclusion

In this chapter we have made a number of suggestions for improving the practice of pre-retirement education. Many of them are of a general nature and will require more detailed examination within the context of a particular company or institution. Their adoption will, we believe, require major changes in the organisation of PRE. Above all, there must be greater willingness to experiment with new approaches, in line with the changing attitudes and circumstances of retired people. A willingness to experiment was characteristic of PRE in its early phases; latterly, it has adopted a rigid stance on key issues of course structure and content. We believe this to have been disastrous in a period when change was essential if courses were to be seen as relevant. The fact that 95 per cent of workers who retire do not receive a course, is a clear sign of this failure to adapt to a changed set of circumstances. We believe that the solutions to these problems will entail: (a) more financial resources devoted to PRE; (b) a closer relationship between PRE and both adult education and the social sciences; (c) a greater understanding of the needs of retired people. Given these changes it may be possible to envisage an improvement both in the quality and quantity of courses. Without these improvements, the outlook for retirement education will remain bleak.

We are sensitive to the argument that many of our suggestions will be difficult to implement, given the shortage of
resources which organisers experience at a local level. However,
we believe this aspect to be less important than the attitudes
which people often bring to the organisation of courses. At
present, many of those concerned with PRE are overly modest in
their packaging and presentation of programmes, accepting that
a three or four day model, a few months prior to retirement,
is the best that can be achieved. Perhaps it is time that we
became more assertive and insistent on demanding better quality
and standards in PRE. People now entering retirement, as well as
future cohorts will resent being 'lectured at' and will press
for greater longer-term planning. If the movement is still
heavily comprised in its pursuit of short courses then we shall
continue to discourage many of the 95 per cent who do not receive
a programme. The consumer must be made to feel that he or she
is missing something of real benefit if PRE is unavailable. At
present, there is very little evidence that such feelings are
being articulated on a large scale; indeed, many people are quite
unaware that such a facility may exist in their community.[22]
Retirement education has been in existence for over 20 years, yet
it has made only a modest impact on people's attitudes and expectations about their life after full-time work. New directions for
pre-retirement education are undoubtedly needed, we hope that this
report will provide some arguments towards the present debate.

CHAPTER 9

Footnotes and References

1. Coleman, A., edited by Groombridge, J., Preparation for
   Retirement in England and Wales: a National Survey., NIAE
   in association with the Pre-Retirement Association, 1982.

2. See, for example, Atchley, R.C., The Sociology of Retirement, Schenkman, 1976.

3. An Introduction to how groups function is found in Douglas,
   T., Basic Groupwork, Tavistock, 1978; see also Stephens,
   M. D. and Roderick, G.W. Teaching Techniques in Adult Educ-
   ation, David and Charles, 1971.

4. For a discussion on this area see, Glendenning, F. 'Another
   Turn of the Screw', in Cheetham, J. et al. Social and Comm-
   unity Work in a Multi-Racial Society, Harper and Row with the
   Open University Press, 1981. pp. 225-231.

5. See, for example, Bolger, A.W., 'Counselling in Retirement'.
   Journal of the British Association for Counselling, No. 37.
   July, 1981, pp.5-9; Manion, U.V., 'Pre-Retirement Counselling,
   The Need for a new approach', Personal and Guidance Journal,
   November 1976, pp. 119-121.

6. Manion, ibid., pp. 120-121.

7. O'Rourke, J.F., and Friedman, H.L., An Inter-union Pre-
   Retirement Training Programme: Commentary and Results.
   Industrial Gerontology, Vol. 13, Spring, 1972, p.61.

8. See Tidmarsh, M., 'New Approaches to Pre-Retirement Preparation' in Preparation for Retirment, Glendenning, F. (ed),
   A Beth Johnson Foundation Publication, in association with
   the Department of Adult Education, University of Keele and
   the Pre-Retirement Association; Hunter, W., 'Pre-Retirement
   Education and Planning', in Grabowski, S.M., and Mason, W.
   D., (Eds). Learning for Ageing, Adult Education Association
   of the U.S.A. and Eric Clearinghouse on Adult Education,
   1974.

9. Hunter, W., ibid., p. 187.

10. See, for example, Self-Help and the Over-Sixties, Beth
    Johnson Foundation, in association with the Department of
    Adult Education, University of Keele, 1978.

11. Lumsden, D.B., 'Educational Implications of Research on
    Retirement', Educational Gerontologist, Vol. 3 , No.4. 1978,
    p.380.

12. Walker, A., 'The Social Creation of Poverty and Dependency
    in Old Age'. Journal of Social Policy, Vol.9., No.1.1980,
    pp, 49-75.

13.   Parker, S., <u>Older Workers and Retirement</u>, OPCS, Social
      Survey Division, HMSO., 1980.

14.   Tiberi, D.M., et al., 'A Comparative Analysis of Four
      Pre-Retirement Models' <u>Educational Gerontology</u>, Vol. 3.,
      No. 4., 1978, p.374.

15.   Cited in Parker S., <u>Work and Retirement</u>, Allen and Unwin,
      1982, pp.76-77.

16.   For a discussion on this type of approach, see Bolton, C.,
      'Humanistic Instructional Strategies and Retirement Educ-
      ation Programming', <u>The Gerontologist</u> Vol. 16., No. 6. 1976.,
      pp.550-555.

17.   For a discussion on mid-life changes see Nicholson, J.,
      <u>Seven Ages</u>, Fontana Paperbacks, 1980.

18.   Tidmarsh, M., <u>op.cit</u>.

19.   Townsend, P., and Davidson, N., <u>Inequalities in Health</u>:
      <u>The Black Report</u>, Pelican Books, 1982.

20.   Layard, R., et al. The Causes of Poverty: Background
      Paper No. 5. <u>Royal Commission on the Distribution of Income</u>
      <u>and Wealth</u>, 1978; for an extensive review of economic inequal-
      ities in old age, see Walker, A., <u>ibid</u>.

21.   Tuckett, D., 'Choices for Health Education. A Sociological
      View' in Sutherland, D., <u>Health Education: Perspectives and</u>
      <u>Choices,</u> Allen and Unwin, 1979.

22.   Parker, S. <u>op.cit</u>.

A P P E N D I X   I

STATISTICAL GLOSSARY

STATISTICAL GLOSSARY

CHI-SQUARED (χ^2) TEST

The chi-squared test is used to establish whether there are significant differences between two or more <u>independent</u> samples. For example, we might be interested in seeing if men and women differed in their satisfaction with the timing of a particular programme. To examine this question, we would count the number of responses from each sex which fell into the categories of "too early", "too late" and "right time". Male and female responses would be compared for each of these categories. The χ^2 test allows us to test the observed distribution against the expected frequency (a hypothetical distribution where the sexes are equally divided in their pattern of response). Thus, the chi-squared test indicates whether the gap between the expected and actual scores could have occurred by chance or whether it indicates real (i.e. significant) differences in satisfaction between men and women.

Further Reading:

Rowntree, D. Statistics without Tears: A primer for non-mathematicians, Pelican Books, 1981.

CHI-SQUARED TEST FOR LINEAR TREND IN PROPORTIONS

The conventional chi-squared test detects any departures from the null hypothesis (that there are no significant differences between sample groups). However, if we are interested in a particular departure from the null hypothesis, additional tests are at our disposal. These can be achieved by sub-dividing the total chi-squared statistic into portions which follow chi-squared distributions on reduced numbers of degrees of freedom. One interesting example occurs where a number of groups give responses to a particular question which appear to follow a certain order or sequence. This might occur, for example, when we ask people to indicate whether they have any health problems. We might want to use this trend to see if it influenced responses to some of our other questions. Table Al provides an example of what we mean:

TABLE Al   No. reporting health problems and not planning to work.

% Reporting health problems	JAGUAR	NCB	MARS	BA	BRISTOL	SHELL	GLASGOW
% Reporting health problems	64%	58%	57%	43%	35%	26%	17%
Plans to look for work	3	3	11	21	15	13	13
Does not plan to look for work	11	21	19	19	14	14	15
Total	14	24	30	40	29	27	28
Proportion Positive	21%	13%	37%	53%	52%	48%	46%

Conventional χ^2 = 14.9   d.f. = 6   5% significant
χ^2 Linear Trend = 7.9   d.f. = 1   1% significant

    With a conventional chi-squared, the groups show significant
differences on whether they are planning to look for work.
However, we have proceeded to re-order the groups on this question,
using the proportion in each who report health problems. The
resulting chi-squared for linear trend statistic suggests that
there could be approximately equal increases in the proportion
of individuals planning to go back to work as we move through the
range from a high proportion to a low proportion of health
problems.

Further Reading:

Armitage, P. Statistical Methods In Medical Research,Blackwell,
            1971.

CRONBACH'S ALPHA COEFFICIENT OF RELIABILITY

    When dealing with any attitude scale we must concern our-
selves with its reliability: assuming no change in the attitude
under study, to what extent will repeated measurements made under
constant conditions produce the same results? Reliability is an
indication of the extent to which a measure contains variable
errors, that is, errors that differed from individual to individual during testing, and that varied from time to time for a given
individual measured twice by the same measurement. In practice,
it is possible to calculate a reliability coefficient, ranging
from zero to one, to gain some indication of reliability.

    Specific attitudes towards work and retirement were measured
in our study, with several multiple-item (Likert-type) scales
being used. These had already been used in a number of studies
on retirement and pre-retirement. In order to gauge their reliability we used Cronbach's Alpha Coefficient. This was calculated using eighty individuals from the National Coal Board, Bristol
and Shell groups. Three scales were used: 'orientation to work',
'attitudes to work' and 'resistance to retirement'. The Alpha
Coefficient for all three was 0.7.

Further Reading:

    For another study using two of the above scales, see Glamser,
F.D. The Efficacy of Pre-Retirement Preparation Programmes, Ph.D.
Thesis, Pennsylvania State University, 1973.

DEGREES OF FREEDOM:

    This is a measure of the opportunities available for data to
vary. For example, suppose we have five numbers 5, 8, 9, 12, 16:
the mean is 10. If the mean is kept constant, only four of the
numbers are "free to vary" because the sum of the five numbers
must remain at 50 and once four of the numbers are known, the fifth
can only have one value. With N numbers only N-1 are free to vary
within the restriction that the mean remains constant.

    The reason for this concern with freedom to vary is that the
laws of chance are only valid when observations are independent.
In the case of N numbers, only N-1 of them are independent for the
same total sum.

McNEMAR'S TEST

This test is particularly applicable to "before and after" designs in which each person is used as his or her own control. In our research, for example, we analyse the attitudes towards retirement of a group of subjects. Following this, each person receives a pre-retirement course. We then analyse the response to the course (have attitudes changed? If so, has this been in a positive or negative direction?). In effect, we are testing the null hypothesis that for those individuals who change attitudes, the probability of changing from a negative to a positive attitude is equal to the probability of changing from a positive to a negative view. McNemar's test analyses the extent of change between the pre- and post-course interviews, allowing us to confirm or reject the null hypothesis.

Further Reading:

Sprent, P., Quick Statistics, Pelican Books, 1981.
Siegal, S., Nonparametric Statistics for the Behavioural Sciences, McGraw-Hill, 1956.

STATISTICAL SIGNIFICANCE

In any statistical analysis there is a range of possible values of the test statistic which is so improbable that we can reject the null hypothesis as a plausible explanation of results and accept the alternative hypothesis, e.g. that there are 'significant' differences in pre- and post-test attitudes. But how do we define "improbable"? What risk are we willing to take in rejecting the null hypothesis when it is really true?

We can declare at the outset what level of risk we are willing to take by setting the level of significance. If the probability of occurrence of the test statistic assuming the null hypothesis is equal to or less than our pre-set level of significance, we reject the null hypothesis and declare the result to the significant. Otherwise the result is non-significant. If we set the level of significance too small, we shall reduce the risk of rejecting the null hypothesis when it is true (i.e. declaring a significant result when we should not) but we also increase the risk of not rejecting it when it is false (i.e. not declaring a significant result when we should). A balance can be struck between these two types of risk and it is customary to use the 5% and 1% level of significance.

Further Reading:

Rowntree, D.   Statistics without Tears: A primer for non-mathematicians, Pelican Books, 1981.

t-TEST

The t-test is typically used when data is normally distributed. If this is not the case, then the non-parametric equivalent (the Wilcoxon Matched pairs signed ranks test) may be used. Secondly, parametric tests such as the t-test generally requires data to be measured on an interval scale (having equal intervals between its units and having the property of being continuous).

The t-test was used in a design where the same groups acted as their own controls in pre- and post-course interviews. Attitudes about work and retirement were represented by single scores, the t-test examined group means (or averages) and indicated whether pre- and post-course responses were significantly different.

Further Reading:

Rowntree, D. "Statistics without Tears". Pelican 1981.

WILCOXON MATCHED PAIRS SIGNED RANKS TEST.

The Wilcoxon test has been used to analyse changes in work attitudes or knowledge about retirement issues in pre- and post-course interviews. The Wilcoxon test compares pre- and post-course responses, taking both direction and magnitute of change into account by giving more weight to a pair of responses showing a large difference than to a pair showing a small difference, and indicates whether there are significant differences between the two attitude or knowledge scores.

The Wilcoxon test requires data on an ordinal scale (where units can be referred to as "greater than" or "less than" each other) and more importantly, does not require data to be normally distributed. As fewer restrictions are imposed upon the use of the Wilcoxon test, it was used in all analyses of attitude and knowledge scale scores.

Further Reading:

Siegal, S. "Nonparametric Statistics for the Behavioural Sciences", McGraw-Hill, 1956.

A P P E N D I X   2

SAMPLING

SAMPLING

There were three important variations in the way our samples were formed.   In the case of Shell International, Mars and Jaguar, we simply took those people eligible for a given number of courses (eligibility was usually defined by the company as people retiring within a certain period).   In these instances, therefore, our sample population consisted of those who could have attended a pre-retirement course.   Individuals were contacted by letter asking if they would be willing to take part in the survey.   The Retirement Councils posed greater problems for drawing a sample. The courses we studied drew participants both from a wide geographical area and from a large number of organisations. Postal questionnaires were used for people we were unable to contact, these providing useful data as to the representativeness of our sample.

In the case of British Airways, National Coal Board and EMI, a more experimental approach was adopted.   British Airways was a case of unsuccessful randomisation, and we have discussed the difficulties we encountered in some detail.   NCB provided a successful quasi-experimental situation;   EMI a successful experimental approach.

NATIONAL COAL BOARD - EXPERIMENTAL GROUP

The background to the sample population is discussed in Chapter 4 of the report.

27 individuals attending one course

1 unable to be interviewed because of illness.
1 going at statutory retirement age.

25 Phase 1 Interviews

1 unable to attend course.

24 Phase 2 Interviews

1 still in full-time employment.

23 Phase 3 Interviews

CONTROL GROUP

The control group of miners were drawn from pits in the North Nottinghamshire region of the NCB.   The emphasis, as in South Notts., was on those taking voluntary early retirement. Letters were sent to all those retiring between April and September 1980, asking if they would be prepared to participate in a survey of PRE.   Included with the letter was a stamped addressed card asking people to state whether or not they were interested in helping with the study or whether they would be remaining in work with the NCB.

<u>55 individuals eligible for survey</u>

15 refused to participate in the research
11 failed to respond to original letter
 3 unable to be interviewed because of illness
 1 unable to be interviewed because of language
   difficulties.

<u>25 Pre-Retirement Interviews</u>

1 refused a second interview.

<u>24 Post-retirement Interviews</u>

<u>MARS</u>

The sample population consists of 57 individuals eligible
for three courses held during 1980. Two problems which arose
during our work were (a) language difficulties with some of
the respondents; (b) pressures towards early retirement. These
difficulties served to reduce the numbers either willing or able
to participate in the research.

<u>57 eligible for Pre-Retirement Education</u>

10 declined to attend course
 7 refused to participate in research
 2 unable to attend interview because of illness
 1 unable to attend interview because of work
   conditions.

<u>37 Phase 1 Interviews</u>

 2 refused a second interview
 4 had language difficulties
 1 was an administrator for the pre-retirement course.

<u>30 Phase 2 Interviews</u>

<u>BRISTOL RETIREMENT COUNCIL</u>

The sample population consists of 48 individuals who
attended two courses held in April and June 1980.

<u>48 individuals attending two courses</u>

11 applications too late to be included in survey
 7 refused to participate.

<u>30 Phase 1 Interviews</u>

(Postal questionnaires sent to late applicants, 9 of
 these were returned).
1 not interviewed due to death of spouse.

<u>29 Phase 2 Interviews</u>

1 deceased
1 refused a third interview.

27 Phase 3 Interviews

JAGUAR

The sample population consists of 34 individual eligible for a course beginning in October 1980.

34 individuals eligible for Pre-Retirement Education

5 long-term sick
3 refused to participate
4 declined to attend course
2 permanent night-shift.

20 Phase 1 Interviews

4 voluntary redundancy and did not attend course
1 did not attend all eight sessions of course
1 unable to attend interview because of illness

14 Phase 2 Interviews

BRITISH AIRWAYS

Several factors prevented successful randomisation. First, employees were not concentrated into convenient work units but were spread over a very large airport where communication was often difficult. Secondly, the possibility of redundancies was beginning to loom as we entered the field-work stage, this may have affected views on whether to participate in the research. Depsite this environment (and because of the level of co-operation from the organisation) we did think a randomised trial of PRE might be feasible. A sample of 100 subjects was proposed, participants being divided equally into four groups: two of these would consist of individuals who had expressed willingness to enter a randomised trial of PRE; the remaining two would consist of individuals who either (a) expressed a definite wish to attend courses; (b) expressed a definite wish not to attend courses.

Our failure to achieve randomisation ultimately reflects the well-established nature of PRE inside the organisation. As a result, it was difficult to provide a justification for individuals to enter a randomised trial (where there was a possibility that they would not receive a course until after leaving work). In this situation most of those who were seen (each individual had an initial interview where the purpose of the research was explained) expressed a definite wish to attend a programme. This point is illustrated when we analyse how we eventually arrived at our sample.

Males

Initially, it was planned to restrict the sample to male British Airways groundstaff (all grades) who were eligible to retire between August 1980 and March 1981. The 277 eligible men were sorted into the following categories:

	Compulsory retirement	Normal retirement
Excluded	41	15

(reasons for exclusion: retiring later than March 1981; geographical location; ill at time of initial interview; already attended a course; untraceable).

	Compulsory retirement	Normal retirement
Interviewed and participated on project	53	19
Non-appearance at interview or failed to reply to invitation to initial interview	31	53
Refused and not interviewed	14	51
	139	138

The number of refusals and non-replies amongst the normal retirees is inflated by the fact that in some cases individuals were three years away from retirement and may have felt that a pre-retirement course was premature.

The group of 72 willing to participate in the research broke down into the following categories:

Definitely attending course	48
Randomised – experimental	11
Randomised – control	10
Definitely not attending course	3

Females

In an attempt to complete the original plan of 25 subjects in each of the four groups, female groundstaff were contacted. On sending the initial contact individuals outside London were excluded, this reduced the eligible group from 94 to 84 (71 compulsory retirees and 13 normal retirees).

	Compulsory retirement	Normal retirement
Definitely attending PRE Course	21	1
Randomised-Experimental	1	–
Retiring later than March 1981	–	7
Untraceable	4	1
On leave	2	–
Ill	1	–
Replies – but too late to be interviewed	3	–
	32	9

(No reminder letters were sent it was apparent that the
planned 25 subjects in each group was unlikely to be achieved).

Groups:		Males	Females	Total
(1)	'Definitely attending PRE course'	48	22	70
(2)	'Randomised – Experimental'	11	1	12
(3)	'Randomised – Control'	10	–	10
(4)	'Definitely not attending PRE course'	3	–	3
		72	23	95

Groups (1) and (2) were reduced in size by selecting every
alternate individual and assigning them to one of the two
retirement courses run in May. This gave a total of 40 individuals who were interviewed and attended a pre-retirement course.
We were unable to contact four individuals at Phase 3.

EMI EXPERIMENTAL AND CONTROL

The sample population consists of 86 individuals who were
due to retire between June 1981 and June 1982.

86 Individuals eligible for Survey

21 refused to participate in the research (at least half
   were classified as 'long term sick').
 1 caring for sick relative.

Allocation to the experimental and control groups was made
by toss of a coin. After individuals were told which group they
were in, the following changes occurred:

Two individuals were unhappy about being allocated to the
control group and were put in the experimental. Four individuals
switched from experimental to control because they were unable to
attend the course. Ideally, given larger numbers, these individuals would have been excluded from the research. However, the
relatively small size of our samples meant that they had to be
retained. Because of the shorter time period between Phase 1 and
Phase 3 interviews (compared with our other groups) Phase 2 information was collected through a postal questionnaire. Finally, one
individual could not be interviewed at Phase 1 due to illness of
spouse.

29 Experimental Phase 1 Interviews   34 Control Phase 1 Interviews

 4 failed to return postal question-   2 refused a post-retirement
                            naire   interview

24 Experimental Phase 2 Interviews

 4 interviews with the group
   not returning postal interviews
   at Phase 2
 4 refused third interview.

24 Experimental Phase 3 Interviews   32 Control Post-Retirement
                                                        interviews

SCOTTISH RETIREMENT COUNCIL

Chapter 5 outlines the background to our sample
population.

78 individuals attending three courses

18 working outside Glasgow
10 refused to participate in the research
 5 permanent night-shift
 9 unable to contact
 2 did not attend full programme
 1 late applicant
 1 unable to attend interview because of illness
 1 had language difficulties.

31 Phase 1 Interviews

(Postal questionnaires sent to remaining 47, 35 of these
were returned)
 2 refused second interview.

29 Phase 2 Interviews

 3 refused a third interview
 1 unable to contact
 2 deceased.

23 Phase 3 Interviews

(21 completed questionnaires from postal group).

SHELL INTERNATIONAL

The sample population consists of 39 individuals eligible
for three courses held during 1980.

39 individuals eligible for Pre-Retirement Education

 7 refused to participate in research
 1 uncertain about whether they were retiring
 1 leaving on voluntary redundancy
 1 unable to attend interview because of illness

29 Phase 1 Interviews

 1 refused a second interview
 1 unable to attend interview because of illness.

27 Phase 2 Interviews

 6 unable to be seen for third interview because still in
   full-time employment at Shell
 1 deceased.

20 Phase 3 Interviews

A P P E N D I X 3

Questionnaire Development

QUESTIONNAIRE DEVELOPMENT

In developing the questionnaire we drew upon the main American retirement and Pre-Retirement Studies. The attitudinal scales in our research were drawn from these sources.

Drafts of the questionnaire were tested in both pre-pilot and pilot surveys. The former helped to clarify the type of questions we would need to ask in our survey; the latter was used to refine the structure of the questionnaire, e.g. to check on word-order, lay-out and overall length. The pre-pilot investigation was carried out with nine employees at a manufacturing company in Stoke-on-Trent. Thirty-six interviews were then completed, using a draft Phase 1 questionnaire. Several important issues arose from this pilot investigation: first, there appeared to be problems in the method of assessing respondents' views on retirement preparation. For example, we asked people: "Do you think that planning and preparation will reduce any problems you may come up against in retirement?" This was closely followed by: "Do you think it necessary for people to plan their retirement?" The first question might provoke biased answers; the second is probably repetitious. These difficulties were resolved by simply asking: "Some people feel that you can plan and prepare for retirement, do you feel this way, or not?" Depending on the response, a range of supplementary questions were asked, clarifying specific aspects of preparation.

A number of questions were found to be unreliable or misleading and were taken out of the questionnaire. Other items were taken out and put into a self-completion booklet, this helped to reduce the overall length of the interview.

A draft Phase 2 questionnaire was tested with 21 pilot interviews. The Phase 3 questionnaire was tested with 25 interviews. Both men and women and manual and non-manual workers were interviewed.

A small number of the interviews were conducted by the Keele team, the rest were done by interviewers from Social and Community Planning Research. SCPR also advised on the wording of many of the questions as well as designing the final lay-out of the final draft of the questionnaire.

An example of the Phase 3 questionnaire is provided for the reader.

1.   The following were particularly helpful:

Hunter, W. A Longitudinal Study of Pre-Retirement Education, Division of Gerontology, University of Michigan, 1968; Streib, G.F. and Schneider, S.J. Retirement in American Society: Impact and Process, Cornell University Press, 1971; Glamser, F. The Efficacy of Pre-Retirement Preparation Programmes for Industrial Workers, Pennsylvania State University, Ph.D. Dissertation, 1973.

Further reading: Hoinville, G., et al. Survey Research Practice, Heinemann Educational Books, 1978.

SOCIAL & COMMUNITY PLANNING RESEARCH

Main Office: 35 Northampton Square London EC1V 0AX Tel: 01-250 1866

STUDY OF PRE-RETIREMENT EDUCATION

QUESTIONNAIRE (3)

P.616

		Col./ Code	Skip to
	Record number	(101-103)	
	Card 1 589	(104-107)	
Sample issue number		(108)	
	Org. Serial number Phase		
	(109) (110-112) (113) 3		
Time interview started			

1a) I'd like to start by going back to the time just before you retired.

Could I ask first, on what date did you retire?

ENTER DATE

Day	Month	Year

(114-119)

b) So for how long have you been retired?

ENTER NUMBER OF MONTHS ☐☐ (120-121)

2a) In the 2 years before you retired, did you have any change in the kind of work you did?

		(122)	
Yes, job changed	1		
No	2	} Q3
Can't remember	3		

IF JOB CHANGED AT a)

b) How did the work you were doing change?
PROBE FOR CHANGES IN NATURE OF WORK OR LEVEL OF RESPONSIBILITY

(123)

c) What job were you doing immediately before you retired?

i) Job title _____

ii) What did the work involve? _____

		Col./ Code	Skip to

3a) When you retired, was there any special event or occasion, like a leaving party or a presentation from your employer?

		(124)	
Yes	1		
No	2		Q4

IF YES AT a)

b) Was this organised (mainly) by the firm, your workmates or by yourself?

	CODE ALL THAT APPLY		
	Firm	(125) 1	
	Workmates	(126) 1	
	Self	(127) 1	
	Other - SPECIFY	(128-130)	

4a) Have you been back to _____ (NAME ORGANISATION) for any reason since you left?

		(131)	
Yes	1		
No	2		Q5

IF YES AT a)

b) Why did you go back?

5a) Is there a club or association for retired members at _____ (NAME ORGANISATION)?

		(132)	
Yes	1		
No	2	} Q6
Don't know	3		

IF YES AT a)

b) Have you taken part in any of it's activities?

		(133)	
Yes	1		
No	2		

		Col./Code	Skip to
6a)	Did you retire because of a fixed retirement age, or did you retire for some other reason ?	(134)	
	Fixed retirement age	1	
	Mentions early retirement	2	
	Retired for other reasons	3	Q7
	IF EARLY OR FIXED RETIREMENT AGE		
b)	Do you now feel you would like to have stayed on working longer at (NAME ORGANISATION), or not ?	(135)	
	Yes	1	
	No	2	Q7
	IF YES AT b)		
c)	Why do you now wish you could have stayed on longer there ?		
7	It takes some people a little while to get used to not working full-time. About how long would you say it took you to become used to not working ? Would you say it was ..... READ OUT	(136)	
	.... No time at all	1	
	A few weeks	2	
	or a few months	3	
	(Still not adjusted to retirement)	4	
	(Never stopped/continued in full-time employment)	5	
	Other specify	6	

		Col./Code	Skip to
8	Are you doing any kind of paid work at present ?	(137)	
	Yes	1	
	No	2	Q10
	IF YES AT a)		
b)	What work are you doing ?		
	i) Job title	(138)	
	ii) What does the work involve ?		
	iii) What is the nature of the industry or business in which your firm is engaged ?	(139)	
c)	Is the job full-time, part-time, or is it casual work ?	(140)	
	Full-time (30 weeks or over)	1	
	Part-time (under 30 weeks)	2	
	Casual work	3	
d)	What is the most important reason for your wanting to work in retirement ?		

		Col./Code	Skip to
9a) If you didn't work do you think you would worry about not having a job to do, or not?		**(141)**	
PROBE WHETHER DEFINITELY OR PROBABLY	No, definitely	1	
	No, probably not	2	
	Don't know/Can't say	3	
	Yes, probably	4	
	Yes, definitely	5	
b) Do you think you would miss being with other people at work?		**(142)**	
PROBE WHETHER DEFINITELY OR PROBABLY	No, definitely	1	
	No, probably not	2	
	Don't know/Can't say	3	
	Yes, probably	4	
	Yes, definitely	5	
c) Do you think you would miss any feelings of usefulness of achievement which work can provide?		**(143)**	
PROBE WHETHER DEFINITELY OR PROBABLY	No, definitely	1	
	No, probably not	2	Q13
	Don't know/Can't say	3	
	Yes, probably	4	
	Yes, definitely	5	
10 IF NOT IN PAID EMPLOYMENT (CODE 2 AT Q8) Do you do any kind of unpaid work at all such as voluntary or community work?		**(144)**	
	Yes	1	
	No	2	Q11
IF YES AT a) **b)** What sort of unpaid work do you do?			
c) Are any of these things that you have taken up since you retired?		**(145)**	
	Yes	1	
	No	2	
	Other SPECIFY	3	

		Col./Code	Skip to
11a) Since you retired, have you looked for any kind of paid work at all?		**(146)**	
	Yes	1	
	No	2	c)
IF YES AT a) **b)** Are you actively looking for a job at the present time?		**(147)**	
	Yes	1	
	No	2	d)
IF NO AT a) **c)** Are you planning to look for a paid job in the next 6 months?		**(148)**	
	Yes	1	
	No	2	f)
IF YES AT b) or c) **d)** What type of work are you looking for?/ will you look for? PROBE FOR DETAILS OF JOB ACTIVITY/INDUSTRY		**(149)**	
e) What is the most important reason for you wanting to work now that you've retired?		**(150)**	
		NOW SKIP TO Q12	
IF NO AT b) or c) **f)** Would you like to get a paid job again or not?		**(151)**	
	Yes	1	
	No	2	
	Don't know	3	

		Col./Code	Skip to
12a)	Do you worry about not having a job to do?	(152)	
	Yes, all the time	1	
	Yes, occasionally	2	
	No	3	
	Don't know/can't say	4	
b)	Do you miss being with other people at work?	(153)	
	Yes, all the time	1	
	Yes, occasionally	2	
	No	3	
	Don't know/can't say	4	
c)	Do you miss any feelings of usefulness or achievement which work may have provided?	(154)	
	Yes, all the time	1	
	Yes, occasionally	2	
	No	3	
	Don't know/can't say	4	
	TO ALL		
13a)	Thinking now about when you first retired, how did you spend the first few days of your retirement?		
	Don't remember	0	
b)	On the whole would you say you felt happy, unhappy or had mixed feelings during these first few days?	(155)	
	Happy	1	
	Unhappy	2	
	Mixed feelings	3	

		Col./Code	Skip to
14	Have you taken up any new hobbies or interests since you retired?	(156)	
	Yes	1	
	No	2	Q15
	IF YES AT a)		
b)	What hobbies or interests have you taken up?		
15	Have you attended any evening or day classes at all since you retired?	(157)	
	Yes	1	
	No	2	Q16
	IF NO AT a)		
b)	Have you thought about attending any evening or day classes?	(158)	
	Yes	1	
	No	2	
16	Before you retired, had you thought about any interests, hobbies or any other things which you would like to do in retirement?	(159)	
	Yes	1	
	No	2	Q17
	IF YES AT a)		
b)	Are there any things which you thought you would like to do but haven't yet done?	(160)	
	Yes	1	
	No	2	Q17
	IF YES AT b)		
c)	What sorts of things are these?		

		Col./ Code	Skip to

17a) Have you found times since your retirement when it has been difficult to keep occupied ?

Yes   1 (161)
No   2
Can't say   3 } Q18

IF YES AT a)

b) Has this been .... READ OUT ....

... Often   1 (162)
occasionally   2
or hardly ever   3

18 When you think about your retirement, do you think of it as ... READ OUT INDIVIDUALLY ....

	Yes	No	Can't say	
An extended holiday	1	2	3	(163)
A new phase of your life	1	2	3	(164)
The beginning of old age	1	2	3	(165)
A life rather similar to when you were working	1	2	3	(166)
A rejection by society	1	2	3	(167)

19 Taking everything into account, how well prepared do you think you were for retirement ? Would you say you were .... READ OUT ....

Very well prepared   1 (168)
Fairly well prepared   2
Not very well prepared   3
or not prepared at all?   4
(Can't say)   5

20a) Some people feel you can plan and prepare for retirement. Do you feel this way, or not ?

Yes   1 (169) Q21
No   2
(Can't say)   3

IF NO AT a)

b) Why do you say that ?

NOW SKIP TO Q22

		Col./ Code	Skip to

IF THINKS CAN PLAN FOR RETIREMENT (CODE 1 AT Q20)

21a) For what sorts of things do you think planning and preparation can be particularly beneficial ?

b) How long before retirement do you think people should start their planning and preparation ?

c) Can you think of any particular things you did to plan for retirement which you have found beneficial ?

Yes   1 (170)
No   2

IF YES AT c)

d) What sorts of plans have you found beneficial ?

Yes   1 (171)
No   2 Q22

22 TO ALL Now that you are retired, do any of the following matters worry you ? READ OUT INDIVIDUALLY

	Yes	No	Can't say	
Your income in retirement	1	2	3	(172)
Income tax	1	2	3	(173)
Your health	1	2	3	(174)
Your housing	1	2	3	(175)
Your relationship with family or friends	1	2	3	(176)
The effect of retirement on you personally	1	2	3	(177)

Blank (178-180)
Duplicate (201-207)
Card 2 (208)

		Col./Code	Skip to

23a) What are the aspects of retirement that you have found particularly pleasurable?

None — 0

b) What aspects of retirement have you disliked?

None — 0

24 Taking everything into account, how would you say retirement has worked out for you? Would you say it was .... READ OUT ....

(209)
Better than you expected — 1
worse than you expected — 2
or about the same as you expected — 3
Not sure/Can't say — 4

25 IF ATTENDED PRE-RETIREMENT COURSE (1st Digit of Serial Number = 1)
OTHERS SKIP TO Q29

I'd like now to talk about the pre-retirement course you attended.

In relation to when you retired, do you think the course came .... READ OUT .....

(210)
too early — 1
too late — 2
or was it at about the right time — 3
(can't say) — 4

		Col./Code	Skip to

26a) Did your retirement course cover anything on .... NAME SUBJECT ENTER IN COL. a)

FOR EACH COVERED ASK

b) Thinking about the advice you received on ....(NAME SUBJECT) during your course, can you think of anything specific you have done as a result of this advice? ENTER IN COL. b)

IF YES AT b)

c) What have you done as a result of the advice? ENTER IN COL. c)

Subject	a) Covered Yes No	b) Done anything as a result of advice Yes No	c) What done
Finance /money matters	(211) 1 2	(212) 1 2	
Health/ Diet in Retire-ment.	(213) 1 2	(214) 1 2	
Leisure	(215) 1 2	(216) 1 2	
Employ-ment/ voluntary work	(217) 1 2	(218) 1 2	

		Col./Code	Skip to
27a)	Apart from these four areas, did you cover any other areas or subjects?	(219)	
	Yes	1	
	No	2	
b)	IF YES AT a)		
	Can you think of anything specific you have done as a result of the advice you received for these other areas?		
	Probe for subject and action.		
	Can't remember	3	} Q28
28	From your initial experience of retirement, can you suggest any ways in which the pre-retirement course could be improved?	(220)	
	None	0	
29	TO ALL		
	I'd like to move on to talk about your health.		
	Do you have any particular physical or health problems at present?	(221)	
	Yes	1	
	No	2	Q30
b)	IF YES AT a)		
	Do these health problems keep you from doing ... READ OUT		
	A lot of things you wish you could do	1	
	Just certain things	2	
	Or can you do almost anything you wish	3	
	(Can't say)	4	
30	On the whole, would you say your health was ... READ OUT	(222)	
	Good	1	
	Fair	2	
	or Poor	3	
	(Can't say)	4	

		Col./Code	Skip to
31	Do you ever worry about your health?	(223)	
	Yes	1	
	No	2	Q32
b)	IF YES AT a)		
	How frequently do you worry? Is it ..... READ OUT	(224)	
	Often	1	
	Occasionally	2	
	or Hardly ever	3	

32	During the last 2 weeks, have you taken any medicines or tablets for any of the following? I mean both medication prescribed by your doctor or anything which you have bought for yourself. Have you taken anything ... READ OUT INDIVIDUALLY.....	Yes	No	
	To help you sleep at night	1	2	(225)
	As a tonic to buck you up	1	2	(226)
	Anything for your nerves (including tranquillisers)	1	2	(227)
	Anything to get relief from pain	1	2	(228)
	Any tablets or medicines for anything else (SPECIFY CONDITIONS FOR WHICH TAKEN)	1	2	(229)

		Col./Code	Skip to
33a)	Did you have a routine health check with for example, your company doctor or a doctor from your own practice in the period before you retired?	(230)	
	Yes	1	
	No	2	
b)	Have you had a routine health check with a doctor since you retired?	(231)	
	Yes	1	
	No	2	
34	How long ago did you last consult your doctor for yourself either at home or at the surgery?	(232)	
	INCLUDE ANY DOCTOR AT RESPONDENTS PRACTICE		
	Less than 2 weeks ago	1	
	2 weeks but less than 1 month	2	
	1 month but less than 3 months	3	
	3 months but less than 6 months	4	
	6 months but less than 1 year	5	
	1 year ago or more	6	

15

35 I am going to read out some problems which some people have with their health. Could you tell me whether, during the last 6 months, you have had frequent difficulty with any of the following .... READ OUT INDIVIDUALLY ....

	Yes	No	Can't say	Col./Code
Problems with sleeping	1	2	3	(233)
Loss of appetite	1	2	3	(234)
Always feeling tired	1	2	3	(235)
Indigestion	1	2	3	(236)
Shortness of breath	1	2	3	(237)
Spells of depression	1	2	3	(238)
Arthritis/Rheumatism	1	2	3	(239)

36 During your last 12 months at work, did you have any time off work because of ill health, apart from minor things like colds or coughs?

	Col./Code	Skip to
Yes	1	
No	2	Q37

(240)

IF YES AT a)

b) What were you off work for? RECORD NATURE OF ILLNESS/HEALTH PROBLEMS

37 Do you think leaving work has ... READ OUT ...

	Col./Code
Improved your health	1
Made your health worse	2
or Not make any difference to your health	3

(241)

38 HAND RESPONDENT LADDER SHEET

I'd like you now to think about your life in general. Consider the top of the ladders as the best possible life for you and the bottom the worst possible life for you. I'd like you to mark with an X the position where you think you were 5 years ago, where you are now and where you will be in 5 years from now.

(242)	(243)	(244)
9	9	9
8	8	8
7	7	7
6	6	6
5	5	5
4	4	4
3	3	3
2	2	2
1	1	1
5 YEARS AGO	NOW	5 YEARS FROM NOW

RECORD RESPONDENTS ANSWERS ABOVE

16

TO ALL

39a) I'd like to ask you a little about your financial position.

How would you describe your present financial position? Would you say you ... READ OUT ...

	Col./Code
Find it difficult to make ends meet	1
Have enough to get by on	2
Are well off	3
or Are very well off	4

(245)

b) Could you tell me into which of these groups your net income falls including your pension or any benefits but excluding tax and other deductions? GIVE SHOW CARD A

ENTER LETTER [ ]

Not given 0 (246)

40 I'd like to ask you now about your family?

a) First are you .... READ OUT ....

	Col./Code	Skip to
single	1	
married	2	
divorced	3	Q41
widowed	4	
or separated	5	

(247)

IF DIVORCED/WIDOWED/SEPARATED AT a)

b) For how many years have you been divorced/widowed/separated?

ENTER NUMBER OF YEARS (248-249)

41 May I ask, who lives with you in this household?

No one, lives alone 0 (250) SEE Q42

ENTER DETAILS OF HOUSEHOLD MEMBERS IN GRID BELOW

Relationship to respondent	OUO	M	F	Age	Marital status M S W/D/S			Employment status FT/Emp PT/Emp H/W Ret Other					Col./Code
		1	2		1	2	3	1	2	3	4	5	(251-256)
		1	2		1	2	3	1	2	3	4	5	(257-262)
		1	2		1	2	3	1	2	3	4	5	(263-268)
		1	2		1	2	3	1	2	3	4	5	(269-274)
		1	2		1	2	3	1	2	3	4	5	(275-280)
		1	2		1	2	3	1	2	3	4	5	(309-314)
		1	2		1	2	3	1	2	3	4	5	(315-320)
		1	2		1	2	3	1	2	3	4	5	(321-326)

Duplicate 301-307

Card 3 308

		Col./Code	Skip to
42a)	IF EVER MARRIED (CODES 2-5 AT Q40) IF SINGLE, SKIP TO Q44		
	Do you have any (other) children ? (apart from those living with you at home)	(327)	
	Yes A	0	
	No	0	
	IF YES AT a)		
b)	How many children do you have who have now left home ?	(328)	
	ENTER NUMBER LEFT HOME		
c)	INTERVIEWER TO COMPLETE		
	ENTER NUMBER OF CHILDREN STILL LIVING AT HOME (FROM HOUSEHOLD BOX)		
	None	0	
	ENTER NUMBER →	(329330)	
	Yes A		c)
	No	00	
	IF HAS ANY CHILDREN		
d)	Do you have any grandchildren ?		
43a)	IF ALL CHILDREN LEFT HOME (SEE Q42 b & b) OTHERS SKIP TO Q44		
	Thinking about your son or daughter living nearest, approximately how long does the journey take for you to go and see them ?		
	RECORD TIME OF ONE-WAY JOURNEY BY USUAL FORM OF TRANSPORT	(331)	
	Less than 10 mins.	1	
	11-30 mins.	2	
	31-60 mins.	3	
	Over an hour	4	
	Other (SPECIFY) _____	5	
b)	When did you last see one of your children ? Was it	(332)	
	Within the last week	1	
	Over 1 week ago, up to 4 weeks	2	
	Over 1 month ago	3	
	Other (SPECIFY) _____	4	
44	When did you last have a visit from, or go to see, one of your relatives ?	(333)	
	Within the last week	1	
	Over 1 week ago, up to 4 weeks	2	
	Over 1 month ago	3	
	Other (SPECIFY) _____	4	
	No relatives	5	

		Col./Code	Skip to
45	Do you have any friends you see regularly who are retired or about to retire ?	(334)	
	Yes A	0	
	No	0	c)
	IF YES AT a)		
b)	About what proportion of your friends are retired or about to retire ?	(335)	
	Almost all	1	
	More than ½	2	
	About ½	3	
	Less than ½	4	
	Other (SPECIFY) _____	5	
c)	Do any of your friends, whether retired or not, live in your neighbourhood or very close by ?	(336)	
	Yes	1	
	No	2	
	Can't say	3	
d)	Have you made any new friends since you retired ?	(337)	
	Yes	1	
	No	2	
46a)	Is there anyone in particular you confide in to talk about yourself or your problems ?	(338)	
	Yes	1	
	No	2	SEE Q47
	IF YES AT a)		
b)	May I ask who that is ?		
	Husband/Wife	1	
	Brother/Sister	2	
	Friend	3	
	Other (SPECIFY) _____	4	

P.616

589 (401-403)

Record Number (404-407)

Card 4 (408)

(409) (410-412) (413) [ ] [ ] 3

Org.   Serial Number   Phase

STUDY OF PRE-RETIREMENT EDUCATION

SELF-COMPLETION BOOKLET

		Col./ Code	Skip to
47	IF LIVING WITH SPOUSE OTHERS GO TO Q48		
	In general, what effect do you think retirement has had on your relationship with your wife/husband ?		
	PROBE FULLY		
	No effect	0	Q48
	b) So, on the whole, do you think the effect of your retirement has been good or bad ?	(339)	
	Good	1	Q48
	Bad	2	
	Mixed	3	
	IF BAD OR MIXED EFFECT AT b)		
	c) Is there anything you think you can do to overcome this ?		
48	Finally, I would like you to answer some questions about retirement and attitudes towards life in general by completing this short booklet yourself.		
	GIVE RESPONDENT SELF COMPLETION BOOKLET		
	INTERVIEWER TO COMPLETE		
	Sex of respondent	(340)	
	Male	1	
	Female	2	
	Time interview ended _____ (including time for self-completion)		
	Length of interview _____ Minutes	(341-43)	
	Date of interview _____		
	Interviewer name _____		
	Authorisation number	(344-47)	

A. Below are 5 statements about retirement. For each one we would like you to show, by <u>ringing</u> the appropriate number, whether you strongly agree, agree, agree, disagree or strongly disagree with what is said.

	Strongly Agree	Agree	Not sure/ Undecided	Disagree	Strongly Disagree	Col.
i) People should not be made to retire solely because of their age.	1	2	3	4	5	(414)
ii) I enjoy the time off that retirement allows.	1	2	3	4	5	(415)
iii) If it were up to me alone, I would have kept on working as long as possible.	1	2	3	4	5'	(416)
iv) I think that things have gone well for me in retirement.	1	2	3	4	5	(417)
v) Retirement is mostly good for a person	1	2	3	4	5	(418)

B. We would like you to consider the statements below about life in general. For each one we would like you to say whether you personally agree or disagree, by ringing the appropriate number.

	Agree	Disagree	Not sure/ Undecided	Col.
i) I am just as happy now as when I was younger.	1	2	3	(419)
ii) My life could be happier than it is now.	1	2	3	(420)
iii) These are the best years of my life.	1	2	3	(421)
iv) The things I do now are as interesting to me as they ever were.	1	2	3	(422)
v) I would not change my past life even if I could.	1	2	3	(423)
vi) Compared with other people of my age, I've made a lot of foolish decisions in my life.	1	2	3	(424)
vii) When I think back over my life, I didn't get most of the important things I wanted.	1	2	3	(425)
viii) Compared with other people, I get down in the dumps too often.	1	2	3	(426)
ix) I've got pretty much what I expected out of life.	1	2	3	(427)

C. Below are listed some activities which people do in their spare time or as part of their normal week. For each one we would like you to show whether you now do more, less, or about the same amount of this since you retired. If the activity is something which does not apply to you, that is something which you did not do either before or since retirement, please tick in the final column.

	Do more since retired	Do less since retired	About the same amount	Not applicable - not usual activity	Col.
Gardening	1	2	3	4	(428)
Housework (cooking, shopping etc.)	1	2	3	4	(429)
Watching TV, listening to the radio	1	2	3	4	(430)
Reading books, magazines or newspapers	1	2	3	4	(431)
Woodwork or other handicrafts	1	2	3	4	(432)
Taking part in sports	1	2	3	4	(433)
Bingo/whist drives	1	2	3	4	(434)
Out to cinemas/theatres /concerts	1	2	3	4	(435)
Out to clubs	1	2	3	4	(436)
Out to pubs	1	2	3	4	(437)
Attend church	1	2	3	4	(438)
Family outings	1	2	3	4	(439)
Driving	1	2	3	4	(440)
Voluntary or community work	1	2	3	4	(441)
Other Activites (Please describe):	1	2	3	4	(442)
	1	2	3	4	(443)
	1	2	3	4	(444)

D. Please tick your replies to the following questions:-

i) On the whole, how satisfied would you say you are with your way of life today?
very satisfied (445) 1
fairly satisfied 2
not very satisfied 3
not satisfied at all 4

ii) Do you ever find yourself feeling 'blue' or depressed?
often (446) 1
sometimes 2
hardly ever 3

iii) In general, how would you say you feel most of the time, in good spirits or in low spirits?
I am usually in good spirits (447) 1
I am in good spirits some of the time and in low spirits some of the time 2
I am usually in low spirits 3

iv) IF WHOLLY RETIRED. Do you think stopping work altogether has made you less satisfied with life?
Yes (448) 1
No 2
Undecided 3

v) IF WHOLLY RETIRED. Alternatively, do you think stopping work has made you feel your life is not particularly useful?
Yes (449) 1
No 2
Undecided 3

vi) IF STILL WORKING, do you think stopping work altogether may make you less satisfied with your life?
Yes (450) 1
No 2
Undecided 3

vii) IF STILL WORKING, do you think stopping work may make you feel your life is not particularly useful?
Yes (451) 1
No 2
Undecided 3

E. Finally, we would like you to say whether the statements shown below are true or false. If you are uncertain about any, please say whether you <u>think</u> the statement is true or not.

		True	False	Col.
i)	For people in their 60's and 70's, regular exercise can restore physical activity and reduce heart rate and blood pressure.	1	2	(452)
ii)	At least 1 in 10 of people past 65 live in long stay institutions (ie homes for the aged, geriatric hospitals).	1	2	(453)
iii)	Nearly three quarters of people aged 65 or more in England and Wales live in a household without a car.	1	2	(454)
iv)	Most older workers cannot work as effectively as younger workers.	1	2	(455)
v)	The majority of older people are healthy enough to carry out their normal activities.	1	2	(456)
vi)	Most older people are set in their ways and are unable to change.	1	2	(457)
vii)	Old people usually take longer to learn something new.	1	2	(458)
viii)	It is almost impossible for most old people to learn new things.	1	2	(459)
ix)	One third of old people live alone.	1	2	(460)
x)	In general most old people are pretty much alike.	1	2	(461)
xi)	People aged 60 and over make up 20% of Great Britain's total population.	1	2	(462)
xii)	When a person retires his health usually gets worse.	1	2	(463)
xiii)	A majority of pensioners in Great Britain live in households below, at, or just above the official poverty line.	1	2	(464)

A P P E N D I X   4

COURSE TIMETABLES

NATIONAL COAL BOARD - SOUTH NOTTINGHAM AREA: PREPARATION FOR RETIREMENT SEMINAR

Three Sessions - One per week
Over Three Weeks

Monday 18th January 1982 - Week 1

9.30 a.m.   Welcome and course arrangement.
            Head of Manpower (1)
            Assistant Manpower Officer (2)

9.45 a.m.   Introduction - Why Prepare for Retirement?
            Chairman, Pre-Retirement Committee and
            Course Leader

10.30 a.m. Coffee

11.00 a.m. "National Pensions and Social Security"
            Department of Health & Social Security
            representative

12.noon   Lunch

1.15 p.m.   "Enjoying Leisure and Food for Thought"
            Sen. Youth and Community Officer (Training)
            (Retired)

2.30 p.m.   "Unemployment Benefits"
            Department of Employment

3.15   Tea - Disperse

Monday 25th January 1982

9.30 a.m.   "Money and Retirement"
            Banking Services Officer, Trustee Savings Bank

10.30 a.m. Coffee

11.00 a.m. "Safety in the Home"
            NCC Fire Services

12.noon   Lunch

Monday 25th January 1982 - Week 2 contd.

1.15 p.m.   "Health in Retirement"
            Health Visitor

2.15 p.m.   "Income Tax Problems"
            Income Tax Officer, Inland Revenue

3.15 p.m.   Tea - Disperse

Monday 1st February 1982 - Week 3

9.30 a.m.   "Fitness in Retirement"
            Keep Fit Association representative

10.30 a.m. Coffee

11.00 a.m. "Security in the Home"
            Police Officer, Notts. Constabulary

12.noon   Lunch

1.15 p.m.   NCB Pensions and Early Retirement
            Benefits
            NCB Pensions & Insurance Scheme Manager

2.30 p.m.   Course Conclusion/Discussion Session
            (Incorporating Tea and Biscuits)
            Chairman, Pre-Retirement Committee
            and Course Leader

MARS: PREPARATION FOR RETIREMENT SEMINAR
Maidenhead & Bray Sports Club Pavillion

21st-22nd May, 1980

Wednesday - 21st May 1980 (Day 1)

9.15 a.m.   Assemble
            Course Leader

9.30 a.m.   The Philosophy and Need for Pre-Retirement
            Training
            Course Leader

10.00 a.m. Social and Personal Adjustment
            Course Leader

10.45 a.m. Coffee

11.00 a.m. The Financial Maze
            Administration Superintendent

11.45 a.m. Budgeting for the future

12.30 p.m. Buffet Lunch

1.30 p.m.   Self Examination and Attitudes
            Course Leader

2.30 p.m.   Project

3.30 p.m.   Discussion

Thursday - 22nd May 1980 (Day 2)

9.15 a.m.   Meet at Slough Social Centre

9.20 a.m.   The Marsters Club
            Club Manager

9.30 a.m.   Benefits of Membership
            Club Secretary

10.15 a.m. Move to Bray

10.30 a.m. Coffee

10.45 a.m. Safely into the Future
            (accommodation problems)
            Plant Safety Officer

11.45 a.m. Your Personal Health and Preventive
            Medicine
            Medical Services Manager

12.45 p.m. Buffet Lunch

1.45 p.m.   Your Rights
            Senior Welfare Officer

2.30 p.m.   Activities and Interests for Your New Career
            Area Welfare Officer

3.30 p.m.   Practical Appreciation
            Course Leader

BRISTOL RETIREMENT COUNCIL: PREPARATION FOR RETIREMENT SEMINAR

4th - 5th December, 1979

"As for Retirement - embrace it, it abounds with pleasure, if you know how to use it".

Tuesday - 4th December, 1979 (Day 1)

9.15 a.m.   Assembly and Welcome
            Introduction

10.00 a.m. Coffee

10.20 a.m. Film: "A Time to Look Forward"

11.10 a.m. Retirement Pensions and other State Benefits.
            Speaker: Department of Health & Social
                      Security representative.

            Lunch

2.00 p.m.   Personal Adjustment to Retirement

3.00 p.m.   Tea

3.20 p.m.   A Safe Home in Retirement
            Speaker: Home Safety Adviser, Bristol
                      Corporation.

Wednesday - 5th December, 1979 (Day 2)

9.30 a.m.   A Healthy Retirement
            Speaker: Nurse, SRN.

10.30 a.m. Coffee

10.50 a.m. Wise Eating in Retirement
            Speaker: Health Education Officer,
                      (Nutrition)
                      Avon Area Health Authority

11.50 a.m. Learning and Leisure in Retirement
            Speaker: Warden of Folk House

            LUNCH

2.00 p.m.   Money Matters in Retirement
            Speaker: Manager, Trustee Savings Bank.

            Tea

3.20 p.m.   Open Forum: in which outstanding questions
            may be answered and the value of the
            Course assessed.

4.00 p.m.   Course ends.

BRITISH LEYLAND (JAGUAR): PREPARATION FOR RETIREMENT SEMINAR

Eight Sessions Over Eight Weeks
One day per week

August 1st 1980 - Session 1

1.30 p.m.   Introduction to Course
            Course Tutor

2.00 p.m.- Retirement and Medical Pratitioner's Viewpoint
3.25 p.m.   Company Doctor

August 8th 1980 - Session 2

1.30 p.m.   Physical Health in Retirement

2.30 p.m.- Holidays for the Retired
3.25 p.m.   Saga representative

August 15th 1980 - Session 3

1.30 p.m.   Money Matters
            Retired Bank Manager

2.30 p.m.- My Approach to Retirement (Leisure)
3.25 p.m.   Retired School Master

August 22nd 1980 - Session 4

1.30 p.m.   State Pensions
            Department of Health & Social Security
            representative (1)

2.30 p.m.- Supplementary Benefits
3.25 p.m.   Department of Health & Social Security
            representative (2)

August 29th 1980 - Session 5

1.30 p.m.- Crime Prevention in the Home
3.25 p.m.   Police representative

September 5th 1980 - Session 6

1.30 p.m.   Food and Diet
            Dietician Coventry & Warwickshire
            Hospital
2.30 p.m.- Welfare in Retirement
3.25 p.m.   Company Welfare Officer

September 12th 1980 - Session 7

1.30 p.m.   Know Your Area
            Retired Public Relations Officer

2.30 p.m.- Safety in the Home
3.25 p.m.   Chief Safety Adviser (Jaguar)

September 19th 1980 - Session 8

11.00 a.m.

11.15 a.m.- Time to Spare
12.30 p.m.

            Lunch

            END OF COURSE

BRITISH AIRWAYS: PREPARATION FOR RETIREMENT SEMINAR

(Two Days)

First Day (Monday)

9.00 a.m.   Course assembles

9.05 a.m.   Course Introduction
             Head of Welfare Services

9.10 a.m.   Airways Pension Scheme
             Admin. Officer, Airways Pension Scheme

10.00 a.m.   Money Matters
             Financial Consultant, Pre-Retirement
             Association

12.noon   Lunch

1.30 p.m.   Taxation
             Staff Taxation Officer

2.00 p.m.   Post-Retirement Employment
             Unemployment Benefits
             Job Centre representative

3.00 p.m.   Social Security Benefits
             Department of Health & Social Security
             representative

(Morning Coffee and Afternoon Tea will be served)

Second Day (Tuesday)

9.00 a.m.   Retirement Action
             Retired Staff Association
             Pensioner Contact Scheme
             Welfare Officer - Retired Staff

9.30 a.m.   Health and Happiness in Retirement
             Deputy Director, Medical Services

10.30 a.m.   Housing/Social Arrangements
             Film
             Manager, Hillingdon Housing Advice Centre

12.30 p.m.   Lunch

2.00 p.m.   Film - "A Time to Look Forward"

2.30 p.m.   Leisure/Hobbies
             Staff Policy Officer

3.30 p.m.   Rebate Travel in Retirement

4.00 p.m.   Conclusion

E.M.I./LEGAL & GENERAL: PREPARATION FOR RETIREMENT SEMINAR

25th/26th June, 1981

Thursday - 25th June, 1981 (Day 1)

9.30 a.m.   Arrival and Coffee

10.00 a.m.   Introduction
             EMI Representative

10.10 a.m.   Adjustment to Retirement
             Legal and General Retirement
             Counselling Manager.

11.00 a.m.   Coffee Break

11.20 a.m.   State Benefits
             DHSS representative

12.30 p.m.   Buffet Lunch

2.00 p.m.   Fitness
             Medical Officer

3.00 p.m.   Tea Break

3.20 p.m.   The Company Pension

4.10 p.m.   Local Benefits in Outline
             Legal & General Retirement
             Counselling Manager

4.30 p.m.   Course ends for day

Friday - 26th June, 1981 (Day 2)

9.30 a.m.   Re-assemble over coffee

10.00 a.m.   Financial Considerations
             Financial Consultant

11.15 a.m.   Coffee Break

11.45 a.m.   Leisure Activities
             Legal & General Retirement
             Counselling Manager

12.30 p.m.   Buffet Lunch

2.00 p.m.   Holiday Time

2.45 p.m.   Tea Break

3.05 p.m.   Voluntary Work

3.45 p.m.   Safety in the Home
             Safety Officer

4.20 p.m.   Course Summary and Close

SCOTTISH RETIREMENT COUNCIL: PREPARATION FOR RETIREMENT SEMINAR

1979-80

Courses for Men

First Day

9.30 a.m.   Introduction to Course

11.00 a.m.   Coffee

11.20 a.m.   Money Matters: Pensions.

12.45 p.m.   Lunch

1.45 p.m.   Money Matters: Supplementary Pensions

3.00 p.m.   Tea

3.20 p.m.- Security in the Home
4.45 p.m.   Course ends for day.

Second Day

9.30 a.m.   Keeping Mentally Alert
            (coffee break included)

12.45 p.m.   Lunch

1.45 p.m.   Visit: Penilee Centre

3.00 p.m.   Tea

3.20 p.m.- At Home with Electricity
4.45 p.m.   Course ends for day.

Third Day

9.30 a.m.   Opportunities for Social Service

11.00 a.m.   Coffee

11.20 a.m.   Books and Libraries

12.45 p.m.   Lunch

1.45 p.m.   Keeping Physically Fit

3.00 p.m.   Tea

3.20 p.m.- Interests Out of Doors
4.45 p.m.   Course ends for day.

Fourth Day

9.30 a.m.- Visit: Langside Geriatric Unit/University Geriatric
12.45 p.m.   Unit, Southern General Hospital and Home for
                    the Elderly.

12.45 p.m.   Lunch

1.45 p.m.   Eat Well and Keep Well

3.00 p.m.   Tea

3.20 p.m.- Gardening
4.45 p.m.   Course ends for day.

SCOTTISH RETIREMENT COUNCIL: PREPARATION FOR RETIREMENT SEMINAR CONTINUED

1979-80

Courses for Men

Fifth Day

9.30 a.m.   Holidays for the Retired.

11.00 a.m.   Coffee

11.20 a.m.   Visit: David Cargill Club/St. Mungo's Club,
                    Dixon Halls Day Centre

12.45 p.m.   Lunch

1.45 p.m.   Income Tax

3.00 p.m.   Tea

3.20 p.m.- Painting and Decorating Hints
4.45 p.m.   Course ends for day.

Sixth Day

9.30 a.m.   Aspects of Social Living

11.00 a.m.   Coffee

11.20 a.m.   Balancing the Budget.

12.45 p.m.   Lunch

1.45 p.m.   Visit: Museum of Transport

4.45 p.m.   Course ends for day.

Seventh Day

9.30 a.m.   Opportunities in Adult Education

11.00 a.m.   Coffee

11.20 a.m.   Consumer Problems

12.45 p.m.   Lunch

1.45 p.m.   Enjoy Your Retirement

3.00 p.m.   Tea

3.20 p.m.   Appraisal of Course

4.45 p.m.   COURSE ENDS

SHELL: PREPARATION FOR RETIREMENT SEMINAR

21st - 28th November, 1980

Friday - 21st November, 1980 (Day 1)

9.30 a.m.   Welcome and Introduction

9.45 a.m.   Retirement Perspective: Discussion on the
nature of retirement and the changes involved
with a review of the more interesting
research projects, the nature of work,
individual motivation, etc.

12.30 p.m. LUNCH

2.30 p.m.   Retirement Perspective (Contd.): including case-
studies on videotape.
(tea break included).

4.30   Course ends for day.

Monday - 24th November, 1980 (Day 2)

9.30 a.m.   Shell Pension Administration
Speaker: Shell representative.

10.15 a.m. Coffee

10.30 a.m. Unemployment and Related Benefits
Speaker: Department of Employment representative.

11.30 a.m. Employment Prospects
Speaker: Job Centre (Bermondsey) representative.

12.30 p.m. LUNCH

Monday - 24th November, 1980 (Day 2 contd.)

2.30 p.m.   National Insurance
Speaker: Department of Health & Social
Security representative.

3.30 p.m.   Tea

3.45 p.m.   Retirement Perspective: Film and
Discussion.

4.30   Course ends for day.

Tuesday - 25th November, 1980 (Day 3)

FINANCIAL PRESENTATION: by Investment
Advisers.

9.30 a.m.   Part One: The Investment Scene - Glossary -
Where to go for Advice - Crucial
Decisions - Alternatives.

12.30 p.m. LUNCH

2.30 p.m.   Medical Matters: Emphasising the positive
aspects of health and retirement.
Speaker: A Medical Doctor.
(tea break included).

4.30   Course ends for day.

SHELL: PREPARATION FOR RETIREMENT SEMINAR CONTINUED

21st - 28th November, 1980

Wednesday - 26th November, 1980 (Day 4)

9.30 a.m.   Financial Presentation Part Two:
Strategies: Examples - case studies.
(coffee break included)

11.30 a.m. Retirement Perspective.

12.30 p.m. LUNCH

2.30 p.m.   Syndicate Groups: Briefing and Discussions.
(tea break included)

4.30 p.m.   Course ends for day.

Thursday - 27th November, 1980 (Day 5)

9.30 a.m.   Retirement Perspective: Syndicate Reports.

10.15 a.m. Coffee.

10.30 a.m. Financial Matters - Taxation: Income Tax,
Capital Transfer Tax, Capital Gains Tax, etc.
Speaker: Shell Representative.

12.30 p.m. LUNCH.

2.30 p.m.   Medical Matters: A General Practitioner's
view of retirement.
Speaker: Medical Doctor.
(tea break included).

4.30 p.m.   Course ends for day.

Friday - 28th November, 1980 (Day 6)

9.30 a.m.   Voluntary Work
Speaker: Voluntary Services Organiser,
St. Thomas' Hospital.
(coffee break included)

11.00 a.m. Retirement Perspective: Adult Education
and Training.
Speaker:

12.30 p.m. LUNCH

2.30 p.m.   Pensioner Facilities: Including details
of the Pensioner Liaison Scheme.

3.30 p.m.   Tea.

3.45 p.m.   Course Review and Assessment.

4.30 p.m.   COURSE ENDS.

APPENDIX   5

SELECTED   RESEARCH

PROJECTS ON PRE-RETIREMENT EDUCATION.

SELECTED RESEARCH PROJECTS ON PRE-RETIREMENT EDUCATION.

Bolton, C. R.   'Humanistic Instructional Strategies and Retirement Education Programming', The Gerontologist, Vol.16, No.6., 1976, pp 550 - 555.

Bowman, D. L.   A longitudinal comparison of attitudes and activity involvement of persons who have completed a pre-retirement planning program, Iowa State University, Ph.d. Thesis, 1974.

Burgess, E. W.   Retirement preparation: Chicago plan.   Patterns for progress in aging.   (Series) Case Study No.5. U.S. Department of Health, Education and Welfare, Special Staff on Aging, 1961.

Charles, D. C.   'The Effect of Participation in a Pre-Retirement Program', The Gerontologist, Vol.11, Part 1, 1971, pp 24 - 28.

Fitzpatrick, E. W.   'Evaluating a New Retirement Planning Program - Results with Hourly Workers', Aging and Work, Vol. 2, No.2, 1979, pp 87 - 94.

Glamser, F.D.   The Efficacy of Pre-Retirement Preparation programmes for Industrial Workers, Pennsylvania State University, Ph.D. Thesis, 1973.

Glamser, F.D.   'The Impact of Pre-Retirement Programs on the Retirement Experience'. Journal of Gerontology, Vol. 36, No.2, 1981, pp. 244 - 250.

Hunter, W.   Preparation for Retirement of Hourly Wage Employees in Niagara Falls, New York. University of Michigan, Division of Gerontology, Mimeo, 1957.

Hunter, W.W.   A Longitudinal Study of Pre-Retirement Education Div. of Gerontology, The University of Michigan, 1968.

Mack, A.   'An Evaluation of a Retirement-Planning Program', Journal of Gerontology, Vol.13, 1958, pp. 198 - 202.

Miller, P.R.   Retirement Education: A factor in retirement adjustment.   Ph.D. Thesis, University of Maryland, 1973.

Tiberi, D.M.   Boyack, V.L. and Kerschner, P.A. 'A Comparative Analysis of Four Pre-Retirement Education Models', Educational Gerontology, Vol.3, No.4, 1978, pp 355 - 374.